BEST *of the* MIDWEST™

Rediscovering America's Heartland

INSIDERS' GUIDE ®

Cover photos: Bob Stefko
Cover design: Terri Ketcham
Text and layout design: Geri Boesen, Terri Ketcham
Map illustrations: Bill Reynolds

Photo credits: Dennis Cox (p. 71 top left); Brian Confer (p. 71 top right); Robert J. Dole Institute of Politics, University of Kansas (p. 53 top center); Hulton Archive/Getty Images (p. 52, p. 53 top left); Iowa Tourism Office (p. 47 top); Mike Klemme/Golfoto (p. 175 bottom right); Jason Lindsey (p. 3 bottom, p. 5); Doug Smith (p. 44, p. 45, p. 47 bottom left and bottom right, p. 48); Peter Tubbs (p. 46, p. 142); Michael Vaughn (p. 33). All other interior photos by Bob Stefko.

Editorial credits:
Midwest Living® magazine: Deputy Editor, Travel/Special Publications: Barbara Morrow. Special Publications Copy/Production Coordinator: Kathy Roberts. Project Manager: Joan Lynch Luckett. Contributing Editors: Barbara Humeston, Christine Ricelli. Photo/Research Assistants: Lisa Schumacher, Jenny McCuen, Katie Knorovsky, Angela Kennebeck, Tory Thaemert, Tara Losee.

Library of Congress Cataloging-in-Publication Data is available.

ISBN 0-7627-3781-6 (Hardcover); 0-7627-3699-2 (Paperback)

Printed in China
First Edition/Second Printing

BEST *of the* MIDWEST™

Rediscovering America's Heartland

Written by Dan Kaercher • Photography by Bob Stefko

INSIDERS' GUIDE ®

GUILFORD, CONNECTICUT
AN IMPRINT OF THE GLOBE PEQUOT PRESS

Contents

This book is more than a collection of written and visual essays about the places I visited on my journey. It's also intended as a practical travel guide. Please consult the "Travel Journal" pages at the end of each chapter for trip-planning advice. My route did not allow me to revisit every one of my Midwest "bests" in person. So, I included a brief "More Favorites" section for every state. We've taken great pains to make sure everything recorded here is accurate, but prices and circumstances change. Be sure to call ahead before you visit.

Finally, the delicious food was a delight throughout my journey. To help you experience those flavors at home, I've included a recipe from each state that you can try. My sincere thanks to those who shared the secrets of their specialties with me.

—Dan Kaercher

■ Key to lodgings prices:
$ $70 or less
$$ $70–$100
$$$ $100–$150
$$$$ more than $150

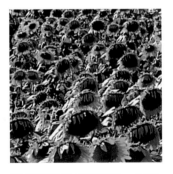

Dan's route covered 10,605 miles through 12 Midwest states
over an eight-week period during the summer of 2004.

Half Lost, Half Found in America's Heartland

This book is the record of an amazing journey that filled one complete season of my life. When I left my driveway in Des Moines, Iowa, one morning in early June 2004, the corn in the fields I passed was barely ankle high. When I returned in late September from the final leg of my sojourn, the harvest was ready to begin. In between, I'd driven 10,605 miles through the 12 states that make up America's Heartland, and revisited almost 60 of my favorite places—from Zoar, Ohio to St. Paul, Minnesota . . . Abilene, Kansas to Mackinac Island, Michigan . . . Indianapolis, Indiana to Stanton, North Dakota . . . and dozens of communities in between, both large and small.

Some of the destinations in this book are familiar to you; others are known best by only a few locals and, now, me and you. Each has its own piece of America's story to tell. Along the way, I also discovered many new gems that have joined my list of Midwest favorites. I dined at small-town cafes and gourmet restaurants, toured little-visited historic sites and modern research facilities, prowled the hidden galleries of world-famous museums and cheered with the fans at major-league ballparks. At night, I laid my weary head to rest at lodgings from grand resorts and big-city hotels to basic motels along the interstates and tiny bed and breakfasts.

What prompted this daunting journey? First, as editor-in-chief and founding editor of *Midwest Living* magazine, I'm constantly asked to share my personal recommendations with travelers. After 18 years at the helm, I wanted to return to many of those places that have provided me with so many happy memories. Were they still as good as I remembered them being? (In almost every instance, the answer was—"better.") Further, my evolving role at *Midwest Living* has required me to spend more and more of my time representing the magazine outside the Midwest, in cities such as Los Angeles, New York and Atlanta. I yearned deeply to reconnect at the grassroots with my region and to reaffirm our magazine's overriding mission: to celebrate everything that is the very best of the Midwest. My trip allowed me to do just that. Since my return, my greatest challenge has been to sort out the thousands of mental snapshots that crowd my brain—some hilarious, some that move me to tears. Many of those moments are recaptured to the best of my ability on these pages.

At various times, I felt curiously half lost and half found on the back roads and byways I followed. As always, I loved the sense of adventure that travel brings. Yet, wherever I was on any given day in the Midwest, I knew I was somehow home, where I belonged. Upon reflection, my compressed view gave me fresh perspectives on our region, in many respects a microcosm of all America. I found that most of the Heartland is prospering, if cautiously, after the national traumas of the past few years. Erstwhile farming communities on the Great Plains are seeking new identities, many with heartening success.

Wherever I was on any given day in the Midwest, I knew I was somehow home, where I belonged.

Once-forlorn industrial centers are coming to life thanks to intrepid entrepreneurs, computer technology and bioengineering miracles. The downtown cores of many Midwest cities are experiencing a dazzling renaissance, not only in terms of sleek office towers and new green spaces, but also by welcoming urban pioneers who are flocking to new loft developments. Ethnically, our region is becoming far more interesting, thanks primarily to a new influx of Hispanic and Asian immigrants and refugees. The surge of new Midwesterners has posed some challenges, but from what I observed, it's brought far more in terms of vitality and cultural diversity.

This is a time of change in the Heartland, and yet the hallmarks of life remain: cozy cafes serving some of the world's best pies; bountiful farm fields, orchards and pastures that seem to belong in a Grant Wood landscape painting; lively city neighborhoods that cling to their rich ethnic traditions; old-fashioned soda fountains; out-of-the-way country inns. The man-made monuments such as Mount Rushmore in South Dakota and Chicago's awesome skyline, the breathtaking natural ones including the forest-rimmed beaches of Michigan's Upper Peninsula—even the oft-derided, flat, wide-open plains and prairies that I love, which define the

Midwest more than any other single topographical emblem.

I wanted to find what's still good and true about everyday life in the heart of America, and I believe I did just that. Was I reassured? Yes, most definitely. Midwesterners still are enjoying enviably rich, full and abundant lives in their cities, towns and farms. Their characteristic unpretentiousness belies a deep, quiet pride in their roots, their families, their homes and their communities. I didn't return home feeling heartened because the Midwest is remaining static or because life here is problem-free. I was uplifted because the dynamic rhythms of change and transformation are happening within the context of touchstones that remain constant. I only hope this book in some small way conveys that sense of continuity in the Heartland.

How can I ever begin to thank enough the Midwesterners I met along the way—travel industry professionals who facilitated my visits, fellow tourists and travelers who accommodated my photo requests, and scores of people from all walks of life who kindly interrupted their daily routines to chat when I came to call? Perhaps what you see depicted here of yourself and your special place in this Midwest in some small way will help repay the debt I owe each of you.

I was accompanied on my sojourn by Bob Stefko, the photographer whose stunning visual images appear on these pages, and by Peter Tubbs, who documented the journey for public television (see page 182).

To each of them, I owe my most sincere thanks—for their patience and their fearless determination to risk absolutely anything to get the photo or video segment we needed.

I also owe more gratitude than I can express to a host of others who made my trip possible: my management at Meredith Corporation, publishers of *Midwest Living*; Barbara Morrow, the talented and perseverant wordsmith who edited my essays and strategized our efforts; art directors Geri Boesen and Terri Ketcham, who married prose and photos into the pleasing product you're holding in your hands; Joan Lynch Luckett, the logistical wizard who coordinated my daily itinerary; copy/production coordinator Kathy Roberts; executive editor Mary Norris and the staff at Globe Pequot Press; the management and staff of Iowa Public Television; and the team at my office who kept things running flawlessly in my absence, notably *Midwest Living* executive editor Greg Philby.

Most of all, as always, I owe my deepest thanks for her unflagging support and understanding to my wife, the world's best traveling companion. Julie wisely sat out most of this frenetic trip, but has been by my side on a hundred other Midwest adventures we'll share forever in our memories.

Dan Kaercher

Dan Kaercher,
Editor-in-Chief
Midwest Living Magazine

Illinois

■ If there's a Heartland state with multiple identities, this one is it. Without Chicago, Illinois probably would be a lot like my home state of Iowa: a pleasant capital city at its heart, corn and soybean fields spilling on forever. But add that amazing metropolis along Lake Michigan to the mix and you have the most complex state in the Midwest. Which aspect of Illinois do you prefer? The historic communities along the mighty Mississippi, Illinois and Ohio rivers . . . the irresistible small towns such as once-forgotten Galena . . . or that teeming megacity and its endless suburbs, each with its own attractions? In Illinois, you can take your pick, because they're all here waiting for you.

The Chicago skyline,
looking south from the John
Hancock Center
Observatory

Classic Chicago

Sports, theater, shopping, dining, museums and the arts—all spread like a grand feast along Lake Michigan. There are many reasons Chicago is my favorite big city, not the least of which is that it's pure Midwest at heart.

Having lived most of my life in midsize cities, I used to be intimidated by Chicago, simply because of its 9.1 million metro population clustered in America's third largest urban area. (Don't even ask how I feel about New York City, where I also travel regularly.) But on repeated visits to the Windy City, I've learned to relish the Chicago scene. In fact, I'm such a Chicago fan that my only problem planning an itinerary is narrowing down my list of stops. This time, I resolve to focus on true Chicago classics. And I make a strategic decision that pays off: I park the car at my hotel, leave my keys with the attendant and rely exclusively on taxis.

The Chicago I love most includes the downtown Loop (defined by those clacking "el" trains), the museum and parks district east and south of the Loop along the lake, and the classy North Michigan Avenue shopping district.

'Big John'

Because I'm billeted at my favorite hotel here, the Art Deco south tower of the Inter-Continental Chicago along North Michigan Avenue, the ultratony shopping district known as the Magnificent Mile, I decide to start at the rooftop of the city (almost): the John Hancock Center Observatory just up the street. At 100 stories and 1,502 feet (including huge insectlike broadcast antennae on top), "Big John"—as it was fondly dubbed during construction—was the

world's tallest building for an instant back in 1970. Then, it was eclipsed by Chicago's Sears Tower and even yielded second-place status to the Amoco building (now the AON Center). Yet, this remains my favorite high-rise view anywhere. One of the world's fastest elevators, at 23 miles per hour, zooms me up to the 94th floor.

There have been some improvements in recent years. The observatory experience begins on the lower level of the Hancock building via its handsome outdoor plaza along North Michigan. Dramatic photos document the construction phase, which required 5 million man-hours to complete in 1970. The still-classy charcoal-color Hancock, soaring from a long-ago landfill known as Streeterville, was conceived by architect Bruce Graham as two separate towers stacked into one modified pyramid, with a distinctive X-shape exterior framing.

Approximately 1,000 feet up in this vertical city within a city, the first thing that enters my post-9/11 brain is security, but I think back to that thorough screening procedure downstairs, and I breathe easy. Then, I wonder 'What do they do up here when it gets really windy in the Windy City?'

Observatory General Manager Randy Stancik says the building can withstand gusts of up to 132 miles per hour, swaying a maximum of five to eight inches in a bad storm. Supposedly, you can see water gently sloshing in the loos on a really breezy day.

It's rather cloudy, but I don't mind. The most fun I ever had up here was with my family on an overcast day when we felt we were smack in the middle of a huge cottony cloud, which, in fact, we were. On a clear day, you can see all the way across Lake Michigan—69 miles. Four states lie within an 80-mile optimum viewing radius: Illinois, Wisconsin, Indiana and Michigan. I cautiously look down at the glistening green lake on the east and at Chicago's burly skyline to the south.

One of the new additions at the observatory, the skywalk, resembles a screened-in porch that lets visitors get up close and personal with the weather gods. Randy tells me he just loves it on a windy day. I'll take his word for it. And, speaking of wind, Randy sets the record straight about the real reason they call this the Windy City. It has nothing to do with breezes. The local politicians who pitched, and won, Chicago as the site of the 1893 World's Fair earned their city that nickname with their loquacity.

Midwest Masterpieces

I could spend days at The Art Institute of Chicago. The little boy in me loves all those medieval suits of armor. And, because I'm a fan of the French Impressionists, I can lose track of time wandering through one of the world's premier collections.

Judith Barter, the institute's Field-McCormick curator of American art, sheds

(Clockwise, from opposite) Crown Fountain in Millennium Park. Upscale shopping along North Michigan Avenue's Magnificent Mile. The lively scene outside Wrigley Field before a game. *Cloud Gate* glistens in Millennium Park.

new light on probably our most parodied masterpiece ever: Grant Wood's *American Gothic*. This dour-looking painting is a well-known icon of the Midwest and Midwesterners. Wood, a native of Cedar Rapids, Iowa, returned to his home state to teach and work after studying in Europe. He used his sister and his dentist as models for the famous portrait. Judith explains that it's about a 19th-century rural father and daughter, and a way of life that already was rapidly vanishing when Wood created it in 1930. The role of an unmarried daughter in that day was to care for her parents.

The painting is ingeniously organized,

when I was a third-grader, and I brought my own youngsters here several times as well. It still fascinates me.

Kurt Haunfelner, vice president of exhibits and collections, says MSI's mission is "to inspire the inventive genius that lurks in all of us." I'm just here because those exhibits are so darn much fun! There's an incubator with chicks hatching, a coal mine to explore, a John Deere combine to climb into, a United Airlines 727 you can walk through, and even a mini factory where you can design, manufacture and market your own toy top.

But it's that monster train set that really

have a pricey seat in a rooftop bleacher on a building directly across from third base.

Stepping out of my cab, I feel I've landed smack-dab in the heart of the midway at the Iowa State Fair back home. Barkers hawk every item imaginable with that blue-and-red Cubs logo. Future all-stars preen in their miniature Cubs uniforms. A hopeful suburban-type couple holds up a hand-lettered sign: "Need three bleacher seats this Thursday." A multitude of vendors shout: "Peanuts!" . . . "Scorecards!" . . . "Programs!" . . .

Chicago's beloved Cubs are playing the Cincinnati Reds today. For a team that hasn't won a pennant since 1945 or a series since 1908, there sure seems to be an abundance of devoted fans here. "What is it about the Cubs?" I ask Patti Purcell, director of Beyond the Ivy Rooftops, the company that manages three of these cushy, outside-the-park vantage points. This one alone accommodates 125 fans. Patti theorizes that it's the appeal of rooting for an underdog and about hope springing eternal every new baseball season. Plus, Chicagoans clearly just plain love baseball.

Frank Gehry's amazing outdoor band shell, the Jay Pritzker Pavilion, crouches like a huge crablike creature from a *Star Wars* movie.

taking its structure from an arched Gothic window of a house you still can see in Eldon, Iowa. The daughter's side of the painting reflects her domesticity (plants on the porch, curtains in the windows, her apron and brooch). The father's side of the painting shows a man's world: farming and the land (the pitchfork, overalls, barn in the background). All those satirists have done a great Midwest artist a terrible disservice.

Outside, along South Michigan Avenue, huge greenish lions guard the institute's front steps like oversize bronze bookends. They were created by Chicagoan Edward Kemeys, a self-taught sculptor, in 1894 and fabricated right here in the city. There's a major expansion under way on the opposite, east side of The Art Institute.

South along the lakeshore stands a sentimental favorite, the 1933 Museum of Science and Industry (MSI). My parents introduced me to this pioneering attraction

grabs me: a re-creation of the route from Chicago to Seattle, complete with scale models of major downtown buildings in both cities and landscape depictions of the Great Plains and the Rocky Mountains in between. Twenty-four trains of all types run concurrently on some 4,200 feet of track. Exhibit technician Doug Drummond tells me the team took lots of photos and looked up old blueprints in city halls to get the building models just right. Hooked on model railroading ever since he got an American Flyer set at age four, Doug confesses that he still unwinds with a hobby setup at home—but it's a much simpler layout than this one.

Perfect Afternoon

If there's a better-loved major-league ballpark here in the Midwest, I'm sure I don't know it. However, I'm not even setting foot inside Wrigley Field on this trip because I

I chomp a freshly grilled brat—smothered in mustard, kraut, onion and pickles—and sip a brew in these penthouse bleachers, surely the best seats outside the ballpark. Despite the threat of rain, there's almost a full house in Wrigley today (38,761 fans, to be precise)—from young T-ballers wearing their team uniforms to diehard old-timers accepting assistance to their seats. I think of the late gravel-voiced Chicago sportscaster Harry Caray and can almost hear his immortal "Holy Cow!" and his trademark off-key rendition of "Take Me Out to the Ball Game."

To my left, in the ivy-walled Wrigley outfield, is one of the few hand-operated signboards in the majors, along with those

Millennium Park's
Jay Pritzker Pavilion

legendary Bleacher Bums seats. It looks like serious rain on the way this afternoon, but everyone's staying put. Somehow, even though I can step downstairs for a posh indoor picture-window view of the game if it gets wet up here, I wish I were with the fans in the bleachers inside the stadium.

Before dinner, I head back to the Inter-Continental for a swim. One of the reasons I love this hotel is its classy pool area, reminiscent of a 1920s spa, with the beautiful tile, yellow walls and ornate wrought-iron light fixtures. I swim laps regularly back home, but this pool is my absolute favorite anywhere. How often do you get to do your backstroke looking up at an incredibly ornate baroque ceiling, surrounded by an exotic mélange of 1920s Moroccan, Spanish and Egyptian decorating motifs? Plus, the hotel pool staff keeps the water really clean and just the right temperature.

As I towel off, Brian Winston, the director of sales and marketing at the Inter-Continental Chicago, gives me a history lesson. Olympic swimmer and, later, big-screen "Tarzan" Johnny Weismuller trained here back in the Roaring Twenties, when this was the luxurious Medinah Athletic Club. Back then, an indoor pool on the 13th floor was quite an architectural feat.

After the stock market crash and several changes of ownership, the Inter-Continental chain arrived on the scene in 1988, renovated the hotel, married the historic south tower with a neighboring hotel to the north and emerged with an 807-room world-class facility. The south tower retains its tycoon-era amenities: big rooms, marble baths, classy furnishings and that fantastic pool.

Even with Chicago's more than 7,000 restaurants, I know exactly where I want to have dinner: Erwin, an American Café, on North Halsted Street. My wife, Julie, and I

(From left) Inside Oak Park's Frank Lloyd Wright Home and Studio. An exterior view of the studio. The pool at the InterContinental. Lion sculptures guarding The Art Institute of Chicago.

first met Erwin Drechsler during a *Midwest Living®* event that celebrated great cooks and great cooking, with special emphasis on Heartland food products and ingredients. We even got to meet the late Julia Child and Alice Waters of California's pioneering Chez Panisse. It was energetic, enthusiastic Erwin Drechsler, however, who lured us to an unforgettable dinner that featured the freshest ingredients and inventive twists on classic dishes.

The burgundy-color building, not far from the scene of my afternoon Wrigley Field adventure, offers a bar and some booths with street views in front. But my guest and I settle in the quiet dining room. Gentle jazz and Latin standards waft through the sound system, and ceiling-height murals of Midwest farm scenes set the eclectic mood here. It's clear from the relaxed customers that this is a place where people in the know come back, again and again. White tablecloths, but nothing pretentious—just classy, comfortable and surprisingly affordable.

Erwin prides himself on hearty yet sophisticated American dishes. He's known for prowling Chicago farmers markets, sometimes with cooking students. I

could write an entire chapter about the dinner my companion and I shared. Where else but here would I have the courage to revisit my mother's weekly standard, calf's liver? But Mother never cooked her variation with creamy turnips and shallots and apple-wood-smoked bacon. My friend has the pan-roasted Great Lakes whitefish with green beans, prosciutto, shallots and marinated grape tomatoes.

We dutifully exchange samples of everything on our plates. Fresh flavors and aromas seem to explode in Erwin's inventive dishes: The herbs, greens, cheeses, nuts, onions, beets, tomatoes and root vegetables are all so flavorful. For balance, we just *had* to order three totally decadent desserts: sour cherry pie with ice cream, an ice cream sandwich with banana cake and a double-brownie fudge sundae.

Design Centers

There's a lot to explore in metro Chicago outside the heart of the city. On my second day, I'm restricting myself to just one suburban shrine that must be visited, especially here in America's cradle of modern architecture.

There's a distinctive building on the

corner of Forest and Chicago avenues in Oak Park, one of Chicago's oldest suburbs directly west of downtown. From the Forest side, it looks like many other dark-stained, massively gabled homes from the 1880s. From the Chicago Avenue side, though, the house is a monument to genius. Long planters, high clerestory windows and pillars etched with symbols—cranes, ancient scrolls, a tree of life—hint at what we'll find inside.

From 1889 to 1909, Frank Lloyd Wright, his first wife, Kitty, and their six children lived in this house. Then, Wright fell madly in love with another Oak Park woman and moved out. The struggling architect was well-liked, even if he was temperamental, and his pioneering Prairie School designs were well-received, although they represented a total departure from the ornate Queen Annes of the day. Many clients later recalled the period they spent working with Wright on their revolutionary homes as the most exciting times in their lives—despite the fact that the talented Wright could be controlling and extravagant with his clients' funds.

Joan Mercuri, president and chief executive officer of the Frank Lloyd Wright

Preservation Trust, guides us through both the architect's home and the adjoining studio. Innovations abound. This house and its Wright-designed furnishings appear contemporary, even today: a cozy two-bench inglenook in front of the fireplace; straight high-back oak chairs in the dining room; contrasting ceiling heights that define some areas and open others; stained-glass skylights; natural interior colors, especially the greens that seem to melt into the outdoors; richly grained quartersawn oak everywhere.

Classical friezes, elaborate plasterwork, geometric patterns in leaded glass and Japanese and Native American motifs all blend naturally and artistically, creating a pleasing and comfortable mix. My head is spinning as I search for every detail. The only room untouched by Wright's design genius was the kitchen, in which Joan says he had absolutely no interest.

As his business grew, Wright added his studio in 1898. Draftsmen occupied the main floor of the firm's creative nerve center, while sculptors and muralists worked on the open balcony above. Classical sculptures add flourishes to the spare horizontal lines and high windows.

Most of Wright's projects were residential, although he influenced every facet of modern architecture and design. He often created furnishings and arranged them in the homes he designed and, divalike, demanded that they not be tampered with. He sometimes checked back years later to be sure every piece was intact!

The playroom that Wright added to his home in 1895 fascinates me most. Before visiting this room, I'd never thought of the eccentric iconoclast as a young family man, even though his children later recalled him as a loving father during those Oak Park years. Wright designed the vaulted-ceiling playroom and scaled its furnishings for his small children. He even tucked into the wall a grand piano with a keyboard that extended out into the room.

Kitty Wright conducted a kindergarten class for neighborhood children here. There's a balcony, built so adults could watch children's productions. The room also has ample and durable storage for toys, musical instruments, games, costumes and books. This is the work of a man who cared.

We return to downtown for another take on Chicago's architectural legacy. From a double-decker boat on the Chicago River,

the buildings seem a bit larger, the perspective a bit different. The tour boat wends its way through the heart of downtown for a look at the birthplace of the skyscraper (Louis Sullivan, Wright's one-time boss, built the world's first, right here in 1885). Art Deco, Beaux Arts, International, Minimalist, Modern, Prairie School—all the great schools of architecture are represented.

In addition to Sullivan, our guide points out works by Ludwig Mies van der Rohe, Helmut Jahn, Frank Gehry and Eliel Saarinen: The Wrigley Building, the Tribune Tower, Marina City, Merchandise Mart and the Sears Tower. Even New York's Manhattan would have a hard time topping this collection of landmarks.

I'm the only one still standing on the deck in the rain, dripping wet, craning my neck in every direction. I try to envision what Donald Trump's new 90-story towers will do to the skyline when completed in 2008 near the Michigan Avenue bridge.

In one sense, you can thank Mrs. O'Leary's cow for the town's architectural riches. After the tragic 1871 conflagration left 300 dead and 100,000 homeless, Chicago rose from the ashes as the avant-garde city of its day. The most dramatic and accessible recent evidence of that lakefront vision, and the latest proof of Chicago's architectural design muscle, is the new 25-acre Millennium Park along South Michigan Avenue near The Art Institute.

Officially unveiled in 2004, the park is a contemporary masterpiece with an array of sculptures and performance spaces replacing what was a disparate collection of parking lots and unused railroad tracks. The badly needed parking hasn't been eliminated; it's just gone underground.

I'm drawn first to The Crown Fountain created by Spaniard Jaume Plensa. Two 50-foot glass-block towers face each other, spouting water, across a reflecting pool that's just an eighth inch deep. But it's the visages on the towers that mesmerize me: a constantly changing parade of some 1,000 Chicagoans from all walks of life. On this steamy day, youngsters in swimsuits stand under those gigantic faces, squealing in the spray. Wish I could do the same.

Then, there's "The Bean." That's what some Chicagoans affectionately are calling a 66-foot-long, 33-foot-wide jelly-bean-shape sculpture made of seamless stainless steel. Officially, sculptor Anish Kapoor calls his creation *Cloud Gate*, but "The Bean" definitely fits. Like a kid in front of one of those contorting mirrors at a carnival, I view the Chicago skyline—and my own waistline—reflected in all sorts of crazy ways. The 3-year-old standing next to me is just as tickled by what she sees.

Frank Gehry's amazing outdoor band shell, the Jay Pritzker Pavilion, crouches, resembling a huge crablike creature from a *Star Wars* movie. How do builders get steel to bend that way? Draped over the lawn, a huge lattice disguises the theater's sound and lighting devices.

Another Frank Gehry creation, a snake-like walkway, links the new space to Grant Park across Columbus Avenue. As I look over my shoulder, Millennium Park's wondrous sculptures inspire awe from this new perspective, sprawling playfully at the foot of Chicago's signature high-rises.

Lakeshore Drive skirting green parks and sandy beaches

Taste of Illinois

Ike Sewell's Original Chicago-Style Deep-Dish Pizza

Bake this generous pizza in a pan at least 2 inches deep.

Olive oil or cooking oil
1 package active dry yeast
1 cup warm water (110°F to 115°F)
3 to 3½ cups all-purpose flour
⅓ cup cooking oil
½ teaspoon salt
6 ounces bulk mild Italian sausage
12 ounces sliced mozzarella cheese
1 14½-ounce can whole Italian-style tomatoes, drained and cut up
1 tablespoon snipped fresh oregano or 1 teaspoon dried oregano, crushed
1 tablespoon snipped fresh basil or 1 teaspoon dried basil, crushed
¼ cup grated Parmesan cheese or Romano cheese
Sliced mushrooms or chopped green sweet pepper (optional)

Generously grease a heavy 10x2-inch round cake pan or 10-inch springform pan with olive oil or cooking oil and set aside.

For crust: In a large mixing bowl, dissolve yeast in the 1 cup warm water. Let stand for 5 minutes. Stir in 1½ cups of the flour, the ⅓ cup cooking oil and salt. Beat with an electric mixer on low speed for 30 seconds, scraping the bowl constantly. Beat for 2 minutes on high speed, scraping the bowl frequently. Using a wooden spoon, stir in as much of the remaining flour as you can.

Cover; let rise in a warm place until double (50 to 60 minutes). Punch down. Cover; let rest for 5 minutes.

No. 1 Chicago Dish

Turn dough into prepared pan. Using oiled hands, press and spread the dough evenly over bottom and 1½ inches up the side of pan. Cover; let rise in a warm place until nearly double (30 to 35 minutes).

For meat filling: In a medium skillet, cook Italian sausage until meat is brown. Drain fat. Pat with paper towels to remove additional fat.

To assemble: Arrange mozzarella cheese over dough. Spoon meat filling and tomatoes over cheese. Top with oregano and basil. Sprinkle with Parmesan cheese.

Bake in a 500° oven for 20 to 25 minutes or until edges of crust are crisp and golden brown and the filling is hot. If you like, sprinkle the pizza with sliced mushrooms or chopped green pepper during the last few minutes of baking time. If necessary, cover crust with foil the last 10 minutes of baking to prevent overbrowning. Cool on a wire rack for 10 minutes. If using, remove side of springform pan. Cut into wedges. Makes 6 to 8 servings.

I can't leave my favorite big city without a taste of one of its specialties: a doughy, cheesy pan of deep-dish Chicago pizza. It's waiting at Pizzeria Uno in the neighborhood known as River North, west of the Magnificent Mile. When I want a carb fix in Chicago, this is where I head. Texan Ike Sewell, eager to start a business serving the pizza he'd learned to love in Italy during World War II, founded the place when he came to Chicago in 1943. Sewell died in 1990, but his pizzeria, nearly engulfed by high-rises and parking lots, does a multimillion-dollar business. There's also Pizzeria Due right down the street, and 185 Uno franchises around the globe. It's not very big, this high altar of the deep-dish cult: a bar, booths and small tables for about 75 diners. The requisite old-time Chicago photos (Al Capone, Comiskey Park, Loop scenes) adorn the green walls.

The restaurant serves about 500 pizzas on an average day. That's sixteen 50-pound boxes of mozzarella and almost 20 huge batches of yeast dough fermenting in enormous cylindrical pots. Worldwide, Uno goes through 7 million pounds of mozzarella and 1 million pounds of sausage annually. Part of the secret, I learn, is the two ovens that bake every pizza for a total of 45 minutes to one hour: one for cooking the doughy crust, the other for burnishing the toppings. Joanne, the cook, splashes some olive oil in the bottom of a round cake-type pan for my sausage and mushroom pizza, smooshes the dough on the bottom and up the sides, then adds mozzarella, Italian sausage, tomatoes, Romano and the final seasonings and toppings. At this point, it's pure torture. I just wanna eat!

I particularly like one of the slogans I see posted over the bar: "Fill the glass if it's empty; empty the glass if it's full. Never leave it empty, and never leave it full." As I exit through the vestibule, other patient "pilgrims" look at me expectantly. They'll wait about an hour. I tease one: "They just ran out!" Not funny, especially when you can smell the yeast and see people inside wiping delectable strings of cheese from their chins. Pizzeria Uno (866/600-8667, www.pizzeriauno.com).

In Lincoln's Footsteps

What propels a man with little formal education, from a poor frontier background, to become possibly the greatest American who ever lived? That question haunts me as I explore the 16th president's Illinois.

Abraham Lincoln landed in the settlement of New Salem in 1831 as a 22-year-old drifter, when a flatboat filled with cargo on its way to New Orleans that he was riding in got hung up on the local gristmill dam. Nearly the entire village turned out to witness the commotion. Lincoln liked what he saw, and New Salem grew to like young Lincoln. He returned to make the settlement his home for six years before he moved approximately 20 miles south to practice law and pursue his political career in then-burgeoning Springfield—the path that eventually led him to the presidency.

Most schoolchildren know the story of Lincoln's log-cabin boyhood in Kentucky and Indiana: how he lost his mother (Nancy Hanks) when he was only nine, and how he read by the light from the log-cabin hearth. At the time Lincoln arrived here as a young man seeking his fortune, this was a frontier village of 25 families on the Illinois prairie. What factors shaped Lincoln's character and fueled his ambitions in New Salem? A thousand historians have asked that question. I'd like to find some clues firsthand.

The hills and woods of the Sangamon River Valley are a visual break from central Illinois' level green cornfields. A wooded path leads to a re-created 1830s village of more than 20 log homes, shops and stores.

The original New Salem had vanished by 1840, supplanted by Petersburg 2½

miles north. During its brief existence, New Salem bustled in a quiet sort of way. Each of the rustic one- to three-room log homes doubled as a family business, it seems: the cooper, the blacksmith, the hatter and the doctor. A one-room Baptist church also housed the village school. The largest structures were the oxen-powered wool-carding mill and the tavern, actually a rustic hotel (37½ cents a night, including a meal; gentlemen slept in the attic loft).

There wasn't much Lincoln *didn't* do in New Salem when he lived here from 1831 to 1837. Farmhand. Whiskey-still fire tender, although he was temperate. Railsplitter. Shopkeeper. Soldier. Postmaster. Surveyor. Legislator. He was well-liked, friendly, funny and hardworking. He had a passion for learning and wanted to advance himself. Shortly after settling here, it's said he walked seven miles north to the Vance farm to acquire a grammar book.

Lincoln was rather shy around women his own age, except, as the legend goes, with Ann Rutledge, who tragically died in 1835 from typhoid fever, leaving him devastated. In one of Lincoln's two unsuccessful general-store ventures (his business partner was a bit fond of the bottle), Lincoln sold dishes, shoes, tools, whiskey and rum, tobacco and cornmeal to area farm families. In the back of one of his stores are the tiny cubbyholes that constituted New Salem's post office. Here, Lincoln took the

liberty of reading his postal customers' incoming newspapers and journals to stay abreast of the outside world.

Charles A. Starling, my guide this afternoon who's dressed as a village man might have been in those days, caught the Lincoln bug as a Boy Scout, often walking the 21-mile trail from New Salem to his family's home in Springfield. Charles pursued a career as a veterinarian, but kept studying Lincoln and later earned an MA in history. Upon retirement, he signed on as an interpreter at New Salem. If you grew up in Springfield, Charles tells me, Lincoln is like a member of your family.

Lincoln worked hard in New Salem, but on Saturdays, he and friends gathered on porches to "set, sip and spit." That is, if Lincoln wasn't himself participating in a wrestling match, footrace, horse race or cockfight. It also was a chance to practice his oratorical and storytelling skills on a tree stump, in front of anybody who cared to listen. I wonder if anyone in the audience had an inkling they were listening to a future president?

Meet Mr. Lincoln

The curving roads of the Sangamon Valley lead me next to Springfield, the capital of Illinois. It's a quiet city, except, I'm reminded, when legislators gather from March until May or later each year. Lincoln arrived in 1837 to practice law. His

(Clockwise, from opposite) "Lincoln's" hat on a Springfield courtroom table. Pottery displayed in the Hill-McNeil store in New Salem. Fritz Klein as Abraham Lincoln. Reenactors near the Lincoln Home in Springfield.

ambition yielded the onetime drifter a prosperous business, a substantial home, a vivacious and attractive wife—Mary Todd—and four sons. Springfield was his home until he and Mary left for the White House in 1861.

Lincoln achieved his upper-middle-class life here by sheer hard work, a passion for education and a deep understanding of human nature. He'd travel for months arguing cases for clients before the circuit court, as it convened in various central Illinois communities. He continued his political career as a legislator and ultimately as a U.S. congressman and president.

Today, Springfield is a comfortable Heartland city of 112,000. The population was only 10,000 when Lincoln left.

Springfield for 23 years, many of them with William H. Herndon. At the office, I meet a man who seems to bring Lincoln to life: Fritz Klein, a star among many Lincoln impersonators across the county.

Fritz's story must be one of the more unusual. He grew up in southern California and was working as a landscaper in Hawaii when he played Lincoln in a Bicentennial amateur production. He was asked to reprise the performance again and again, and finally decided to pursue a career as "Lincoln" right here in Springfield, where he and his wife have raised four children.

It helps the illusion that six-foot-three-inch Fritz looks uncannily like Mr. Lincoln. He uses a few makeup tricks, but the

was a Whig when he first served in the Illinois legislature and U.S. Congress. He delivered his landmark "House Divided" speech here in 1858. And it was here, after his assassination in 1865, that 75,000 citizens filed past his bier for 38 hours.

At Home with the Lincolns

At Lincoln Home National Historic Site near the heart of town (the edge of Springfield in Lincoln's day), I find more clues about the great man and his family life. Mary Lincoln was petite, well-bred, vivacious and opinionated. Yet, she often is characterized as vain, disagreeable and, sometimes, insane. I'm asked to keep in mind that this was a woman who ultimately lost three of her four sons, was maligned for her Confederate family ties and saw her husband murdered. By all accounts, however, the Lincolns were happy here.

A boardwalk leads from the visitors center past picket fences toward the brown-and-green Greek Revival house, part of a four-block historic site that includes 13 homes. Most have been restored on the exterior only, painted the rich colors of the era.

The Lincolns purchased their story-and-a-half home for $1,500 in 1844 and spent approximately $2,000 adding onto it. Eventually, they enlarged it into a handsome two-story. A guide points out the well-researched decorating touches in the parlor. The house is true to the era, although only about 50 items actually belonged to the Lincolns—some china and, upstairs, Mary Lincoln's nighttime commode.

As I write this, Springfield is looking forward to the opening of the $150 million Abraham Lincoln Presidential Library & Museum. Clearly, Springfield and central Illinois take their Lincoln ties seriously. I leave town satisfied that I've picked up at least one clue to the origins of Lincoln's greatness: He came from this place.

> Lincoln achieved his life here through hard work, a passion for education and a deep understanding of human nature.

I'm staying on an upper floor of the Springfield Hilton, by far the tallest building in town at 23 stories. The former Route 66, perhaps America's most fabled highway, runs through the middle of town. Ornate Victorian storefronts not only still stand, but also are carefully maintained. A few funky shops and eateries mingle with traditional businesses along neat downtown sidewalks. Victorian-era Maldaner's restaurant, in a high-ceilinged 1890s building near the Old State Capitol, is the oldest, and I think the best, eatery in town.

Lincoln's presence is simply everywhere in this easy-to-navigate city, and many of the shrines are in close proximity. My first stop is the Lincoln-Herndon Law Office Historic Site just across the plaza from the Old State Capitol. Lincoln practiced law in

classic Lincoln profile is pure Fritz Klein. He's studied Lincoln's writings extensively, and when out of character even plays songs from Lincoln's era on the banjo. Beyond appearance, it's his voice that snags me. Of course, there's no recording of Lincoln speaking, but many wrote about his backwoods inflection ("cheer" instead of chair, "thar" instead of there).

I ask Fritz the same question I've been asking others: What was the source of Lincoln's greatness? Some credit his mother, his innate genius and his determination to learn. Fritz cites still more qualities: Lincoln's pragmatism in pursuit of higher goals, his understanding of human foibles, his deep faith and his genuine humility.

Just across the plaza stands Illinois' Old State Capitol, now a historic site. Lincoln

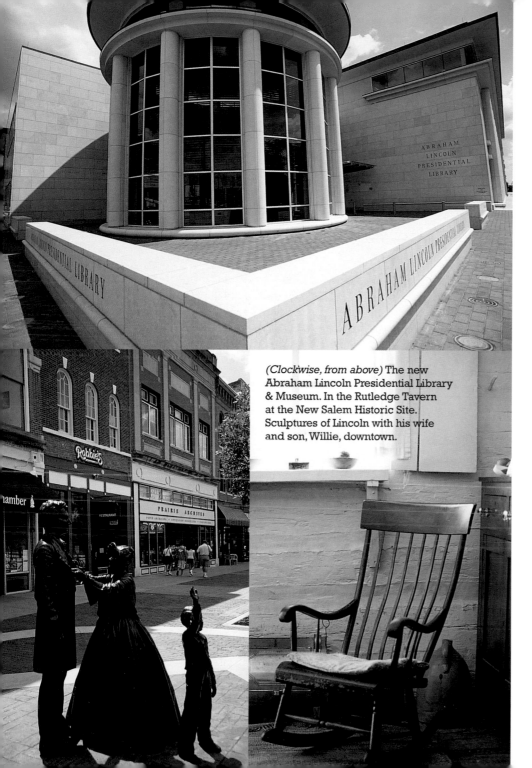

MARIGOLD CITY

Abraham Lincoln wasn't the only great political leader central Illinois gave to America. I find myself on a sunny morning standing beside a flower-encircled statue overlooking the beautiful lagoon at Mineral Springs Park in Pekin, Illinois (population 35,000).

The town is named for China's capital, which apparently is perched at nearly the same latitude on the opposite side of the globe. The most famous native son is eloquent U.S. Senator Everett Dirksen, who died in 1969 at age 73. And the most famous flower is the sunny little marigold.

Here's the story: Everett Dirksen was the son of a local baker. He served Pekin as a councilman and finance commissioner, then became a U.S. Representative (1933–1948) and finally rose to prominence in the U.S. Senate from 1950 to 1969, the final 10 years as minority leader. (It's said young Everett used to practice his legendary oratorical skills expounding to a cow in the Dirksen family barn.) Known as a bipartisan coalition builder, he helped end the filibuster that threatened to block passage of the Civil Rights Act in 1964.

Among Dirksen's many causes was the marigold. He lobbied to have the humble blossom designated as the national flower. Why the marigold? Dirksen likened its hardiness, resilience and diversity to that of the American people.

Dirksen didn't win his marigold campaign, although his spirit lives on in the Pekin Marigold Festival. Since 1972, Pekin has thrown this huge party every September. Proceeds go to local charities. Pekin Area Chamber of Commerce (309/346-2106, www.pekin.net).

(Clockwise, from above) The new Abraham Lincoln Presidential Library & Museum. In the Rutledge Tavern at the New Salem Historic Site. Sculptures of Lincoln with his wife and son, Willie, downtown.

The General's Town

President Ulysses S. Grant is just one colorful chapter in the story of Galena. Once, this northwestern Illinois town was a frontier metropolis. Now it's booming again, thanks to antiques hunters, golfers and history buffs.

I discovered the charm of Galena not as a travel writer, but as a Boy Scout dad accompanying my son, Adam, and about 10,000 other scouts at the U.S. Grant Pilgrimage that's held here every April. That weekend, when it wasn't raining, the temperature was atypically sweltering. We were camping. In spite of the circumstances, I fell in love with Galena.

The town's white church steeples graced the first Christmas-issue cover of *Midwest Living®* in 1987, a best-seller on the newsstands. Over the years, on much quieter return visits during every season, my appreciation of Galena has only grown deeper.

An Enchanting Escape

Back home, Julie and I have a framed series of richly detailed architectural watercolors by local artist Carl Johnson. Each depicts a Galena building or streetscape. Johnson once told me he was a commercial artist in Chicago when he stumbled onto the town in 1969. That visit inspired him to pursue his life's dream of painting watercolors.

Three months later, Johnson and his wife, Marilyn, moved their family here. Since then, his passion has taken him around the globe, painting and sketching the world's most beautiful buildings. After his travels, Johnson returns to Galena and the apartment above his gallery on Main Street. He says: "Every time I come back, I'm still enchanted by this place."

Johnson's love affair with the town is a familiar story. A quiet and secluded farm community 50 years ago, Galena now attracts 1.3 million visitors annually, many of them Chicagoans who own or rent vacation or retirement homes in the area (downtown Chicago is about three hours east). One lure is the rare architectural legacy that energized Carl Johnson. With 85 percent of its buildings on the National Register of Historic Places, the town is a living museum of 19th-century design: Federal, Greek Revival, Gothic Revival, Italianate, Second Empire and Queen Anne.

The community's history began with lead—*galena* in Latin. Native Americans mined the malleable, corrosion-resistant mineral here long before Europeans began settling in the 1820s. Because this area wasn't affected by glaciers, lead and other minerals are closer to the surface and easier to mine. Bullets, gunshot and cannonballs were made from lead. It also was used in pipes, glass and crystal, and even in burial-vault liners.

Just three miles from the Mississippi River, Galena and the river that runs alongside downtown welcomed convoys of riverboats laden with goods and fortune-seekers. Wealth spawned wealth. The mines provided money to build mansions and classic churches that still pepper the hillsides. At one time, 85 percent of the lead mined in the U.S. came from Galena.

Then, things changed. Lumbering and farming of surrounding postcard-pretty Jo Daviess County eroded the hillsides. That, in turn, silted in the Galena River, making it unnavigable for riverboats, which were by then being eclipsed by railroads. Demand for lead declined dramatically after the Civil War. Galena's population, which had peaked at 14,000 in the 1850s, dwindled by more than 10,000 (the current population is 3,500).

As the 20th century unfolded, the nearly forsaken town was so down at its heels that it didn't bother to widen streets or put up new buildings. And that became Galena's salvation. In the 1970s, a preservation-minded mayor, Frank Einsweiler, led a campaign to keep Galena's collection of 19th-century homes and businesses intact. Antiques dealers, bed-and-breakfast owners and artisans began streaming to town. About six miles east, investors built the sprawling, 6,800-acre Galena Territory mega development, which includes Eagle Ridge Resort & Spa.

Today, the Galena area boasts some 50 inns, 189 golf holes, 2,500 guest rooms, and more than 100 shops, including Carl Johnson's gallery. The 1855 DeSoto House Hotel, where Lincoln once spoke from the balcony, has been elegantly refurbished.

As I set out on foot, I'm struck by the irony that this idyllic town, where today's only conflicts seem to arise when parking

(Clockwise, from opposite) Home accessories in one of more than 100 shops found in downtown Galena's historic buildings. Shopping in downtown Galena. Inside the stately, preserved Ulysses S. Grant home. Period homes and churches dotting Galena's steep bluffs.

gets scarce on weekends, supplied the raw material for the Civil War. Galena's most famous citizen would have understood.

Citizen Grant

Ulysses S. Grant didn't grow up here, nor did he live here long, although he's associated with Galena more than with any other town. And Galena certainly remembers U. S. Grant. The home that the town presented to him after his success as a Civil War general has been preserved as a historic site, and Grant Park features a bronze statue of the general with the inscription "Grant, Our Citizen" at its base.

The stately five-bedroom Grant house presides at the top of Bouthillier Street, overlooking the rambling river, downtown Galena and the steeples rising from the bluff on the opposite side of the valley. Built in 1860, the red brick Italianate with white roof brackets and trim was purchased for $2,500 and presented, completely furnished, to Grant in 1865, when he returned from the Civil War. The general was welcomed by 25,000 wildly cheering admirers and a triumphal arch.

The future president first arrived in Galena in 1860 at the age of 32, a seeming failure. He'd attended West Point and served 15 years in the U.S. Army, which included service during the Mexican War. In St. Louis in 1848, he married Julia Dent, the love of his life. They had four children. Despondent over being separated from his family, Grant resigned his captain's commission and attempted several unsuccessful careers, including farming and real estate, before joining his father and brothers in Galena. During his Galena interlude, Grant traveled a wide area for his family's leather-goods business.

When the Civil War came in the spring of 1861, Grant helped train troops here and left for Springfield with an Illinois infantry regiment. With the backing of his commander-in-chief, fellow Illinoisian Abraham Lincoln, Grant rose quickly to the rank of major general, one of nine Civil War generals from Galena. In April 1865, he accepted Lee's surrender at Appomattox and returned to his Galena welcome.

Then came the presidency and more adulation, followed by criticism. Grant ran his 1868 presidential campaign from the DeSoto House Hotel. A hard-drinking cigar smoker, he went on to the White House for eight scandal-tainted years. Then, the Grants made an astonishing 29-country global tour and settled in the New York City area. He visited Galena occasionally, for the last time in 1880.

His Galena home has light butternut and maple woodwork, understated trimmings for the style of the era. Items from the family's world tour still decorate the rooms: an urn from Yokohama, Japan; vases from Bulgaria; a painting from Mexico. In Grant's study, I see his personal cigar stand.

From the front porch, I survey a view Grant reportedly loved: down the valley to the placid Galena River, toward the hillside churches and homes on the other side. I'm told that Grant used this home as a retreat, similar to presidents today who find refuge at Camp David.

Mark Twain encouraged Grant, who'd suffered financial reverses, to write an autobiography. He completed his still-praised *Memoirs* in June 1885 and died the following month, after an agonizing battle with throat cancer (blame the cigars). In 1897, Grant's tomb was dedicated in New York City, with one million people attending, including President McKinley. When Julia died in 1902, Grant's heirs deeded the house to the town.

His tarnished presidency notwithstanding, "Grant was a quiet man with a reputation for getting things done," Terry Miller, the manager here, tells me. It's an epitaph that, I suspect, would have pleased Galena's most famous citizen.

DeSoto House Hotel

Fanciful
Belvedere
Mansion

Memorial in
Grant Park

More Favorites

BISHOP HILL

Swedish roots run deep in this western Illinois colony (about 30 miles southeast of the Quad Cities) founded more than 150 years ago by 1,200 religious dissidents from Sweden. Before disbanding in 1861, the colony was the largest of its kind in the U.S.

You can imagine you've returned to the mid-1800s along the streets of this once-thriving community. At the Heritage Museum in the 1853 Steeple Building, a film details the colony's history. Pick up a free brochure to guide you on a walking tour. On the lower level of the huge Colony Church, visitors can peek into little apartments of early settlers. At the Bishop Hill Museum, a gallery displays artist Olof Krans' paintings of village scenes and portraits of residents.

Costumed interpreters, some descendants of original settlers, welcome visitors to restored buildings, many facing the shaded town square. Swedish crafts and baked goods fill small shops. Bishop Hill (309/927-3345, bishophill.com).

NAUVOO

Although the Mormons who built this village headed west, their spirit lingers in Old Nauvoo, down the hill from Main Street in this Mississippi River town of 1,100. At the imposing, modern visitors center, a film recounts the restoration of some two dozen buildings in what once was home to some 20,000 residents. Guides dressed in mid-1800s costumes lead tours.

The towering limestone Mormon temple that once loomed above the river has been rebuilt at Temple Square, on the site where it burned years ago. Adjacent to the temple, a handful of antiques shops and specialty boutiques extends along Mulholland Street, downtown's main thoroughfare. Nauvoo Tourism (877/628-8661, beautifulnauvoo.com).

QUAD CITIES

Linked by the Mississippi, this sprawling metropolitan area of 400,000 is defined by four cities: Rock Island and Moline in Illinois, and Davenport and Bettendorf in Iowa. Along the riverbanks, parks and paths for hiking and biking connect landmarks and attractions. Barges, pleasure craft and three glittering casino boats share the broad channel.

Gardens surround the Quad City Botanical Center's seven-story conservatory along the Rock Island riverfront. Nearby, you can explore the eight-block Arts and Entertainment District.

Parklike John Deere Commons follows the river in Moline. The striking John Deere Pavilion houses vintage and modern machinery and hands-on exhibits. Stop at the nearby Collectors Center, a replica of a 1950s Deere dealership. Nearby, restaurants and pubs fill 1880s buildings around the Mark, a concert and sports arena.

In Davenport, visitors head for galleries, eateries and shops in the 1830s Village of East Davenport. On Museum Hill, tour the hands-on Putnam Museum of History and Natural Science.

Visitors of all ages love Bettendorf's fanciful Family Museum of Arts and Science, part of a $12 million project that includes a cultural arts center. Quad Cities Convention & Visitors Bureau (800/747-7800, visitquadcities.com).

Travel Journal

CLASSIC CHICAGO

Visitors find more of almost everything in the nation's third largest city, including world-class museums and attractions, top-notch performing arts and cultural institutions, acclaimed restaurants and great shopping. More information: Chicago Office of Tourism (877/244-2246, 877chicago.com).

Chicago Greeters Program City-wise locals sharing their knowledge and love of the city, showing visitors 25 different neighborhoods, and basing tours on 40 different themes, from sports and music to shopping or architecture. Free, limited to six guests each, lasting two to four hours and using public transportation (CTA transit card provided). All tours originating at the Chicago Office of Tourism at the Chicago Cultural Center Visitor Center. Allow two weeks to preregister (312/744-8000).

Featured Stops

Architecture River Cruise Narrated river cruise spotlighting more than 50 architecturally significant sites. Ticket charge. Walking, bus and bicycle tours also available. Chicago Architecture Foundation (312/922-3432).

The Art Institute of Chicago One of the world's leading art museums, with more than 300,000 works. Donation suggested (312/443-3600).

Beyond the Ivy A rooftop view of the Cubs from across the street over the third-baseline fence. Beverages and grilled sandwiches (847/825-8686, ext. 12).

Erwin, an American Café Unforgettable food featuring the freshest ingredients and inventive twists on classic dishes (773/528-7200).

Frank Lloyd Wright Home and Studio The home where the famous architect lived and worked from 1889 to 1909 in Oak Park (10 miles west of the Loop). Admission charged (708/848-1976).

Oak Park Besides the Home and Studio, two dozen other Wright-designed homes and buildings; Ernest Hemingway Birthplace and Museum, the Victorian-style home where the Nobel Prize-winning author spent his early years; art galleries, an eclectic mix of shops and a variety of restaurants. Oak Park Area Convention & Visitors Bureau (888/625-7275, visitoakpark.com).

InterContinental Chicago With a Byzantine-lavish indoor pool, located along the Magnificent Mile. $$$$ (312/944-4100).

John Hancock Observatory Atop the John Hancock Center along North Michigan Avenue, 94th-floor views of up to 80 miles, including four states, plus Chicago's only open-air skywalk. Admission charged (888/875-8439).

Millennium Park Opened in 2004, 24½-acre area in Grant Park, with a Frank Gehry-designed 4,000-seat outdoor performance pavilion, sculpture collection by acclaimed artists, landscaped promenade and fountain with water cascading from two 50-foot-high glass-block towers, ice-skating rink in winter, and the award-winning Park Grill Restaurant (312/742-1168).

Museum of Science and Industry Compelling collections and exhibits spanning a maze of tiers and balconies at this popular museum (seven miles south of downtown). Opening in spring 2005, the U-505, a relocated and restored 700-ton German submarine captured on June 4, 1944, off the coast of Africa, forming the centerpiece of an underground exhibit that immerses visitors in the story of the sub's capture by the U.S. Navy. Other top exhibits: the Great Train Story, a 3,500-square-foot dynamic model-train display; the Coal Mine, taking visitors down 50 feet in a real hoist to the bottom of a mineshaft. Admission charged (800/468-6674).

Wrigley Field North Side landmark that's home to the Chicago Cubs. Built in 1914, old-fashioned field with ivy-covered outfield walls with no advertising, a hand-operated scoreboard and a statue of Harry Caray, the Cubs' late, legendary broadcaster (773/404-2827).

More Great Stops

Museum Campus A parklike space along Lake Michigan surrounding the Field Museum, John G. Shedd Aquarium and Adler Planetarium & Astronomy Museum, each among the world's best of its kind. Admission charged at each. Field Museum (312/922-9410). Shedd Aquarium (312/939-2438). Adler Planetarium (312/922-7827).

Navy Pier A former military dock, now a mile-long complex of shops, restaurants and attractions jutting into Lake Michigan near the southern end of the Magnificent Mile. Highlights including an 18-hole miniature golf course, an amusement park with a 15-story-high Ferris wheel, lakeside dining, the Chicago Children's Museum and the Chicago Shakespeare Theater. Concerts, plays and other events throughout the year (312/595-7437).

Shopping

Magnificent Mile More than 400 shops and boutiques, plus some 200 restaurants and 50 hotels, along flower-lined North Michigan Avenue north of the Chicago River. Also, five high-rise shopping malls, anchored by top retailers such as Bloomingdale's, Saks Fifth Avenue and Nordstrom (312/642-3570).

State Street In the downtown Loop area, Chicago's original top shopping district anchored by Carson Pirie Scott and the flagship 11-story Marshall Field's. Plus independent bookstores, discount outlets, galleries and retail giants including Old Navy (312/782-9160).

Lodging

Hotels in Chicago, especially downtown, tend to book up early and cost more. Be sure to ask about packages and discounts. Parking also is expensive.

Embassy Suites Downtown Lakefront Convenient location between the Magnificent Mile and Navy Pier, with family-friendly suites and full breakfast. $$$$ (866/866-8094).

Hotel Allegro In the Loop, a renovated landmark blending a vibrant color scheme with original Art Deco design. $$$–$$$$ (866/672-6143).

Dining

The Berghoff Family-owned and -operated for more than 100 years. Both traditional German fare and contemporary cuisine, from Wiener Schnitzel and sauerbraten to ahi tuna and Asian pear salad. In-house bakery featuring European-style desserts and the Berghoff's rye and brewers breads (312/427-3170).

Frontera Grill Authentic Mexican cuisine prepared by acclaimed chef Rick Bayless. Ingredients often organic and custom-grown (312/661-1434).

Gino's East Downtown Famous deep-dish pizza made by hand and loaded with fresh ingredients (312/943-1124).

Gold Coast Dogs For classic Chicago-style hot dogs topped with bright green relish and a sprinkling of celery salt (312/578-1133). Several locations throughout the city and suburbs.

Harry Caray's Restaurant Named for the late Hall of Fame baseball announcer, legendary Italian steak house serving the finest prime, aged steaks and chops in a truly warm Chicago atmosphere (312/828-0966).

Heaven on Seven Tasty gumbo and Cajun and Creole favorites in a lively setting. On the Magnificent Mile (312/280-7774), in the Loop, Wrigleyville and Naperville.

Shaw's Crab House Chicago's premier seafood restaurant, really two restaurants in one: The Oyster Bar featuring regional oysters on the half shell, clams, lobster and crab dishes in a casual setting; the Main Dining Room, serving more than 40 fresh seafood entrées, as well as chicken, prime steaks and pasta dishes (312/527-2722).

IN LINCOLN'S FOOTSTEPS

Springfield, the Prairie State's capital, was Abraham Lincoln's home for 24 years. Today, this city of 112,000 people in central Illinois preserves the 16th president's legacy with museums and carefully restored historic sites. Downtown, 33 outdoor interpretive exhibits provide a glimpse of what the city was like during Lincoln's time. The exhibits, called "Here I Have Lived," are part of the "Looking for Lincoln" tourism program, which weaves together Lincoln-related sites and attractions throughout central Illinois. Currently, 12 communities participate in the multifaceted project. More project information: lookingforlincoln.com. More Springfield information: Springfield Convention & Visitors Bureau (800/545-7300, visitspringfieldillinois.com).

Featured Stops

Lincoln-Herndon Law Offices Now a historic site, a brick building downtown where Abraham Lincoln practiced law from 1843 to 1852, with William Herndon becoming his partner in 1844 (217/785-7960).

Lincoln Home National Historic Site Two-story home, the only one that the Lincolns ever owned, where the family lived from 1844 to1861, located in a restored historic neighborhood. Authentically furnished as an upper-middle-class home of the period, with horsehair-upholstered furniture, carpets, rich wallpaper designs, elaborate candelabra on

The InterContinental Chicago

the mantel and portraits of George and Martha Washington on the wall. Some 50 items in the home authenticated as belonging to the Lincolns. Free tickets required; available at the Lincoln Home Visitor Center (217/492-4241, ext. 221).

Lincoln's New Salem State Historic Site Village near Petersburg re-creating young Lincoln's 1830s town (20 miles northwest of Springfield). Costumed interpreters chronicling frontier life, and self-guided walking tours through a tavern, country store, one-room school and timbered houses. Closed Mondays and Tuesdays (217/632-4000).

Maldaner's A Springfield institution since 1884, serving classic American fare such as pistachio-crusted wild king salmon and grilled lamb chops. At lunch, a local signature, the unbelievably rich Horseshoe sandwich. An elegantly decorated upstairs dining room with Victorian-era globe lights. Casual downstairs dining room, with a high tin ceiling, etched glass and original walnut wainscoting creating a warm, historic atmosphere (217/522-4313).

More Great Stops

Dana-Thomas House A 1904 Prairie-style mansion designed by Frank Lloyd Wright. Original art-glass doors, light fixtures and furniture in a 35-room, 12,000-square-foot house. One-hour guided walking tour; donation suggested. Closed Mondays and Tuesdays (217/782-6776).

Illinois State Capitol Opened in 1877, domed building with elaborate murals, paintings and several different kinds of marble. Free tours weekdays on the half hour, and weekends on the hour (217/789-2360).

Abraham Lincoln Presidential Library & Museum Library with the world's largest collection of documents related to Lincoln's life. Scheduled to open in the spring of 2005, Lincoln museum with all sorts of interactive exhibits and multimedia programs chronicling

the 16th president's life. The library and museum, located across from each other near the Old State Capitol, making up the dramatic new center consolidating a trove of some 12 million items including books, artifacts and documents from the era. For example: the Gettysburg Address penned in Lincoln's own hand, and re-creations of scenes in Lincoln's boyhood log home, the Cabinet room at the White House as it looked in Lincoln's day, the box at Ford's Theatre where Lincoln was shot and the Old State Capitol when Lincoln laid there in state. Library (217/558-8844). Museum (217/558-8882).

Lincoln Tomb State Historic Site A towering obelisk and statuary made from melted-down Civil War bronze cannons marking the graves of Lincoln and his entire family (except for his son, Robert, who is buried at Arlington National Cemetery). The nose on the oversize bust of Lincoln in front of the monument has been rubbed bright, a local good-luck tradition. Lincoln had wanted to return in death to his beloved Springfield, where more than 300,000 people annually visit his tomb (217/782-2717).

Old State Capitol Where Lincoln delivered his famous 1858 "House Divided" speech, tried cases before the Supreme Court and studied in the law library. Built in 1839 of a locally quarried, very porous dolomite. With the completion of a new, domed capitol building just down the street in 1876, the original Springfield statehouse served for almost a century as the Sangamon County Courthouse. In 1970, a new courthouse came along and the old building was dismantled stone by stone and returned to its original form (217/785-7960).

Shopping

Flowers With Love Animated scenes of Victorian life on the lower level, plus gifts (217/787-3337).

Prairie Archives Rare and used books, postcards, autographs, records, comics and collectibles (217/522-9742).

Recycled Records More than 75,000 new and used CDs, cassette tapes, vinyl records and VHS tapes (217/522-5122).

Tinsley Dry Goods Lincoln memorabilia and paintings of historic central Illinois landmarks (217/525-1825).

Lodging

In and around the Springfield area, standard hotels and motel chains, including Hampton Inn, Red Roof Inn and Holiday Inn.

The Inn at 835 A landmark apartment house transformed into an elegant bed and breakfast. $$$ (217/523-4466).

Horseshoe sandwich at Maldaner's, Springfield

Mansion View Inn & Suites Motel rooms and suites in a refurbished brick inn across the street from the governor's residence. $–$$ (217/544-7411).

Renaissance Springfield Hotel Full-service hotel with many amenities and an indoor pool. $$$ (217/544-8800).

Springfield Hilton Recently renovated modern hotel, with complimentary full breakfast buffet. $$ (217/789-1530).

Dining

Café Brio Serving inventive Caribbean and Mexican cuisine in a historic brick building downtown (217/544-0574).

Sebastian's Hideout Mediterranean fare such as grilled pork with polenta, as well as steaks and seafood (217/789-8988).

THE GENERAL'S TOWN

Galena is carved into the bluffs above the serene Galena River, not far from the Mississippi River (about 80 miles west of Rockford). In the 1800s, lead mining fueled the town's rapid growth. Today, the historic community is a mecca for artists and shoppers alike. Vintage brick buildings line Main Street, and white-steepled churches and ornate Victorian homes look down from the surrounding hillsides. More information: Galena/Jo Daviess (pronounced Davis) County Convention & Visitors Bureau (800/747-9377, galena.org).

Featured Stops

Carl Johnson Gallery For watercolors, pen-and-ink drawings and more (815/777-1222).

Main Street Galena With more than 100 art galleries, specialty shops and cafes in restored 19th-century buildings along eight-block-long Main Street. Stores stocking the latest home accessories, local artists' works and antiques. Also, inviting coffee shops and a variety of restaurants serving everything from pizza to upscale bistro fare. Galena/Jo Daviess County & Visitors Bureau (800/747-9377, galena.org).

Ulysses S. Grant Home State Historic Site Two-story brick Italianate structure that was Ulysses S. Grant's home from 1865 until 1880, with personal and family possessions, as well as china and silver from the Grant White House. Open Wednesdays–Sundays. Donation suggested (815/777-3310).

More Great Stops

Belvedere Mansion A 22-room, 1857 Italianate mansion featuring opulent Victorian-era furnishings and elaborate furniture from the estate of the late pianist Liberace, including the green draperies from *Gone With the Wind*. Admission charged (815/777-0747).

DeSoto House Hotel Elegant, three-story historic brick hotel along Main Street, where notables stayed and Abraham Lincoln spoke

Interpreters at New Salem

from a balcony. A graceful curving stairway leading from the lobby to 55 guest rooms with an old-time ambience. $–$$$$; ask about packages (800/343-6562).

Eagle Ridge Resort & Spa A full-service resort sprawling across 6,800 acres amid the wooded hills of northwestern Illinois (six miles east of Galena). With four championship golf courses, two restaurants and a spa. Accommodations including 80 lodge rooms and 340 vacation homes and condominiums. Activities and facilities including bicycling, swimming, spa, horseback riding, Camp Eagle for kids, boating and skiing. Inn rooms: $$$–$$$$. One- to eight-bedroom homes and villas: $$$–$$$$. Ask about packages (800/892-2269).

Galena/Jo Daviess County Historical Society and Museum In an 1858 Italianate mansion, with exhibits, artifacts and photographs about lead mining, steamboating, the Civil War, Ulysses S. Grant and other chapters in the Galena story. Admission charged (815/777-9129).

Shopping

Galena's Kandy Kitchen Chocolates made by hand, plus some 100 varieties of hard candies, jelly beans, taffy and licorice, in a shop where tin ceilings and antique candy cases remind you of yesteryear (815/777-0241).

Karen's Neat Stuff Three floors in two buildings packed with all sorts of collectibles, furnishings, plus Christmas trimmings and decorations (815/777-0911).

Main Street Fine Books & Manuscripts Rare editions, autographs, maps, historic documents and more (815/777-3749).

Poopsie's Pottery, decorative glass and all sorts of whimsical home accessories (888/425-3621).

Lodging

Chestnut Mountain Resort A casual, family-friendly resort on a wooded palisade overlooking the Mississippi River (eight miles southeast of Galena). With 19 downhill ski runs, ski lessons, indoor pool and an array of activities. $$–$$$; ask about packages (800/397-1320).

Allen's Log Cabin Guest House Five original 1830s cabins, with wood-burning fireplaces and whirlpool tubs (just west of Galena). $$$–$$$$ (815/777-4777).

The Victorian Mansion Authentically furnished 1856 Italianate bed and breakfast with eight guest rooms. $$$–$$$$; ask about packages (888/815-6768).

Dining

Benjamin's For pizza, sandwiches and bistro dining, plus live music (815/777-0467).

Fried Green Tomatoes Upscale Italian dining with inventive drinks and elegant desserts in a historic downtown location (815/777-3938).

Luna Blu Restaurant Featuring Mediterranean cuisine (815/777-0033).

Perry Street Brasserie With a gold-medal-winning European master chef who's cooked for royalty and celebrities. Local and/or organic products used (815/777-3773). ∎

Indiana

■ What's a Hoosier, anyway? I'm advised I can pick from about 30 different stories. Is the term derived from the frontiersman's greeting of "Who's yere?" Or from an English word for hill people? Or from (ugh) a post-brawl "Whose ear?" For me, after traveling across Indiana for years, Hoosier has come to be synonymous with friendly, down-to-earth people who always seem ready with a warm welcome—just like Midwesterners in general. This is a north-south sort of state. There are more farms and cities in the northern two-thirds. The southern third is hilly, forested and less populated. And at the state's hospitable heart is a vibrant metropolis as the capital. Whether you're a Hoosier or not, you'll feel right at home in Indiana.

A Brown County back road

Winning Indy

The Indianapolis Motor Speedway brings droves of visitors to Indiana's capital. But my favorite places to visit here are situated right downtown—in this welcoming city's reenergized heart.

Indianapolis is America's largest city not on a navigable waterway. Developers tried to rectify that flaw with limited success in the 1830s, when they built the Indiana Central Canal. That waterway, renovated and beautifully landscaped, has been reborn. Almost in the shadow of the capitol, the new Circle Centre mall and the revitalized business district, the canal is the spine of White River State Park and a dazzling lineup of top-notch attractions: the Indianapolis Zoo and White River Gardens, Indiana State Museum, IMAX theater, NCAA Hall of Champions, Eiteljorg Museum of American Indians and Western Art, Victory Field and the Congressional Medal of Honor Memorial.

White River Renaissance

The Indiana General Assembly kicked off this visionary project in 1979, when the area was a gritty industrial district with a meat-packing plant and flour and paper mills. When I visited in 1988, the Indianapolis Zoo was the first new feature in the lineup. I can't wait to explore the most recent addition, the new state museum. Today, although throngs of kids on summer outings with their parents flow through here, the park and its attractions are so well-planned and spread out that it doesn't feel crowded.

Experiencing all the attractions could easily consume a week, but I'm determined to hit the highlights in a couple of days.

First stop: the Indianapolis Zoo. Some 350 species of animals living in five areas that the zoologists call biomes thrive in this state-of-the-art facility. Almost 8,000 plants are scattered throughout the 64 acres, as are habitats for animals from dolphins to white rhinos. I find myself eyeball-to-eyeball with a blue-tongued skink lizard from Australia. He seems to handle the confrontation much better than I do.

There's more to see at White River Gardens next door. I step carefully—very carefully—through two sets of doorways at the Hilbert Conservatory, home during the summer to thousands of butterflies. They're everywhere: over me, around me and on me. A brochure helps identify common morphos, zebra longwings and others.

Past and present, science, art and culture mingle at the new Indiana State Museum nearby. High school basketball. Popcorn. Hoagie Carmichael. More than 400,000 artifacts in all. A massive hands-on exhibit tells the story of Indiana limestone, which is used around the world in many famous structures, including the Empire State Building and the Pentagon.

It's lunchtime, so I sample the signature Creamy Velvet Chicken Soup in the Crossroads Café and step into the re-created L. S. Ayres Department Store Tea Room (circa 1905), which has been reproduced down to the china, silver and period views visible in the windows. Outside, a steam-powered clock marks the quarter-hour by playing the first nine notes of "Back Home Again in Indiana" on eight brass whistles.

College athletes are the stars in the park's NCAA Hall of Champions. Exhibits explain the original mission of the now Indy-based NCAA—football safety in the days before helmets. Visitors can shoot hoops in a re-created 1930s gym, and explore exhibits and three theaters that celebrate 23 sports in all, from football and basketball to riflery.

The park's Eiteljorg Museum puzzles me. What's a showcase for Western art doing in Indianapolis, anyway? I'm told that late Indianapolis businessman Harrison Eiteljorg traveled the West for his coal-mining interests. The museum is a compelling contemporary display of his collections.

At the Congressional Medal of Honor Memorial, I count 27 curved glass walls, each seven to 10 feet tall, etched with the names of more than 3,400 Americans from all states who have been honored, dating to the Civil War. Via recordings, stirring tales of valor are retold throughout the day.

The canal connects all these attractions like a cool, silvery ribbon, looking more inviting as the afternoon wears on. I join the pedal boaters lazily gliding past, looking up at the downtown skyline. Despite being one of the region's largest metropolitan areas, Indianapolis exudes a friendly, welcoming air. This park is an important reason why.

(*Clockwise, from opposite*) A zebra longwing butterfly in the White River Gardens Hilbert Conservatory. Soldiers and Sailors Monument in the circle downtown. On the White River Canal. Daring to pet a boa constrictor at the Indianapolis Zoo.

The Hoosier Poet

I feel more of the city's gracious and welcoming spirit in Lockerbie Square, a National Historic District, just blocks from downtown, surrounding the 1872 James Whitcomb Riley Museum Home. The quiet, compact neighborhood is a shady mix of residential and commercial buildings, grand brick homes and Victorian cottages.

Residents—coffee mugs in hand—walk dogs, and bicyclists bounce over the cobblestone street in front of the Riley home, a stately brick neo-Italianate. The poet lived there for more than two decades and died in 1916.

No Midwest state reveres a poet as Indiana does Riley, who was raised in Greenfield (15 miles east of Indianapolis). He wrote more than 1,000 poems "for the child in all of us," most of them employing a distinctively Hoosier country dialect. Ever heard of "Little Orphant Annie"? Or, "When the Frost is on the Punkin"?

Riley's father wanted him to go into law, but a Tom Sawyer-like streak spurred him to travel his home state with a medicine show instead. Later, the young wanderer tried his hand at poetry. By the early 1900s, Riley was a star on the Chautauqua circuit, reading aloud his heartwarming poems. He even appeared at Carnegie Hall in New York City, and counted Mark Twain among his literary friends.

When Riley died, more than 35,000 people filed past his bier for some six hours at the state capitol. That's how much Indiana loved James Whitcomb Riley. And Riley loved Lockerbie Street.

The poet penned his famous verse about Lockerbie years before he found himself living here. The home was owned by friends, Major and Mrs. Charles L. Holstein. Officially, Riley was a paying guest. Twice spurned by sweethearts, the lifelong bachelor virtually was adopted by the Holsteins.

A poet's spirit at the Riley Museum Home

The home, with its trademark green-striped awning over the entry, is a treasure in its own right, said to be America's finest late-Victorian home open to the public. It's never changed hands since he lived there.

Ornate, high-ceilinged rooms contain exquisite furnishings and rich fabrics, now-rare butternut woodwork, and extensive plasterwork and decorative painting. I also sense that people really lived here. In his bedroom at the head of the stairs, Riley's cane and hat lie on the bed.

I pick up a collection of Riley's poems and reread his tribute to this neighborhood. The verse ends with these lines:

> *For no language could frame*
> *and no lips could repeat*
> *My rhyme-haunted raptures*
> *of Lockerbie Street.*

Taste of Indiana

Creamy Velvet Chicken Soup
Indiana State Museum, Indianapolis

⅓ cup butter or margarine
⅓ cup all-purpose flour
⅛ teaspoon ground white pepper
3 cups chicken broth
⅓ cup half-and-half or light cream
⅓ cup milk
1½ cups finely chopped, cooked
     chicken

In a medium saucepan, melt butter. Stir in flour and white pepper. Stir in chicken broth, half-and-half and milk. Cook and stir over medium heat until mixture is thickened and bubbly. Cook and stir for 1 minute more. Stir in chicken; heat through. Serve immediately. Makes 4 servings.

PRIME CUTS

Indianapolis has its share of long-standing favorite restaurants, but in my book, one of them ranks in a class by itself. Ask NFL and NBA stars and racecar drivers if they know St. Elmo Steak House in Indy. Or ask homegrown celebrities such as David Letterman, Tommy Hilfiger and Jane Pauley. Once, at California's tony Spago restaurant in Beverly Hills, I asked celebrity chef-owner Wolfgang Puck if he'd ever dined at St. Elmo when he was a sous chef in Indianapolis. "I would have loved to have eaten there, but I couldn't afford it!" he said, laughing.

Joe Stahr opened St. Elmo Steak House in 1902 in the vintage storefront where it still resides. Where does the unusual name come from? Joe was a former seaman who called upon St. Elmo, the patron saint of sailors, for luck. The restaurant is beside an alleyway along South Illinois Street, just off Monument Circle, almost in the shadow of the city's Soldiers and Sailors Monument, which was dedicated in the same year.

I feel I'm stepping into that Delmonico's scene from *Hello, Dolly!* as I pass the grand bar and bustling kitchen area on my way to the restaurant's original dining room, which has been expanded over the years. It's all a whir of white tablecloths, waiters in black suits, and nostalgic photos of downtown and the hundreds of celebrities who've dined here. Brass fittings, mahogany paneling and Tiffany lighting fixtures enhance the turn-of-the-last-century atmosphere.

St. Elmo has witnessed its share of ups and downs over its 103 years. During World War II, the owners patriotically opened to serve breakfast to thousands of troops passing through Union Station nearby. Then, downtown Indy faltered, and so did St. Elmo. Now, co-owner Craig Huse says he's riding a wave of

redevelopment that translates into a whole lot of steaks: 3,500 per week to be precise; 65 tons of beef a year.

Salvadore, the waiter, takes my order: filet mignon, medium rare. And, of course, shrimp cocktail. St. Elmo added shrimp cocktail to the menu in 1947, and it's been the star ever since. In fact, 760,000 big, juicy shrimp show up on ice at St. Elmo tables each year. What's the secret to the industrial-strength, eye-crossing sauce that everyone remembers?

"Freshly ground horseradish. That's all I'll tell you," Craig says, with a mysterious smile. Then my host takes me downstairs to Indiana's largest wine cellar, where we make our selection from among 20,000 bottles (mostly reds, of course).

The finale comes over coffee. The packed room falls silent. Salvadore, who's been with St. Elmo 18 years, piles stacks of plates, saucers, glasses, coffee cups and serving trays atop our table. Trancelike with intensity, he kneels, grabs the tablecloth and—whoosh!—yanks it off without so much as rattling a wineglass. The trick? "Just believe you can do it. Then, pull fast, hard and downward," Salvadore says triumphantly. St. Elmo Steak House (317/635-0636).

Pretty as a Picture

Stands of trees line the winding roads, crowd a hilly landscape and all but hide log cabins, covered bridges and split-rail fences. No wonder an artists' colony has thrived for more than a century in Brown County.

The moments I've cherished most as editor-in-chief of *Midwest Living®* have been spent driving down winding country lanes on sunny days, far from any interstate highways, feeling half lost and half found, without another person or car in sight.

It's that way for me in Brown County. Somehow, the glaciers that plowed so much of Indiana and the Midwest took a detour here. After an hour's drive south from Indianapolis, hills suddenly erupt near Nashville, the only town of size. Hardwoods—maple, oak, poplar, beech, hickory, dogwood, redbud, sassafras, sumac—the size of mini skyscrapers make canyons of the roadways. Autumn must be an absolute foliage riot here.

Country Roads

Because state and federal parklands and forests claim more than half of Brown County, it remains blessedly undeveloped outside Nashville, the county seat. In fact, you'll find only three stoplights in the entire county, and the tallest building here is three stories. No billboards block the views, and even lighted signs are rare.

Twisting roads wend past rustic log homes, new and old, nestled into leafy glades. Poor soil means farming never flourished here, not even orchards. The terrain also made carving roads and rail lines difficult. So Brown County was passed over, until the area brought new types of settler: artists and craftspeople. Tourists followed. Now, it's a natural treasure just 55 miles south of Indianapolis.

The inspiring setting began attracting artists more than a century ago. Then came the creative rush derived from living and working around other artists. The result was stunning landscapes, still lifes and portraits of the simple folk who lived in these hills by artists who lived among them. Add to all that pottery, glassware, quilts and other crafts. An artists' colony has thrived here since.

I drive past road signs heralding places such as Bean Blossom, Gnaw Bone, Bear Wallow Hill and Greasy Creek Road. The car rumbles a little ominously through the tunnellike 1880 Bean Blossom covered bridge, one of several of these charming anachronisms still in use here.

Near Bear Wallow Hill just around one bend, I discover the Flower and Herb Barn nursery, which started as a log cabin back in the 1800s. It was moved and restored in 1987, and now is a profusion of flowers, trees and shrubs in the sort of natural setting that big-city nurseries spend fortunes to re-create. A sign says that if the owners aren't around, just dig up what you want and leave a note—they'll send a bill.

I check in at the Artists Colony Inn in downtown Nashville, where they still disagree about whether they want a chain pharmacy in town. Co-owner Ellen Carter (with her husband, Jay) grew up here in an artist's household, lived in New England for a time, then came back, bringing some Yankee ideas: pencil-rail beds, wooden floors, rag rugs and Windsor chairs.

The local artists' names that christen the inn's rooms are pure Brown County. I'm in the suite named for T. C. Steele, who happens to be my favorite Hoosier painter. In the twilight, I catch up on my e-mail and sip coffee on the balcony, gazing down at visitors strolling by. Up the street, I see the studio of glassblower Jim Lawrence, who learned his trade at carnivals as a boy.

The next day, one of those country roads I love to follow leads me to the Story Inn, an ordinary tin-fronted general store that now constitutes the entire town of Story (population 7). I'm here for an inventive lunch that includes a grilled artichoke sandwich and raspberry-ginger cobbler, but first I have to step upstairs and inspect one of the bed-and-breakfast rooms known for its ghost. The famous Blue Lady, believed to have been murdered here by her husband, Doc Story, in the mid-1800s, reportedly haunts this place. I screw up my courage and look into every dark corner, but no luck today (I'm relieved!).

Another two-lane road leads to Brown County State Park, recalling my breakfast conversation with a couple from Fort Wayne that morning. They'd already been out for a daybreak hike in the hills. I asked

(*Clockwise, from opposite*) A potter's work. Rustic bridge along a Brown County back road. Raspberry-ginger cobbler at the Story Inn. Glassblower Jim Lawrence at work in the Quintessence Gallery. At the T.C. Steele State Historic Site.

HORSEPOWER HEAVEN

As soon as I step inside the Auburn Cord Duesenberg Museum in Auburn (about 15 miles north of Fort Wayne), I know I've struck real automotive gold. This 1930s Art Deco car palace, listed on the National Register of Historic Places, housed the showroom and administrative offices of the Auburn Automotive Company (which made Auburns, Cords and those Gatsby-esque Duesenbergs) from 1930 to 1937. It was reopened as a nonprofit museum in 1974.

In the early days of the auto age, before Detroit dominated the industry, cars were manufactured in many locations by small firms. In Indiana, there was Studebaker in South Bend, Stutz in Indianapolis and, of course, the Auburn in Auburn.

More than 100 cars fill eight galleries. The Duesenbergs are the stars. A 1932 Torpedo Speedster once owned by novelist John O'Hara and bazillionaire John Paul Getty, among others, tips the scales at 6,000 pounds and has a wheelbase that measures 142½ inches. Gary Cooper and Clark Gable had two Duesies each. Price tag: $14,000 to $18,000 in 1930s dollars, when a Ford Model A cost $500.

The collection also includes cars not made in Auburn: Packards, Lincolns, Rolls Royces and Cadillacs. There's an L-29 Cord once owned by Frank Lloyd Wright and a 1904 Auburn, the museum's oldest car. Visitors can look into the corner office of visionary industrialist E. L. Cord, Auburn's president from1926 to 1937. After Auburn, the restless Mr. Cord wound up in California, owning most of Beverly Hills before it became Beverly Hills.

Auburn Cord Duesenberg Museum (260/925-1444). Area information: DeKalb County Visitors Bureau (877/833-3282, dekalbcvb.org).

how often they visit Brown County. "Absolutely every chance we get," they quickly reply. I see why.

Artists' Haven

I'm no art authority, but as with most people, I know what I like. High on my list are Impressionist-school paintings that convey the rich textures and hues of the land and the seasons. That's why the art of T. C. Steele captivated me on my first visit to Brown County.

Now I'm back on a sunny afternoon,

appointed apple-green parlor, rambles across a hilltop. The lush summer scene outdoors must have inspired the artist's interior color choice and the inscription the introspective Steele had carved into his white limestone fireplace mantel: "Every morning I take off my hat to the beauty of the world." How fitting.

Outside, I envision what the dark red house looked like when its wraparound porch was screened in. The sound of the hilltop breezes blowing through those screens inspired Steele to call this "The

> The sound of breezes blowing through those screens inspired Steele to call this "The House of the Singing Winds."

revisiting his home and studio at the T.C. Steele State Historic Site west of Nashville. Relatively few people explore this hidden gem each year. That's surprising, because it's one of the most beautiful spots in Brown County, with woods, meadows and views that seemingly roll on forever.

Theodore Clement Steele was an Indiana native who'd studied art in Munich, Germany, and returned to his home state to paint among his fellow Hoosier School artists. He discovered Brown County during a country outing in 1906 and liked what he saw. In 1907 and 1908, Steele and his second wife, Selma, built a summer cottage here. Later, it became their year-round home.

Soon, Steele was the best-known of the then-thriving Brown County art colony. He and his wife entertained both their fellow artists and their sometimes-befuddled Hoosier neighbors. (What must Brown County natives have thought about these eccentric artists in their midst?)

The single-story house, with its richly

House of the Singing Winds."

Standing on the front lawn, I pick out scenes Steele painted with his bold yet somehow delicate strokes. Those canvases hang inside and on the walls of his barnlike studio down a short path from the house.

On the north side of the studio, there's a huge window wall facing his house, designed to welcome the consistent north light he required for painting. Along with landscapes he created, some of Steele's portraits decorate the walls. Outside, Selma Steele's flower gardens explode with color.

T. C. Steele bought his 211 acres for about $2 per acre. When he died in 1926, the property passed to Selma, and she willed it to the state of Indiana just before she died in 1945. It's been one of the state's little-known treasures ever since, rescued from disrepair in the 1980s in a collaborative effort by staff members and volunteers. I purchase a couple of Steele prints in the tiny studio gift shop, hoping to take home reminders of the serenity I feel in this peaceful place.

(Clockwise, from above) On the porch of Nashville's Artists Colony Inn. Hand-woven baskets. The 125-year-old Bean Blossom covered bridge. Some works by glassblower Jim Lawrence.

BEAN BLOSSOM BRIDGE 1880

Living Architecture

If one image captures Columbus, Indiana, for me, it's driving into town. A view of the contemporary cable-stay Second Street Bridge frames the ornate 1874 Empire-style Bartholomew County Courthouse in the distance.

I love great architecture and design, and that's what first brought me to this south-central Indiana community. I never expected to find so much of it in an industrial city of 39,000, though. Now, even knowing what to expect, I'm surprised. Driving and walking through town, the sun breaks through after a rainy afternoon, heightening the visual drama of great buildings shimmering like mirages in sidewalk pools of water.

The needlelike 192-foot spire of North Christian Church, designed in 1964 by Eero Saarinen, seems to soar into the clouds in its parklike setting. Then there are the massive blocklike forms of First Christian Church, a preview of things to follow when Eliel Saarinen of Finland, Eero's father, designed it in 1942.

The list goes on: the local newspaper offices, a pleasing downtown mall, public housing, schoolhouses, private homes designed by the likes of the Saarinens, I. M. Pei, Richard Meier and Cesar Pelli. A plaza surrounds a Henry Moore sculpture near St. Peter's Lutheran Church (Gunnar Birkerts of Latvia, 1988), across the street from the Cleo Rogers Memorial Library (I. M. Pei, 1969). All told, there are more than 60 buildings of national and international note in Columbus, which puts it in an architectural league with New York City and Chicago.

Columbus and the world can thank J. Irwin Miller, architectural patron and the tycoon behind local giant Cummins Incorporated. As his family's company (manufacturers of diesel engines) exploded in the postwar years, Miller knew he'd have to recruit top-notch talent from around the globe. One way to do that, he reasoned, was to create a setting that set Columbus apart from the "ticky-tacky boxes" multiplying like mad everywhere.

It started in 1957 with the schools. The Cummins Foundation agreed to pay architectural fees for any building designed by a world-class architect. Then the fever spread to municipal buildings, churches and private companies, even private homes. Soon, the whole town was a showcase of architectural masterpieces.

Despite all the stunning contemporary designs, Columbus is still a city of tree-shaded residential streets and older buildings lovingly cared for. The most notable is the courthouse, along with its 19th-century commercial neighbors lining Washington Street.

Everywhere I turn, landscaping complements the striking edifices: Columbus is one grand park. As my guide says, "Great architecture is in the water here." I think she must be right, because design takes center stage in this small Indiana city like nowhere else.

More information: Columbus Area Visitors Center (800/468-6564, www.columbus.in.us).

North Christian Church

More Favorites

BLOOMINGTON

This lively university community, about 50 miles southeast of Indianapolis, attracts some of the best and brightest students. Handsome buildings of limestone from nearby quarries distinguish the city of 70,000 and the sprawling, shaded Indiana University (IU) campus.

A massive Beaux Arts-style county courthouse dominates the downtown square, center of an 11-block area of 200 restaurants, music clubs and shops, including Fountain Square Mall in a renovated historic building. There's a bookstore on almost every corner, and the whole family will love the new touch-and-try-it WonderLab science museum. Nearby, browse the Bloomington Antique Mall, the largest of its kind in southern Indiana.

Kirkwood Avenue, lined with galleries, shops and restaurants, links downtown to the campus entrance, which is marked by huge limestone gates. Two 1800s bed and breakfasts, Grant Street Inn and Scholars Inn, are within easy walks of the downtown square. For a special-occasion dinner, try Champman's on the city's eastern edge. Bloomington Convention & Visitors Bureau (800/800-0037, www.visitbloomington.com).

INDIANA DUNES COUNTRY

Towering dunes crown a landscape of beaches and bogs, prairies and forests along northwestern Indiana's 25 miles of Lake Michigan shore. Lake, Porter and La Porte counties share the shoreline, where industry exists alongside nature barely 50 miles beyond Chicago's skyline. Farther inland, inviting towns dot the countryside.

Indiana Dunes National Lakeshore

Centerpiece of the region, the 15,000-acre Indiana Dunes National Lakeshore attracts beachgoers and nature lovers, anglers and bird-watchers. East of Gary, mounds of silvery white sand extend 25 miles to Michigan City. Midway between the two cities is the village of Chesterton, where galleries and antiques and crafts shops line the streets.

Along the lakeshore, you can follow the boardwalk through tamarack pines, tiny orchids and insect-eating plants at Pinhook Bog. Visitors also scale Mount Baldy, one of the tallest dunes, and stroll miles of beach or follow a half dozen trails. The national lakeshore, next to Indiana Dunes State Park, has a nature center and trails.

In addition to chain motels, lodgings range from Spring House Inn, minutes from the lake in Porter, to Creekwood Inn, an English manor house in Michigan City. More information: Indiana Dunes National Lakeshore (800/959-9174, ext. 225, nps.gov/indu). Lake County Convention & Visitors Bureau (800/255-5253, alllake.org). La Porte County Convention & Visitors Bureau (800/634-2650, visitlaportecounty.

com). Porter County Tourism (800/283-8687, indianadunes.com).

PATOKA LAKE

From the traffic-free main channel of Indiana's second largest inland lake, Patoka Lake and the Hoosier National Forest appear nearly untouched by humans (60 miles northwest of Louisville, Kentucky). Among the four state recreation areas bordering Patoka Lake, visitors can camp, bike and hike a 1,000-acre triangular peninsula within the Newton-Stewart Recreation Area, encountering deer, birds and other wildlife in this road-free domain.

The trail's 6½-mile main loop begins at the lake visitors center, where you can find out about special programs from star parties and fishing derbies to guided hikes, along with crafts, music and kids' activities. Two marinas rent houseboats.

Cabins, motel-style rooms and floating cabins along the shore at Patoka Lake Marina are available for rent. More information: Indiana Department of Natural Resources, Patoka Reservoir Office (812/685-2464, www.in.gov/dnr).

Travel Journal

WINNING INDY

The interstate beltway circling Indianapolis resembles the speedway the city is best known for. Indiana's capital and largest city is on the "fast track" for more than just the Indianapolis 500 auto race. Visitors will discover a vibrant, revitalized downtown with an array of world-class attractions including museums, a zoo, a sleek downtown mall, and riverside parks and trails. More information: Indianapolis Convention & Visitors Association (800/958-4639, indy.org).

Featured Stops

Circle Centre Downtown, four-level mall spread over two square city blocks, with more than 100 stores and restaurants, plus a nine-screen movie theater and a video-game theme park (317/681-8000).

Indiana State Museum With two restaurants: L. S. Ayres Tea Room, featuring legendary Creamy Velvet Chicken Soup. The Crossroads Café also serves the soup, as well as made-to-order pizzas and sandwiches, a grill, and soup-and-salad bar (317/232-1637).

James Whitcomb Riley Museum Home The mansion where the beloved Hoosier poet lived, now open for tours, in historic Lockerbie Square (317/631-5885).

White River State Park In downtown Indianapolis, with paved pathways along the river, expanses of shrub- and flower-lined lawns and pedal-boat rides on historic Central Canal. Attractions including the Indiana State Museum, Indianapolis Zoo, NCAA Hall of Champions, Congressional Medal of Honor Memorial, Victory Field Baseball Park, White River Gardens, IMAX theater and Eiteljorg Museum of American Indians and Western Art (800/665-9056, inwhiteriver.com).

More Great Stops

Children's Museum of Indianapolis Five levels of interactive exhibits in the largest museum of its kind in the world (just north of downtown). A limestone wall for youngsters to climb, an antique carousel and a boat they can "sail," plus a new $25 million dinosaur exhibit. Admission charged (317/334-3322).

Indianapolis City Market Downtown historic landmark building bustling with merchants offering a wide assortment of merchandise, from imported groceries to fresh produce and flowers. Closed Sundays (317/634-9266).

Monument Circle In the center of downtown, home to the towering Indiana Soldiers and Sailors Monument and the Colonel Eli Lilly Civil War Museum (317/232-7615).

Shopping

Broad Ripple Village A lively, eclectic older neighborhood about 20 minutes north of downtown, with specialty shops, antiques dealers, restaurants and bars (317/251-2782).

Rocky Mountain Chocolate Fudge, caramel apples and more along Monument Circle (317/687-1322).

Lodging

Chains such as the Hilton, Hyatt Regency and Embassy Suites downtown. In the suburbs and surrounding area, standard motels including AmeriHost, Comfort Inn, Hampton Inn and Holiday Inn.

Canterbury Hotel The ritzy restored downtown landmark where celebrities such as Mick Jagger and Elton John have stayed, adjacent to Circle Centre $$$$ (800/538-8186).

Crowne Plaza Hotel An upscale 273-room hotel in the renovated downtown train station, rebuilt in 1888 in Romanesque Revival style. Rooms resembling refurbished Pullman train cars, decorated around themes inspired by Charlie Chaplin, Amelia Earhart and other notables. $$$ (317/631-2221).

Indianapolis Courtyard Downtown by Marriott On the edge of White River State Park, with a T.G.I. Friday's restaurant and 24-hour fitness center. $$$ (317/635-4443).

Old Northside Bed & Breakfast Near downtown, an 1885 brick mansion with themed rooms, in-suite whirlpool tubs and fireplaces. $$ (800/635-9127).

Dining

Indiana History Center's Stardust Terrace Cafe Beside Central Canal across from White River State Park, serving sandwiches and quiche-of-the-day. Outdoor seating in season (317/232-1882).

Milano Inn A downtown favorite, serving fresh tomato pizza and robust Italian fare (317/264-3585).

Shapiro's Deli An Indianapolis institution since 1905, serving sandwiches, salads, side dishes, soups and desserts (eight blocks south of downtown). Specialties including stuffed cabbage, potato pancakes, short ribs and hot German potato salad (317/631-4041).

PRETTY AS A PICTURE

For more than 100 years, artists have thrived in the wooded hills and hollows of south-central Indiana's Brown County (55 miles south of Indianapolis). In the hub town of Nashville, log cabins and clapboard cottages house more than 300 shops selling art, crafts and antiques. Visitors also can watch artisans work in their studios. More information: Brown County Convention & Visitors Bureau (800/753-3255, browncounty.com).

Featured Stops

Artists Colony Inn and Restaurant In Nashville, 23-room 19th-century-style inn furnished with local crafters' works. $$. Dining room with a large stone fireplace specializing in homemade soups, desserts and sweet-potato dishes (800/370-4703).

Brown County State Park Indiana's largest state park, in the rolling hills southeast of Nashville. Highlights: an 82-mile network of horseback-riding and hiking trails, swimming pool, picnic areas, campsites and a nature preserve, with a self-guided nature trail (812/988-6406).

Flower and Herb Barn Nursery A profusion of flowers, trees and shrubs in a natural setting (812/988-2689).

Story Inn In tiny Story, serving fine European and traditional southern-Indiana cuisine in a tin-fronted former 19th-century general store with a pot-bellied stove, wooden floors and an old player piano (14 miles south of Nashville). Accommodations including cottages and 14 rooms with private baths. Guests tell stories of seeing the Blue Lady, a mirthful, white-robed apparition who supposedly haunts the inn, and each room has its own history. $$ (800/881-1183).

T.C. Steele State Historic Site The 1907 hilltop home and studio of artist T. C. Steele, an Impressionist painter who helped start the Brown County artists' colony (nine miles west of Nashville). On the surrounding grounds, trails winding through woods and wildflower patches (812/988-2785).

More Great Stops

Monroe Lake Indiana's largest reservoir and site of nationally acclaimed fishing tournaments (just south of Bloomington).

With three public beaches, 325 campsites and a full-service marina (812/837-9546).

Shopping

Brown County Craft Gallery In downtown Nashville, showcasing about 30 artisans' works, including weaving, basketry, pottery, jewelry, glass, folk art and other creations (812/988-7058).

Lodging

Abe Martin Lodge Rooms and dining in the main lodge, plus rustic cabins in Brown County State Park. Main lodge built of hand-hewn native stone and timber. $–$$$ (877/265-6343).

Hotel Nashville Resort Family-friendly all-suite hotel (one and two bedrooms) one block from downtown Nashville, with pool and sauna. $$$; ask about packages (800/848-6274).

Dining

The Nashville House A Nashville institution, serving homey favorites including fried biscuits, hickory-smoked ham and homemade apple butter in a cozy setting with red-and-white-check tablecloths, stone hearth and log walls (877/374-3324). ∎

T.C. Steele State Historic Site

Iowa

■ My home state always seems to hover near the middle of the nation in many respects including location, population and size. Low-key and small-town-friendly by nature (the largest city is Des Moines, the capital, with a metro population of 500,000), Iowans dominate national news every four years when their caucuses kick off the presidential race. We Iowans pride ourselves on top-notch schools and universities. The state's erstwhile economic mainstay, farming, has yielded to bioengineering, financial services, manufacturing and insurance. Bordered by the Mississippi and Missouri rivers, the land morphs from majestic bluffs in the northeast to rich, rolling central farmlands to western Iowa's windswept Loess Hills.

The Mississippi River from Pikes Peak

Mississippi Main Street

Everywhere it courses, the Mississippi River leaves its mark. I'm revisiting a spectacular, 100-mile swath of the river valley in northeastern Iowa: towering wooded bluffs, green islands and proud river towns.

Early in the morning, my first vantage point is the lofty overlook at Eagle Point Park, 440 feet above the river in northeastern Dubuque. Far below, a northbound coal-laden barge is about to slip into Lock and Dam No. 11 (one of 29 between St. Paul and St. Louis). Surprisingly graceful turkey vultures waft on the warm air currents. No bald eagles are flying today, but their ranks are growing again in this area, especially during the winter months. From my celestial perch, people and vehicles below appear to silently creep along like tiny insects.

From this perspective, the river looks as awesome as it is: a waterway that courses for 2,500 miles, beginning at a small lake in northern Minnesota and flowing into the Gulf of Mexico, swelling from a mere 12 feet wide and less than two feet deep to 2,500 feet wide and 200 feet deep at New Orleans; a river that drains 1.25 million square miles in 31 states—more land than any river in the world, except the Nile and the Amazon; a river fed by 25 major tributaries, including the Missouri, Ohio and Des Moines rivers; a river that discharges more water than any other on the continent (2.3 million cubic feet per second).

River Town Revival

For me, river towns are special—like eccentric Auntie Mame promising adventures at every turn. Dubuque (population 60,000) is my favorite river town anywhere.

I'm first in line at the new limestone-and-glass National Mississippi River Museum and Aquarium in the redeveloped Port of Dubuque. They call this waterfront enclave the Ice Harbor, because riverboats once sought refuge here when the channel froze during the winter. Now, it's the setting for a $188 million collection of attractions that replaced a shabby industrial neighborhood. In addition to the museum, there's a casino, two excursion boats, river walk, amphitheater, conference center and a hotel with a water park.

The Smithsonian-affiliated museum celebrates the entire Mississippi, north and south, as well as all of America's great rivers. In the wildlife area, I get acquainted with an albino turtle, a fat-lipped 100-pound catfish and a rather scary water moccasin. Playful otters and ducks bob and dive in their own tanks. From downriver, there's a bayou alligator and an alligator snapping turtle.

A wall map, actually a satellite photo, shows the entire Mississippi River Valley from outer space. It's the world's largest composite map. Using a wheel device called a spin browser, I zoom up and down a visual simulation of the river, stopping wherever I want to linger over a view. Another exhibit shows the impact of those huge flood-control walls and how wetlands serve as a sort of safety sponge when the river floods. There's a "dead zone" in the

Gulf of Mexico—5,000 square miles devoid of wildlife and plants thanks to fertilizers that we lavish on farms and lawns.

Other exhibits show yesteryear steamboats, which once plied the river by the hundreds (many of them were fabricated right here at the old Dubuque Boat and Boiler Works). I even get the chance to pretend-pilot a towboat through a lock. Finally, at the National Rivers Hall of Fame in the museum, I "meet" some of the colorful characters associated with this river: Mark Twain, explorers Marquette and Joliet and even musician Louis Armstrong.

For a panoramic view of the city, I head for the 1882 Fenelon Place Elevator west of the museum at the base of a 200-foot bluff. Generations have boarded this endearing curiosity, billed as the world's "shortest and steepest" scenic railway. I ring a bell and an operator at the control house on top starts the green-and-white car that seats eight. Two cars operate on a counterbalance system that requires a single 15-horsepower motor, one car pulling the other up as it glides down.

The original cable car was the brainchild of a local banker and former mayor who simply wanted more nap time when he went home for lunch to his bluff-top mansion—a half-hour carriage ride around that bluff when his bank was just 2½ blocks away. Soon, neighbors were hitching rides, and he started charging five cents (it's now

(Clockwise, from opposite) The Dubuque County Courthouse, a National Historic Landmark. Downtown and the Port of Dubuque. The National Mississippi River Museum and Aquarium. Sister Mary Ann Sullivan, O.C.S.O., at Our Lady of the Mississippi Abbey.

DIVINE CARAMELS

I'm making a quick candy run (for the gang back at the office) to Our Lady of the Mississippi Abbey near Dubuque. I ask the friendly, soft-spoken nun her name. Then, I ask again. Yes, it's true, she assures me. Sister Anne Elizabeth Sweet, O.C.S.O., is in charge of marketing for the Trappistine sisters who create what I consider to be the world's best caramels, right here on their 550-acre organic corn-and-soybean farm overlooking the river. After I make my purchase, Sister Anne Elizabeth takes me on a whirlwind tour of the new candy-factory building, where the 22 sisters (ages 33 to 77) whip up creamy confections—60,000 pounds of caramels and 10,000 pounds of mints and hazelnut meltaways annually; more than 20,000 boxes total.

Although the sisters work hard at candy-making, they labor even more fervently at the contemplative life, starting each day with prayers at 3:45 a.m. and finishing with prayers at 7:15 p.m. The delectable temptations they churn out make their cloister self-supporting.

In the candy-making room, I watch sisters slather the hot, buttery goo onto trays for cooling and cutting. Then, it's off to the mini assembly line, where sisters wrap and box their creations. The Lord is smiling on me today: A kindly sister in charge of culling rejects keeps lobbing defective caramels my way. Pure heaven!

September through December is the busy time here, when Christmas orders are filled to be delivered around the globe by mail and UPS. Things are going so well, the nuns have been able to ship off seven of their number to an island near Trondheim, Norway, to establish a new abbey there. Orders: 563/556-6330, trappistine.com.

$1.50 round-trip). At the top, after a three-minute, 296-foot ride, I linger at the landing to survey restored Victorian homes, red brick warehouses, riverboats and the old Dubuque lead-shot tower.

The city's architectural gems stand out: the courthouse, the ornate clocktower and the grand Five Flags Theater, modeled after the Majestic in Paris. Church steeples are everywhere, and most of them are Catholic. The Dubuque area counts two Catholic colleges, along with nine convents and monasteries.

Founded as a lead-mining center in the 1780s by French fur trader Julien Dubuque, this community has seen its share of ups and downs. The 1980s were mostly "down": Two economic mainstays, meat-packing and agricultural implements, hit the skids. That's when activists mobilized and recharged the riverfront with public and private funding for attractions from a greyhound park to that wonderful river museum. It worked. Now Dubuque, which remains one of the nation's largest cities not located on a federal interstate highway, hums with visitors and new computer-support, telemarketing, insurance and publishing enterprises. One resident tells me: "It's getting so you can't find a place to park downtown anymore." Good.

Vistas—Present and Past

For centuries, travelers have roamed on and along the Mississippi in this area for many reasons: exploration and military dominance, the fur trade, lead mining, and commerce. Now, it's the scenic riches of this valley that attract wanderers like me. I follow the twisting, turning Great River Road National Scenic Byway, a leisurely route that extends almost the entire length of the Mississippi. Marked by signs with riverboat emblems, the route leads to otherwise bypassed hamlets such as tiny Ball-

town (population 39) high on a ridge above the river north of Dubuque.

We're just in time for a late lunch at Breitbach's, Iowa's oldest operating restaurant and bar, dating to 1852. The place looks like a rambling old farmhouse with a big, shady front porch. A sign gratuitously proclaims, "Best food in town." There clearly are no alternatives in greater Balltown.

They serve 2,500 meals daily here during the peak autumn leaf-peeping season. Owner Mike Breitbach darts between the bar and dining room. Mike's wife, Cindy, presides over the kitchen. In between seating guests, tending bar and taking orders, Mike fills me in: He's the fifth generation to run what has served over the years as a stagecoach stop, general store, barbershop, cafe, bar, post office and dance hall. At one time, the Breitbachs lived upstairs. Mike's great-grandfather, grandfather and father all were born and also died in this building. Mike made his own debut here 55 years ago.

Local memorabilia deck the walls, from lanterns to feed-store signs, cooking pots, a quilt, even an old pickup-truck door. The notorious James Gang stayed here incognito on their way to the Great Train Robbery in Northfield, Minnesota, in 1876.

My satisfying lunch is more than adequate, but the pies surpass all my wicked expectations: gooey slices of walnut, Snickers, apple, cherry and raspberry. It's a tough call, but the sweet-sour tang of the raspberry pie gets my vote.

Leaving town, I pull over for yet another awesome view of the Mississippi Valley. Farther north, the twisting route teases me with tantalizing glimpses of the river. Skinny shelves of land packed with riverside vacation cottages on stilts nestle beside the highway and railroad tracks. I weave through river towns, including McGregor, Marquette and German Gut-

(Clockwise, from top left) A fleet of riverboats in the Ice Harbor at the Port of Dubuque. Tracing raised animal forms in the "Marching Bear" mound group at Effigy Mounds National Monument. Gift, import and antiques shops line the street near Dubuque's Fenelon Place Elevator. Breathtaking overlook at Eagle Point Park.

The Mississippi River Valley at Balltown

tenberg, with its historic limestone buildings.

Near McGregor, I'm soon gaping at the view again, this time from Pikes Peak, named for Zebulon Pike, who explored here in 1805 before he headed west. It's the highest point along the Mississippi (500 feet above the river; 1,130 feet above sea level). Across the river, there's the town of Prairie du Chien, Wisconsin, and the mouth of the Wisconsin River. This is where, in 1673, French explorers Marquette and Joliet and their party were the first Europeans to behold the Mississippi. Islands are everywhere, and wooded bluffs reign, untouched by ancient glaciers.

Upriver, more vistas unfold from Effigy Mounds National Monument, but the 2,526-acre preserve's most important mission is guarding more than 200 known Native American burial mounds created from 800 to 1200 A.D.—31 of them effigies. These raised mounds of earth, painstakingly built by native peoples for spiritual reasons, are only four feet high, but can be as long as 200 feet. Although other effigies survive in Minnesota, Wisconsin, Illinois and Ohio, they're disappearing fast. At the turn of the last century, there were more than 10,000 mounds in Iowa alone. Now, fewer than 1,000 remain. The effigies here are special because they depict animals and birds, as well as more typical conical and linear shapes.

Park ranger Merle Frommelt takes me down five miles of remote, winding gravel roads under groves of oaks and maples to the park's most secluded group of effigies. Standing beside me, high above the Mississippi, Merle slowly traces a shape hidden in the grass-covered rises. I finally see it! A bear, 137 feet long and 70 feet wide. I gradually discern bears, eagles and simple geometric shapes. Woodland Indians built these marvels, using just sticks and crude stone implements. In spring, they buried the remains of their dead here, part of the reason no excavations are permitted. At that time, this was oak-studded prairie, so the view must have been even more spectacular and spiritual.

On the Water

Upriver at Lansing, Captain Jack Libbey is waiting to give me a ride on the *Mississippi Explorer I*, one of two excursion boats he operates. Jack has lived in the area for more than 30 years. He's documented Mississippi life for various projects and sponsors, including the Smithsonian Institution. Nobody knows this stretch of water

Taste of Iowa

Best-Ever Berry Pie
Breitbach's Country Dining, Balltown

- 1 recipe pastry for double-crust pie (log on to midwestliving.com for recipe)
- 1 cup sugar
- ¼ cup quick-cooking tapioca
- 4 cups fresh or frozen unsweetened red raspberries
- 1 tablespoon sugar

Prepare pastry and roll out one ball of dough for bottom crust. Line a 9-inch pie plate with rolled-out pastry.

In a large mixing bowl, mix the 1 cup sugar and the tapioca. Add raspberries. Gently toss till coated. (If using frozen fruit, let mixture stand 15 to 30 minutes or till fruit is partially thawed, but icy.)

Transfer the berry mixture to the pastry-lined pie plate. Trim the bottom pastry to edge of pie plate. Cut slits in remaining rolled-out pastry; place on filling, trimming pastry ½ inch beyond edge of pie plate. Fold top pastry under bottom pastry and crimp edge as you like. Cut slits in top of pie pastry, and sprinkle with the 1 tablespoon sugar.

To prevent overbrowning, cover edge of pie with foil. Bake in a 375° oven for 25 minutes for fresh fruit, 50 minutes for frozen. Remove foil. Bake for 25 to 30 minutes more or till top is golden. Cool on a wire rack. Makes 8 servings.

---

the way he does. We shove off and enter the nine-foot channel marked by buoys. Jack explains why the buoy we're passing is inscribed "663.7": we're 663.7 miles north of the confluence of the Mississippi and Ohio rivers at Cairo, Illinois.

Then, we're off the main channel and navigating the river's shallow backwaters. Bluffs soar up to 300 feet on either side. Jack says that the islands we're passing didn't exist until the lock and dam system lowered river levels in the 1930s. Huge floating beds of yellow lotuses perfume the air. Arrowhead plants, with tender, potatolike tubers the Indians once harvested, also crowd sections of the braided, shallow waterways. Many of the bluffs we pass still camouflage effigies like those I saw up close just an hour ago.

Jack reports that more than 40 percent of North America's migrating birds use the Mississippi as a superhighway. We see herons, egrets, cranes, tundra swans, geese, ducks and even a couple of bald eagles. The eagles live to be about 30 years old and mate for life, Jack says. He calls them "beavers of the sky," because their huge nests are made of twigs.

We spot several actual beavers and their lodges. Minks, otters, muskrats and possums also flourish among the silver maples and willows that shade the riverbanks. A heron flaps its huge wings. Jack repeats a river legend: "When a river pilot dies, he comes back as a blue heron and guides other pilots on their way."

Jack tells me he's traveled the world, including other major rivers such as the Yangtze in China. "But," he says, "every time I come back here, I love it more."

Perry's Patron

On the surface, Perry (named for a railroad boss) looks idyllic, popping up as an oasis of trees crowned by a blue water tower floating in an ocean of green corn 40 miles northwest of Des Moines. The big news is the unveiling of "Hometown Perry, Iowa," Roberta Green Ahmanson's latest initiative to reinvent her hometown.

What a story! Roberta grew up here, a class of '67 boomer, the daughter of a railroad man. She found her calling in journalism class. After college, she wound up the award-winning religion writer for the *Orange County Register*. An introduction by a friend to an idiosyncratic bazillionaire philanthropist named Howard Ahmanson changed her life (his father made millions in the savings and loan business). The pair wed in 1986 and have passionately and prayerfully funded their agenda as a team ever since— the arts, as well as conservative religious and social causes. Everything from art exhibits in London to a rescue mission in Orange County to the Hotel Pattee right here in Perry.

After the railroad folded and Perry hit the skids in the early 1990s, meat-packing took up some of the employment slack and brought an influx of Hispanic immigrants. Mexicans and Central Americans now make up almost a third of the population of a town originally settled by Germans, Irish and Swedes. Roberta, who'd maintained her hometown ties through the years, purchased the run-down hotel in 1993 and remade it into a historic treasure— to the tune of $10 million-plus: Mahogany paneling, brass fittings, copper and stone, terra-cotta tiles, Persian carpets. Forty exquisite rooms, each with a different theme reflecting the heritage of this town and the Heartland. A luxurious spa and fitness center, first-class dining in David's Milwaukee Diner, and paintings and murals, many by regional artists.

My favorite place to hang out is the cozy library off the English Arts and Crafts-style lobby. I sit in a leather-covered Gustave Stickley chair and watch the fire glow beneath the huge, hammered-copper mantel hood. Outside, 11 flags flutter in the breeze, each representing a different nationality that settled in Perry.

Back in the library, I chat with Roberta, a tall, sturdy, straightforward woman with bright eyes. She says, "I was looking for something to do. Well, I found it . . . . Who I am was shaped profoundly by growing up in this town."

Roberta recalls for me how the Hotel Pattee project blossomed into the renovation of the entire block: the restored Security Bank building next door, which serves as the project headquarters; a gift shop; a sunny courtyard with head-turning contemporary sculptures. Then came the opportunity to acquire the tiny 1904 Carnegie Library that reposes in the middle of Perry's compact downtown "triangle" across the street from the Hotel Pattee. That led to "Hometown Perry, Iowa," restoring the library, sponsoring seminars, documenting Perry's immigrant history, and recording on audio- and videotape the life stories of 400 Perry residents.

Why bother? Roberta's no-nonsense reply: "When you drink from the well, remember the well digger." Hometown Perry (515/465-2518, www.perryia.org). Hotel Pattee $$$–$$$$ (888/424-4268).

Hotel Pattee

Remaining Faithful

I've visited the Amana Colonies more than a dozen times for the food, the handmade crafts and their pure escape value. This time, I also seek out people who can help me better understand what this area was—and is—all about.

The Amana Colonies consist of seven small villages and 1,600 people, roughly the same number who lived here a century ago. Many of them are descendants of a group of utopians who settled the lush Iowa River Valley in 1855. Originally persecuted in Germany, the colonists opposed the state Lutheran church and formed what they called "The Society of True Inspiration," which still is the basis of their communal lifestyle.

Not to be confused with the Amish, residents of Amana embraced modern technology on their farms and in their factories. In 1932, after several years of the Great Depression and a disastrous fire that destroyed their huge woolen and flour mills, the community navigated what's still known locally as "The Great Change." At that time, they traded communal ownership for stock shares in today's Amana Society, which oversees 26,000 acres of prime farmland and profitable enterprises.

Community Foundations

Faith and business, once intertwined, became separate pillars of Amana life. Both still flourish, thanks to hard work, good business sense, curious visitors and a still-active church. Most visitors come to the villages for the shops that sell artisans' works and restaurants that serve hearty traditional German food. My wife, Julie, and I drove here for an early Sunday morning service in the long brick meetinghouse located in Middle Amana.

The building has two entrances: one for women, one for men. Although Amana residents no longer dress in the uniformly dark clothing they once wore on a daily basis, it's Sunday, and almost all the women are in black dresses, shawls and caps. The men wear dark suits and ties. Rows of hooks for long-ago straw hats and caps line the walls of the men's vestibule, and a distinctive Amana hand-woven rug decorates the floor. "Sprechen Sie Deutsch?" an elderly gentleman asks. "Nein," I reply. "So few do these days," he laments.

A member tolls the bell using a rope that dangles from the ceiling of the compact vestibule. All enter the main room at the same time, single file, each carrying a German Bible and a Psalter Spiel, with men on one side, women on the other. The elders take their seats in front as worshippers slip into long benches facing them. The room is without adornment—no crosses, no stained glass, no altar, no organ. Just a small podium for the presiding elder, who happens to be a young woman.

The service is part German, part English. All hymns are sung by strong voices a cappella in German. What's most apparent to me is the mood of silent prayer and earnest self-reflection. Some worshippers barely look up during the entire service.

Later on, I chat with wiry, bearded Lanny Haldy, executive director of the Amana Heritage Society, which operates the museum in Main Amana. He explains that the word Amana means "remain faithful." How did the villagers live? Everything was provided communally: medical care, housing, food and clothing. Adults were assigned their tasks by the elders. Extended families lived together in the large assigned homes and ate in 50 communal kitchens. For every village there was a church, meetinghouse, bakery, wine cellar, post office and general store.

Those tenets still anchor Amana life. "Just look around," Lanny says. "You see no sprawl. And the church, of course—that's where we still hear the message that the material world isn't what it's all about."

(From top) Community Church Museum in Homestead. Shops lining the streets in Amana.

Paris of the Plains

Near the heart of Iowa, Des Moines represents the best of what many Midwest cities offer— attractions, plus some intriguing surprises. But there are a few quirks you should know about before you visit . . .

It's hard to write objectively about your own hometown—so I won't try. A recent *Des Moines Register* article indicated some self-deprecating locals tend to view the growing ranks of inbound transplants with something akin to disbelief. Why on earth would anyone voluntarily move here? Self-promotion isn't our forte, which is a shame.

My wife, Julie, and I have called Des Moines home for 33 years. I've raised a family and built a career here. Housing is affordable (in a recent survey, the average upmarket four-bedroom home price was more than $100,000 below the national average). Commutes average 18 minutes. People are warm and friendly. It's pretty, and it's clean—all the nice things that I'm convinced make midsize Midwest cities the best places to live in America.

Did you know Des Moines is the nation's second largest insurance center after Hartford, Connecticut? The largest employer in the city and the state is Principal Financial Group, with 7,000-plus number crunchers locally. Des Moines gave the nation three U.S. secretaries of agriculture, one of them later a World War II vice president, Henry A. Wallace, and another, E. T. Meredith, the founder of Meredith Corporation, the national media giant that's my employer. (Ever heard of *Better Homes and Gardens*® magazine?)

Business is booming in Des Moines. Unemployment hovers around two per-cent. A steady stream of corporate transferees from across the nation infuses civic life with energy. In recent years, local insurance and financial-services companies have invested hundreds of millions in office towers that define compact downtown Des Moines' skyline—all linked by more than three miles of skywalks. The once-shabby riverfront, presided over by a lovably fusty, late-Victorian state capitol topped by a stunning 23-karat gold-leaf dome, now is alive with walkways, parks and attractions.

The city boasts a top-notch symphony, as well as an opera company, and the local summer arts festival is one of the nation's most highly regarded. The Des Moines Art Center showcases a first-rate contemporary collection in a striking hilltop building designed in various stages by no less than Eliel Saarinen, I. M. Pei and Richard Meier. Speaking of architecture, Iowa's 1869 governor's mansion, Terrace Hill, is considered the nation's finest example of Second Empire Victorian design.

In the ethnic diversity department, white-bread Des Moines traditionally has been challenged. But, thankfully, growing African American, Asian and Hispanic communities are adding new vibrancy.

All that said, Des Moines does have a quirk or two. First, that name. To some it might sound elegantly French, but nobody quite knows what it means. The best explanation is some corruption of Indian and French words for mounds, monks or "in the middle." Then, there's the state fair: Each August, more than a million visitors dutifully swarm the historic fairgrounds (remember, that's in a state of 3 million and a metro area of 500,000). Everyone, from designer-outfitted suburbanites to pig farmers in overalls, parades past a glass-fronted cooler showcasing a life-size dairy cow carved from butter accompanied by another masterpiece, such as, perhaps, an all-butter rendition of Elvis, John Wayne or *The Last Supper*. Then, we ogle the state's grand-champion boar in a pen in the Swine Barn (last year's winner: Holy Macaroni at 1,183 pounds). Finally, we revel in consumption of fair foods, including some 20 ingeniously served on a stick—meatballs, pork chops and, believe it or not, fried Snickers candy bars and Twinkies.

Agricultural Roots

Despite all the trappings of progress and affluence, I hope we Iowans don't lose sight of our roots, literally and figuratively. More than anything else, our forebears settled here for the chance to grow things in the rich, black soil. Fertile Iowa is one of the nation's most intensively farmed states (an astonishing 90 percent of the land is devoted to farming, although fewer than one in 10 Iowans so much as sets foot on a farm even occasionally these days). Appropriately, Des Moines is the home of the

World Food Prize, brainchild of Iowa Nobel Prize laureate Norman Borlaug and funded by local transportation magnate John Ruan. *Successful Farming*® magazine is published here by Meredith Corporation.

Whenever I need a reminder about where today's Des Moines and Iowa and much of the Midwest came from, I visit Living History Farms, a working agricultural museum that celebrates 300 years of farming with exhibits and hands-on experiences in the northwestern suburb of Urbandale. The museum's 550 acres are a time warp. At the re-created 1875 village of Walnut Hill, I walk along wooden sidewalks and poke around the implement store, newspaper office, lawyer's office, post office and other businesses. At the millinery shop, a costumed clerk shows off a pheasant-feather-festooned hat.

Crowning a hill is the nondenominational Church of the Land, built where Pope John Paul II celebrated Mass in 1979 before 350,000 faithful—the state's largest gathering ever. At the 1850s farm stead, an interpreter, "Farmer Phil," explains how his oxen, Nick and Toddy, help with backbreaking chores such as plowing and harrowing, and shows me a log home similar to one where a pioneer might have lived.

The modern, earth-bermed Henry A. Wallace Exhibit Center helps me figure out how hybrid seed corn, first developed and marketed here, revolutionized agriculture in the 1930s. Other displays communicate how convenience foods have changed our lives, and how scientists constantly brainstorm new and sometimes unexpected uses for Iowa's bumper crops.

Even though farming no longer drives the economy as it once did, I'm reminded that it's part of who we are and what makes Des Moines so representative of the best of the Midwest—and America.

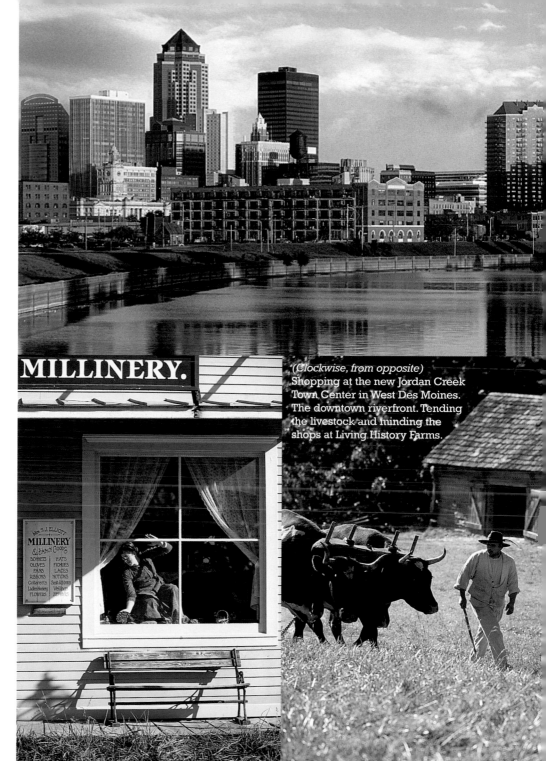

(*Clockwise, from opposite*) Shopping at the new Jordan Creek Town Center in West Des Moines. The downtown riverfront. Tending the livestock and minding the shops at Living History Farms.

More Favorites

DECORAH

Amid the limestone palisades and forested hills of northeastern Iowa's Upper Iowa River Valley—an area that reminded Norwegian settlers of their beloved homeland—this college town of 8,200 could have been the model for a Norman Rockwell painting. Long known as Iowa's "Little Norway," Decorah treasures its legacy.

The Iowa River edges downtown (105 miles northwest of Dubuque). Along Water Street, antiques stores and gift shops brimming with Nordic crafts and Scandinavian imports tuck into vintage buildings. You can't miss the elegantly renovated Hotel Winneshiek, built in 1905, with its Victorian Rose Restaurant.

Spanning most of a downtown block, the Vesterheim Norwegian-American Museum complex includes a onetime luxury hotel, stone mill, church, log school and early homes. Visitors view collections of furnishings and other heirlooms, plus displays about the immigrants' journeys.

Canoeists love paddling the scenic 30 miles of the Iowa River that runs between Decorah and Kendallville.

More information: Winneshiek County Convention & Visitors Bureau (800/463-4692, decoraharea.com).

IOWA GREAT LAKES

Dickinson County in northwestern Iowa claims 13 lakes (about 95 miles northeast of Sioux City). Generations of vacationers have returned year after year to the largest three—West Okoboji, Big Spirit Lake and East Okoboji. Visitors swim, fish, boat waterski or simply loll on beaches.

Resorts, large and small, with lodgings from cabins to condos, dot the lakes' shores. You also can golf, hike and bicycle. Families flock to the area's amusement park, built in 1899, with its wooden roller coaster and other rides. Okoboji Tourism (800/270-2574, vacationokoboji.com).

MANNING

In 1881, immigrants from the Schleswig-Holstein region north of Hamburg, Germany, settled Manning (about 90 miles northwest of Des Moines). German-themed architecture mixes with other buildings along the brick Main Street in this community of 1,500. You can join lively festivals such as Kinderfest, Deutsche Tag, Oktoberfest and Weihnachtsfest.

The main attraction, the Hausbarn, draws visitors from across the U.S. The peaked, thatch-roofed structure in Heritage Park was built in Germany in 1660, disassembled, transported to Manning, and reconstructed five years ago. German families once shared *hausbarns* with their livestock. Inside, you'll see living quarters at one end and stalls and pens at the other, separated by an open hearth.

Thatchers from Germany built the foot-thick roof using 6,500 bundles of reeds from Baltic Sea marshes. The area's German craftsmen completed the brick-and-beam walls, and a volunteer laid the brick floor. The Hausbarn Restaurant next door serves German dishes and beers. A short walk through a pine grove leads to the 1915 Leet/Hassler Farmstead. More information: Manning Heritage Foundation (800/292-0252, www.manningia.com).

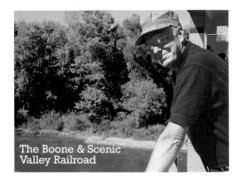

The Boone & Scenic Valley Railroad

ALL ABOARD!

I'm wearing an engineer's hat, hanging on for dear life as I stand petrified on the narrow side landing of a 1,000-horsepower 1942 diesel locomotive—156 dizzying feet over an improbable gorge in central Iowa. The railroad built the massive original bridge here in 1903 from a million board feet of lumber. This steel version replaced it in 1912. Jim Gardner, the volunteer engineer, assures me it's still sturdy—especially when we're traveling only seven miles per hour.

Boone (50 miles northwest of Des Moines, population 12,500) is a railroad town named for the legendary frontiersman. It's also the birthplace of First Lady Mamie Eisenhower. Local boosters decided in 1983 to honor their heritage by creating an excursion line. In 1989, they purchased the last new steam engine of its type from China. Today, the Boone & Scenic Valley Railroad, with a steam engine, six diesels and 20 passenger cars, offers a taste of the glory days of passenger trains.

Excursions start at a reconstructed old-time depot near downtown. On the return trip, I get a chance to play engineer, tooting the whistle. Soon, I spot the Boone water tower down the tracks. Much to my amazement, I wish I could do it all over again, including that heart-thumping view. Boone Area Chamber of Commerce (515/432-3342, booneiowa.homestead.com).

Travel Journal

MISSISSIPPI MAIN STREET

For area information: Allamakee County Economic Development (800/824-1424, www.visitiowa.org). For Dubuque information: Dubuque Area Chamber of Commerce (800/798-8844, www.dubuquechamber.com).

Featured Stops

Breitbach's Country Dining Home cooking and from-scratch pies in Balltown (15 miles northwest of Dubuque, 563/552-2220).

Effigy Mounds National Monument Native American burial grounds (70 miles north of Dubuque, 563/873-3491).

Fenelon Place Elevator The world's shortest and steepest scenic railway (563/582-6496).

Mississippi Explorer **Cruises** In Lansing, river excursions (563/586-4444).

National Mississippi River Museum and Aquarium Centerpiece of the redeveloped Port of Dubuque (563/557-9545).

More Great Stops

Heritage Trail Twenty-six-mile bicycling and hiking trail from just north of Dubuque west to Dyersville. (563/556-6745).

McGregor River town 65 miles north of Dubuque popular with houseboaters. Antiques along old-time Main Street. McGregor-Marquette Chamber of Commerce (800/896-0910, mcgreg-marq.org).

Spirit of Dubuque An authentic old-fashioned paddle wheeler offering Mississippi cruises. Ticket charge (800/747-8093).

Lodging

Grand Harbor Resort and Waterpark On the Dubuque riverfront, new hotel with an indoor water park. $$$–$$$$ (866/690-4006).

REMAINING FAITHFUL

Amana Colony villages cluster two to three miles apart. Shops sell handcrafted furniture, antiques, cheese and sausages. Crafters demonstrate woodworking, basket-making and other old-time skills. Highlights also include restaurants, museums, wineries and Iowa's only operating woolen mill. More information: Amana Colonies Convention & Visitors Bureau (800/579-2294, amanacolonies.com).

More Great Stops

Tanger Outlet Center In Williamsburg (15 miles southwest of the Amanas) along I-80, more than 50 off-price stores such as Liz Claiborne and Ralph Lauren (319/668-2885).

Dining

Ox Yoke Inn Specializing in family-style German dishes, steaks and from-scratch desserts, in an 1856 home (800/233-3441).

PARIS OF THE PLAINS

More information: Greater Des Moines Convention & Visitors Bureau (800/451-2625, seedesmoines.com).

Featured Stops

Des Moines Art Center Including an acclaimed collection of contemporary works. Free admission (515/277-4405).

Living History Farms An agricultural museum. Admission charged (515/278-5286).

More Great Stops

Des Moines Botanical Center Along the Des Moines River, arboretum under a geodesic dome. Major collections of exotic plants and bonsais. Admission charged (515/323-6290).

Iowa State Historical Museum Chronicling Iowa's past (515/281-5111).

Jordan Creek Town Center An upscale new mall in West Des Moines, with retailers such as Pottery Barn and J.Crew. Also restaurants and a 20-screen cinema (515/440-6255).

Valley Junction A compact suburban district of more than 100 antiques and specialty shops in vintage buildings (515/222-3642).

Dining

Bistro Montage American and French cuisine, emphasizing fresh, locally grown ingredients (515/557-1924).

Zanzibar's Coffee Adventure Coffee and other beverages in a casual, inviting atmosphere (515/244-7694). ∎

Breitbach's Country Dining

Kansas

■ Kansas is one of those "topographically challenged" Great Plains states that strives to entice travelers off a main east-west superhighway (I-70, in Kansas' case, but it might as well be I-80 in Nebraska, I-90 in South Dakota or I-94 in North Dakota). Don't count me among those who need to be lured off the interstate. And nobody has to convince me to linger here. Kansas offers perceptive travelers a rich history, colorful frontier traditions and welcoming, well-kept small towns—all with unique stories and down-home friendly people. If you give it a chance, you'll find the Sunflower State beguiling you with the serenity of its vast prairies and broad horizons. I feel close to the land and the sky in Kansas, which is exactly what I like.

Konza Prairie in the Flint Hills

Hometown Heroes

Kansas raises more than wheat and cattle. The Sunflower State has produced a fistful of plucky heroes and heroines. On my journey around the state, I learned more about three of them and their hometowns.

hen Dwight David Eisenhower was a boy playing in the streets of Abilene, the town (90 miles west of Topeka, population 6,500) was a few years beyond its heyday as a rowdy Chisholm Trail cattle center.

Wealth spawned by 3 million cattle shipped east from Abilene funded grand homes, among them the imposing Lebold Mansion, which you can tour. But the Eisenhowers didn't live in one of these palaces. In their small, tidy white frame house, warmhearted Ida and her stern husband, David, a creamery manager, raised six strapping, achieving sons. One of those boys, Ike, boarded a train at the Union Pacific depot downtown in 1911, headed for West Point and, ultimately, a famed military career and the presidency.

Today, that little house is the centerpiece of the 22-acre Eisenhower Presidential Library and Museum, a cluster of limestone buildings that includes a visitors center. The depot serves as the Abilene visitors center, where you can board a trolley bus that takes you to attractions ranging from the American Indian Art Center to the Dickinson County Historical Museum, with its frontier exhibits. One exhibit at the center's museum celebrates Ike's decision to create the nation's interstate highway system, which has had such a profound impact on Kansas and the nation.

The Eisenhowers had more than 25 home addresses during Ike's long career.

But he always remembered Abilene. He revisited his hometown many times. On one of those visits he told an audience: ". . . The proudest thing I can claim is that I am from Abilene."

Robert Dole and Russell

Fewer than 100 miles west of the hometown of his World War II Supreme Commander, Bob Dole was born in 1923 in Russell, Kansas (population 4,700), founded as a railroad water stop. Like the community, the Doles scratched through hard times. Dole's mother, Bina, sold sewing machines door-to-door. His father, Doran, had an egg-and-cream stand.

With $300 loaned to him by a local banker, the future senator and presidential candidate headed to Lawrence to study at the University of Kansas (KU). Then came World War II. Just days before the war ended, soldier Dole was critically wounded in Italy. He remained in bed for six months. Russell's help got him back on his feet.

A worn cigar box is among the many exhibits at the imposing Dole Institute for Politics, dedicated in July 2003 on the KU campus. Russell citizens used the box to gather $1,800 they donated to help their hometown war hero pay his medical bills.

Dole returned to his Russell to kick off his 1976 vice presidential campaign. He wept as he told his old friends and neighbors: "I am proof that you can be from a

small town without a lot of material advantages and still succeed. If I have had any success, it is because of the people here."

Amelia Earhart and Atchison

Aviation pioneer Amelia Earhart helped put Atchison (50 miles northwest of Kansas City, population 11,000) on the map. And the Missouri River community still reveres its hometown heroine.

Nearly 70 years ago, the whole nation was enthralled by the flier's exploits: first woman to fly across the Atlantic Ocean; first woman to make the crossing solo; first aviator to fly from Hawaii to the U.S. mainland. When she disappeared in 1937 two-thirds of the way on a round-the-world flight, the entire country grieved.

Overlooking the Missouri River, the hilltop house where she was born in 1897 now is a historic site. Photos and mementos of the childhood tomboy and dreamer decorate the high-ceilinged rooms.

I'm most interested in looking out one window again. It's always captivated me that Earhart could have gazed down from her bedroom at the Missouri River where, 100 years before, explorers Lewis and Clark traveled on their historic journey. Later, Earhart wrote a poem that she titled "Courage." The first line may help explain what Atchison gave to that free-spirited adventurer: "Courage is the price which life exacts for granting peace."

(*Clockwise, from opposite*) Amelia Earhart, Dwight Eisenhower and Robert Dole. A bronze of Ike at Abilene's Eisenhower Center. Amelia Earhart's girlhood home. Inside the Dole Institute of Politics.

Amelia Earhart Birthplace Museum

Amelia Earhart was born July 24, 1897 In the home of her grandparents, Alfred G. and Amelia Harres Otis. The home was constructed circa 1860.

The Birthplace Museum is owned by The Ninety-Nines, Inc. International Organization of Women Pilots

On the Trail

In east-central Kansas, the vast, grassy Flint Hills ranching country is known for Santa Fe Trail history and Great Plains-style Americana. Council Grove celebrates its colorful past and a very happy present.

As I enter the Flint Hills of central Kansas, the familiar-looking farms and fields of the state's eastern quarter yield to sprawling ranches, where cattle thrive on native prairie grasses that carpet the thin, rocky soil. Driving along a gravel road, I pull off to take in a 360-degree panorama of prairie ridges and valleys punctuated by barbed-wire fences, distant ranch houses and huge, round bales of hay. Over the warble of meadowlarks, my car radio announces tornado warnings for nearby counties. I find myself wondering if those storms deserve the credit for the blazing orange-pink sunset I'm witnessing.

I arrive in Council Grove (50 miles southwest of Topeka, population 2,300) at dusk and follow the red blinking neon arrows on Main Street to the Cottage House Hotel. The turreted, white brick Victorian-style building was built as a blacksmith's home and shop in 1867, then was enveloped by an 1870 addition.

After checking in, I explore the neighborhood on foot. Downtown, window displays of furniture, apparel and other goods remind me of hometown stores in the 1950s. The most commotion I encounter during my stroll is a rumbling pickup driven by a teen talking on his cell phone.

Later, dining on roast beef at the limestone Trail Days Bakery Café, I try to envision this historic restaurant almost a century and a half ago. At that time, the two-story landmark was the Rawlinson House, now known as the Terwilliger House, last sentinel of civilization for bullwhackers coaxing their heavy-laden freight wagons along the Santa Fe Trail.

Trail Days

Council Grove owes much of its rich history to the frontier trail and a mile-wide stand of oaks, maples, hackberries, elms and walnuts nourished by the Neosho River, which winds through town. The community gained its name from an 1825 powwow held in a shady grove between government agents and Osage tribe members to ensure safe passage for Santa Fe freight wagons. From about 1821 to 1880, the trees provided lumber for repairs to wheels and axles of the wagons that rolled between Missouri and New Mexico. Oxen and mules were watered at the river before the dry, two- to three-month journey. Drovers bought beans, bacon and whiskey at the still-standing Last-Chance Store.

The 900-mile length of the Santa Fe Trail was a bustling commercial and military artery. In addition to traders, the trail transported miners, adventurers, trappers, soldiers and immigrants to the arid Southwest. Although the trail's heyday ended with the arrival of the railroads, a wide swale carved by iron-shod wheels of wagons, traveling up to 20 abreast, remains visible five miles west of Council Grove.

Downtown, a paved walkway follows the Neosho River, not far from where wagons once forded the stream. Two nearby statues represent the two cultures that dominate this area's history: the 1928 Madonna of the Trail depicting a bonneted pioneer mother and her children, and a 1998 bronze of a proud Kaw warrior.

As a visiting writer once wryly noted, Council Grove is big when it comes to historic tree stumps. One is the remnant of the massive Council Oak, dating to that 1825 frontier powwow. Another is the stump of an elm commemorating the 1867 visit of General George A. Custer and his ill-fated Seventh Cavalry. Yet another massive stump is the remains of Post Office Oak, where early Santa Fe Trail travelers cached messages about trail conditions. That tree finally died in 1990 at the majestic age of 270 years.

The 1851 Kaw Mission State Historic Site recalls the misguided efforts of early Methodists, who set up a school to instruct native boys in "civilized" ways. The experiment lasted several years, but the school's young charges kept slipping back to their village. In the 1920s, the classic limestone structure was renovated by descendants of the original schoolmaster into an imposing, modernized home. Today, as some Council Grove residents try to heal the wounds of past injustices, they've planted hundreds of bur oak trees at a park southeast of town.

(*Clockwise, from opposite*) Peach pie at the historic Hays House. The Cottage House, built in 1867 as a blacksmith's home. A bronze statue of a Kaw warrior. One big, grassy banquet for the cattle grazing across the Flint Hills.

Each tree memorializes a Kaw who lived here at one time. Kaw descendants from Oklahoma, where the tribe was removed to in 1872, purchased the property a few years ago to develop as a Kaw heritage site.

My companions and I lunch at the Hays House, another historic Santa Fe Trail building along Main Street. (The entire town of Council Grove is listed on the National Register of Historic Places.) The Hays House dates to 1857, making it one of the oldest continually operating restaurants west of the Mississippi River. Like many frontier structures, the restaurant has housed a variety of activities over its colorful existence: church socials, political speeches and frontier courtroom trials.

I have lunch here, indulging in chicken-fried steak with chicken gravy—about as Kansas a meal as you can get—accompanied by ripe, home-grown tomatoes and fried okra. The food is heavenly, and dessert is truly celestial: fresh peach-and-strawberry pie with real whipped cream and homemade oatmeal-cinnamon cookie-dough ice cream.

While I eat, former Hays House owners Helen and Charlie Judd regale me with stories. Helen's family bought the place in 1911, and she and Charlie came back to Council Grove from teaching careers in California to run the Hays House in the 1970s. They explain that the restaurant's builder and namesake, Seth Hays, was a grandson of frontiersman Daniel Boone.

Along Main Street

It's apparent that community spirit and pride run strong and deep in this prosperous county seat town. Historic structures and homes are well-tended. On Tuesday nights during the summer, anyone who cares to can participate in a lively jam session on the sidewalk in front of the barbershop along Main Street.

When the local National Guard unit sent 18 area citizen-soldiers off to duty in Iraq, the high school gym was packed. The band performed, the mayor gave a speech, and local merchants donated items for the guardsmen and guardswomen to carry with them. People stick together here, a trait I notice throughout the plains states.

At the Main Street offices of the *Council Grove Republican*, I meet a trim Don McNeal, age 89, who runs the daily newspaper with his son, Craig (a mere pup at age 64). Don says the newspaper was founded in '72 (that's 1872, he clarifies with a smile). He started here in '36 (that's 1936, Don says with a wink). I suppose when you're 89, you're entitled to qualify centuries that way.

It's a wonder that a newspaper can stay afloat in a town this size, when some dailies struggle in major markets. According to Don, the paper is profitable because it's earned and reciprocated the trust of the community. Along Main Street, an unlocked newspaper rack uses the honor system. I drop in 35 cents and pick up a copy of the *Republican* to read at the hotel.

A Good Life

Besides retirees, history buffs and vacationers looking for the good life on the plains, couples with lifestyles similar to Debbie and Bill Miller's may hold the secret to the future of communities such as Council Grove. About nine miles southwest of town, Bill and Debbie own 1,200 acres where they breed genetically engineered Angus cattle. Bill is a public relations writer for a beef marketing group and works from his computer-outfitted attic office. Debbie is a magazine freelance writer (for *Midwest Living*®, among other titles). Both Kansans, they had lived elsewhere, then returned to their home state in 1991 to raise two daughters.

Why did they pick Council Grove? Debbie says they specifically wanted a ranch with a big foursquare house like the one she grew up in near Abilene, a creek running through the property and accessibility to big airports (the turnpike, about 30 miles away, takes them to either Kansas City or Wichita within two hours). Good schools were a priority, too. They also love the town and its history. Bill serves on several community boards, and Debbie is active in school parents' groups and plays saxophone in the community band.

Wearing jeans, boots and a denim shirt, Debbie takes me on a bumpy pickup ride around their ranch. As we talk, she opens and closes pasture gates and mentally keeps tabs on 125 cow-calf pairs. Does it get lonesome, I wonder? Not at all. Debbie tells me they have potlucks with neighbors at the old one-room schoolhouse down the road. They're only nine miles from town, after all. It's a good life. . . .

Konza Prairie near Manhattan

Prairie Oasis

The single image that defines the Great Plains states to many travelers is the vast treeless prairie, where endless grasslands appear to some as desolate and vacant. Other travelers, me among them, are awed by the prairie.

Less than two centuries ago, this ocean of grass blanketed 170 million acres from Canada to Texas, including most of the Midwest. Kansas' Flint Hills comprise the largest remnant of that wondrous ecosystem.

The prairie survived in these hills because the thin soil covering this nearly 40-mile-wide swath of limestone and shale defied the plow. But it's the world's richest grazing land. The tallgrass prairie, where big bluestem grass can soar to 12 feet tall, nourishes cattle as it once did buffalo.

At the Konza Prairie Biological Station just five miles north of busy I-70, visitors can experience the prairie as it once was—silent, vast and teeming with life. This 8,600-acre preserve, overseen by Kansas State University (KSU), is named for the tribe that once lived here. Though most of the preserve is reserved for research, 14 miles of hiking trails lead deep into the prairie.

Valerie Wright, a KSU naturalist and educator, takes me on a driving tour of Konza. Our journey begins at Hulbert Center headquarters, which was named for the professor who led the 1970s effort to create the preserve. The two-story stone building originally was built as a ranch bunkhouse and barn.

As we jounce along rutted trails, Valerie points out round-headed *lespedeza*, or bush clover, a delicate red-and-white flower. More than 600 species of plants populate Konza. Among them are grasses with no-nonsense names: big and little bluestem, Indian and switch grass, side oats grama, prairie cord and buffalo grass. Wildflowers are more poetically labeled: beard tongue, plains larkspur, gayfeather and prairie coneflower.

Farther along the trail, Valerie suddenly stops: "Sorry, I brake for butterflies," explains the entomologist. There are plenty of butterflies to brake for: In all, 78 species live here.

Konza's lush animal life includes dozens of species of larger creatures. The streams we cross harbor frogs, crayfish and tiny fish. As we drive, five big wild turkeys strut in a line across our path. More than 200 species of resident and migrating birds flit through the grasses, prairie chickens and meadowlarks among them.

Buffalo are the real stars here. Valerie calls them the "lawn mowers of the plains" because of their voracious appetites. Millions once ruled the prairies. Hunted to near extinction, the big, shaggy animals are making a comeback. Currently, a herd of 300 roams Konza.

The prairie requires periodic fires to thrive. Konza markers note when tracts were intentionally burned. Before European settlement, lightning did the job, assisted by tribes who knew new grasses after a burn attracted buffalo.

Leaving Konza, I sense more than ever how this land shaped the character of the people of the Great Plains—including my own forebears. Roots here run as deep as those of the big bluestem. They must, in order to withstand droughts, tornadoes, blizzards, economic crises and isolation. For the self-reliant souls who put down prairie roots, the rewards are rich, like the soil. Konza Prairie (785/587-0441, ksu.edu/konza).

A Free Spirit

This laid-back Midwest university town has a spellbinding history and a funkiness that I love. Besides, where else would you be served great homemade soup and ice cream in a college-hangout microbrewery?

There's something wonderfully fey about Lawrence that I can't quite put my finger on. I do know it's my favorite university town anywhere. Although it has its predictable aspects—new strip malls and boxy suburban housing developments—the Lawrence that I love centers on Massachusetts Street, the 15-block historic downtown district.

Kansas is known as being very straitlaced, conventional and predictable—right? Well, someone forgot to mention that to the folks in Lawrence. Downtown, everyone younger than 30 seems to have at least one body part pierced and is walking a large dog on a leash. Women with long, straight hair and discreet tattoos gracefully glide along in sandals and prairie skirts.

Is this Kansas, Toto, or a flashback to Haight-Ashbury in the 1970s? Well, not exactly, but it's as close as you come in the Midwest, and I love it. Home of the University of Kansas (KU), Lawrence has been called the Berkeley of the Midwest because of its decidedly bohemian air.

That's not the only reason I appreciate this community of 80,000, give or take a few thousand of the 27,000 KU students. Lawrence belies the state's flat stereotype: It's very hilly and wooded—the KU campus sprawls across Mount Oread—nestled in a beautiful valley along the Kaw (Kansas) River. I'm also drawn to Lawrence because of its rich, albeit blood-soaked, history. Nowhere in Kansas does the state's motto—*Ad Astra per Aspera* (To the Stars Through Difficulty)—apply more.

In the 1850s, the Kansas-Nebraska Act made this then territory a battleground between pro- and anti-slavery forces. In 1854, abolitionist New Englanders founded Lawrence. Just 17 miles northwest, proslavery settlers dominated Lecompton, the former territorial capital.

Raids and shoot-outs between the two factions were common. Without warning on the morning of August 21, 1863, about 400 renegade Missourians led by Confederate guerrilla William Clarke Quantrill rode into Lawrence and shot down almost 200 men and boys. The town was left a charred ruin. Gritty survivors, mostly women and children, quickly rebuilt their town, this time of brick and native limestone. Thousands of trees were planted.

Intriguing Brews

After a night in the country at the Circle S Ranch—a very with-it, cowboy-themed hostelry 11 miles north of town—I start my day foraging for breakfast along Massachusetts Street. Milton's is typical of eclectic Lawrence, with six varieties of coffees imported from Ethiopia and Venezuela. You can even get a fried-egg sandwich with chipotle mayonnaise.

Much of downtown Lawrence is a National Historic District. Just west of Massachusetts Street, 126 carefully tended homes, five of which survived the 1863 raid, range from straightforward National-style houses to Disneyesque Victorians.

On one corner downtown, the old Eldridge Hotel still welcomes visitors. It was twice burned, then rebuilt during the Bleeding Kansas era. Across the street, a once-abandoned trolley and bus station holds the Free State Brewery, my favorite microbrewery anywhere. I love the cheddar ale soup and portobello spinach salad, followed by apple crisp with homemade vanilla ice cream. And the beer is good, too.

Thanks to those rather stuffy New England Puritans, Kansas was as dry as the Sahara for decades, enacting its own prohibition against alcohol in 1880. That embargo was only repealed in 1948.

Chuck Magerl founded the Free State in the 1980s, the first brewery to open in Kansas in more than a century. Wearing his usual jeans and a casual shirt, Chuck tells me, "I serve what tastes good to me, whether it's beer or food."

The chalkboard on the wall always touts five to 10 different brews, including standards such as Copperhead Pale Ale and Ad Astra Ale. As you'd expect in the nation's breadbasket, there's a Wheat State Golden. Chuck sells some 2,000 barrels of beer here annually. That's a lot of suds. But this is a university town, after all—and my favorite one at that.

(*Clockwise, from opposite*) Cold ones at the Free State Brewery. Strolling along funky, historic Massachusetts Street downtown. Acclaimed old-fashioned cinnamon rolls at WheatFields Bakery, also serving artisan breads and tempting pastries. Drawing brews at the Free State. On the University of Kansas campus.

Taste of Kansas

Hays House Brisket, *Council Grove*

- 1 3- to 3½-pound beef brisket
- ½ cup chopped onion
- ½ cup liquid smoke
- ½ cup soy sauce
- ¼ cup Worcestershire sauce
- 1 tablespoon celery seeds
- 1 tablespoon bottled minced garlic
- 1 teaspoon ground black pepper
  Hamburger buns, split (optional)

For brisket: Trim fat from meat. Place meat in a large resealable plastic bag set in a shallow dish.

For marinade: In a medium bowl, combine onion, liquid smoke, soy sauce, Worcestershire sauce, celery seeds, garlic and black pepper. Pour over the meat; seal bag. Marinate in the refrigerator for 6 to 24 hours, turning bag occasionally.

Place meat in a foil-lined 13x9x2-inch baking dish; pour marinade over meat. Bake in a 325° oven for 3 to 3½ hours or until it's very tender, turning once. Remove from oven. Carefully transfer meat to cutting board; discard marinade. To serve, thinly slice meat across the grain. Place on a serving platter. If you like, serve in hamburger buns. Makes 8 to 10 servings.

More Favorites

HUTCHINSON

Towering grain elevators frame this bustling commercial center (population 40,000). Founded by a Baptist minister where the Santa Fe Railroad crosses the Arkansas River (about 45 miles northwest of Wichita), Hutchinson was a relatively tame settlement among the Sunflower State's rowdy frontier towns.

Hutchinson teems with visitors in September during the Kansas State Fair. But no matter the month, there's always a crowd at the Kansas Cosmosphere and Space Center, one of the world's top space museums. The Apollo 13 command module occupies an honored spot among scores of spacecraft, a full-scale space shuttle and Blackbird spy plane. The museum houses the largest collection of space artifacts outside the Smithsonian Institution. You'll also love the IMAX theater and planetarium shows.

Downtown, shoppers browse the antiques district, with more than a dozen stores along South Main Street. As many as 125 of the buildings date to the turn of the last century, including the Reno County Courthouse and the refurbished Art Deco Fox Theatre, which hosts concerts and stage shows.

Pack a picnic lunch and drive northeast to the 100-acre Dillon Nature Center. Along three miles of trails, you can view some 300 varieties of trees, as well as birds and several gardens.

Hutchinson sits atop one of the world's largest salt deposits, a 70-mile stretch of huge white caverns. The Reno County Historical Museum chronicles the mines' history. When the Kansas Underground Salt Museum opens in spring 2006, visitors will be able to descend into the caverns.

Hutchinson visitors frequently travel six miles southeast to Yoder, an Amish community of shops, a bakery and restaurant.

More information: Greater Hutchinson Convention & Visitors Bureau (800/691-4282, visithutch.com).

LINDSBORG

Kansas was settled by a colorful quilt of Old World immigrants. Lindsborg (population 3,800) still wears its Swedish American heart on its sleeve as a badge of pride. The cornflower yellow and blue Swedish colors wave from every lamppost along the downtown streets, lined with galleries, restaurants and one-of-a-kind shops.

Cobbled streets pave the way into this lovingly preserved town along the Smoky Hill River (20 miles south of Salina). Local artists' renditions of a Swedish folk art symbol, the *dala* horse, decorate most store windows. You'll also see the horses on many doors in the town's neighborhoods of 19th- and early-20th-century houses.

The 12 historic buildings of the McPherson County Old Mill Museum chronicle central Kansas life in the era after Lindsborg was founded in 1869. Visitors view one of the simple dugout shelters in which settlers often began their new lives.

Dozens of artists showcase their skills at galleries in and around Lindsborg. The Birger Sandzén Memorial Art Gallery displays works of the late, internationally acclaimed painter.

More information: Lindsborg Chamber of Commerce–Little Sweden (888/227-2227, www.lindsborg.org).

Travel Journal

HOMETOWN HEROES

Small-town Kansas produced three famous Americans. President Dwight David Eisenhower hailed from Abilene (90 miles west of Topeka); Vice President Bob Dole was raised in Russell (190 miles west of Topeka); and aviator Amelia Earhart was born in Atchison (50 miles northwest of Kansas City). More information: Abilene Convention & Visitors Bureau (800/569-5915, abilenekansas.org). Atchison Area Chamber of Commerce (800/234-1854, atchisonkansas.net). Russell Chamber of Commerce (785/483-6960, russellks.org).

Featured Stops

Eisenhower Center, Abilene Chronicling Dwight D. Eisenhower's life and legacy (785/263-6700).

The Robert J. Dole Institute of Politics, Lawrence Celebrating the life and career of Senator Bob Dole (785/864-4900).

Amelia Earhart Birthplace Museum, Atchison Hilltop childhood home of the renowned aviator. Admission charged (913/367-4217).

More Great Stops

Amelia Earhart Earthwork, Atchison A stunning one-acre natural portrait of the aviation pioneer (913/367-2427).

The Dickinson County Historical Museum, Abilene Wild Bill Hickok's gun and an operating antique carousel (785/263-2681).

Lebold Mansion, Abilene Ornate, renovated 1880 Italianate home. Admission charged (785/263-4356).

Shopping

American Indian Art Center, Abilene Paintings, sculptures, carvings, beadwork and jewelry (785/263-0090).

Nell Hill's, Atchison Stylish emporium for home accessories and gifts (913/367-1086).

Lodging

Victorian Reflections, Abilene Five rooms in a 1900 mansion. $–$$ (785/263-7774).

St. Martin's Bed & Breakfast, Atchison Panoramic view of the historic town. $$ (877/367-4964).

Dining

Brookville Hotel, Abilene Famous for its fried chicken dinners (785/263-2244).

Kirby House, Abilene Victorian-era mansion, serving steaks and seafood (785/263-7336).

RiverHouse, Atchison Incredible grilled veggie sandwich and elegant entrées, plus a Missouri River view (913/367-1010).

ON THE TRAIL

Council Grove (35 miles southwest of Topeka) once the main staging point for the Santa Fe Trail. Also the location of an 1825 powwow between government agents and Osage tribe for safe passage. More information: Council Grove Convention & Visitors Bureau (800/732-9211, www.councilgrove.com).

Featured Stops

The Cottage House Hotel & Motel Bed and breakfast and motel. $–$$$$ (800/727-7903).

Hays House Restaurant and Tavern Serving fried chicken, beef brisket and homemade pies (620/767-5911).

Kaw Indian Mission Exhibits about the Kaw Indians and Santa Fe Trail (620/767-5410).

Trail Days Bakery Café From-scratch treats in an 1861 Santa Fe Trail landmark. Fresh breads, rolls, cookies, muffins and other goodies made from wheat grown and milled in Kansas (620/767-7986).

More Great Stops

Seth Hays Home Period furnishings in the town founder's 1867 home (800/732-9211).

Tallgrass Prairie National Preserve Two hiking trails (17 miles south of Council Grove) and an 1881 ranch house (620/273-6034).

A FREE SPIRIT

Vibrant Lawrence boasts a rich history (40 miles west of Kansas City). More information: Lawrence Convention & Visitors Bureau (888/529-5267, visitlawrence.com).

Featured Stops

Circle S Ranch and Country Inn Luxurious inn on a 1,200-acre ranch where buffalo graze. $$$$ (800/625-2839).

Free State Brewery Downtown brewpub and restaurant (785/843-4555).

Milton's Breakfast, lunch, dinner and very good coffee (785/832-2330).

More Great Stops

Haskell Indian Nations University Walking tours of this Native American university, founded in 1884 (785/832-6686).

Spencer Art Museum On the University of Kansas campus, 11 galleries of sculptures, photographs and paintings (785/864-4710).

Shopping

Phoenix Gallery More than 100 local and regional artists' works (785/843-0080).

Dining

WheatFields Bakery Artisan breads and great cinnamon rolls (785/841-5553). ∎

Michigan

■ Michigan is rich in contrasts: big cities and rugged forests that teem with wildlife; logging operations and copper mining, and huge auto and chemical plants; tidy farmsteads and remote lighthouses. Its citizenry counts vibrant African American and Middle Eastern communities alongside Old World Finns, Swedes, Germans and Dutch. Then, there's the water, always the water: Four of the five Great Lakes— Michigan, Superior, Huron and Erie— rush against its 3,200 miles of shoreline (that's more than the entire West Coast of the U.S.), plus thousands of inland lakes, rivers, streams and waterfalls. My route through the state yields a series of fascinating snapshots of the many facets of Michigan's pleasantly split personality.

Miners Beach along Lake Superior within
Pictured Rocks National Lakeshore

An 'Almost' Capital

At first glance, Marshall appears to be a typical town of 7,500. But detouring a couple of blocks down Kalamazoo, Grand and Sycamore streets leads me to elegant homes of almost every 19th-century style.

I first visited this quaint community in 1987, when a Michigan writer urged us to feature the historic homes of Marshall in one of our earliest issues. I decided to take a look for myself. I was smitten.

I've never seen, before or since, a small town with so many beautifully preserved Victorian homes—850 in Marshall's National Historic District, the largest such neighborhood in the nation for a community this size. Gothic and Greek Revival, Italianate and Queen Anne with turrets and cornices and curlicues everywhere. Name the style, and you'll find it reflected in immaculately restored Marshall.

Besides all those fabulous homes, Marshall claims what is arguably the state's most legendary restaurant, Schuler's, where I linger over a fabulous Sunday brunch with owner Hans Schuler; and its oldest operating lodging, the 1835 National House Inn, where I'm staying. The inn was once a stagecoach stop; it's now cozily furnished with antiques. There's the Old Stone Livery (now Marshall's Town Hall, complete with clock tower), the governor's mansion that wasn't and the believe-it-or-not Honolulu House.

Marshall's quirky history also sets the town apart. The original village was established in the 1830s by settlers from upstate New York, who parsimoniously gave the resident Potawatomi two rifles and a bag of grain for the land. Soon thereafter,

ambitious entrepreneurs championed the town as Michigan's as-yet-undesignated permanent capital. They built the first of those grand mansions, as well as one for the governor (now home of the local D.A.R. chapter). In 1847, Marshall lost the race by one vote. With Marshall out of the running, several more votes were taken, and more centrally located Lansing, just up the road, became the capital.

Trusses and Patent Medicines

So, plucky Marshall found other callings. The Michigan Central Railroad made this a hub. Then, the town became the world's patent-medicine capital—pills and potions good for whatever ails you (until the Pure Food and Drug Act came along in 1906). Next came hernia trusses. Marshall's most famous citizen, Harold C. Brooks, whose family ran the flour mill, and his wife, a seamstress, devised a garment that helped men in those days of heavy lifting. Marshall's trusses caught on, and Brooks began to donate part of his fortune to acquire and preserve Marshall landmarks.

These days, Marshall residents make their livings working at the local hospital or at small- to midsize manufacturing businesses, or by commuting to jobs in nearby cities such as Lansing and Jackson. But they remain devoted to their town's treasures—such as the Honolulu House.

In the 1850s, Michigan Supreme Court Chief Judge Abner Pratt of Marshall was appointed U.S. Counsel to the Sandwich Islands, as Hawaii was known at that time. He returned home with a passion for all things Polynesian. Pratt even dined on Hawaiian-style food and affected island attire. The result of his obsession was a home that was an extravagant fusion of Victorian and Hawaiian design, now restored and home to the historical society.

The Honolulu House had to be one of the most unusual residences of its day. Not that it isn't lovely. It's just so . . . unexpected. Oriental and Victorian embellishments. A huge central tower outside and a grand winding staircase inside. Extravagant decorative paintings that all but smother the walls and 15-foot ceilings.

On a Saturday evening when I, frankly, find myself dead-tired and a bit homesick, I head out for a stroll around the town square and its colorfully lit fountain, just steps away from my big corner room at the National House. Couples hold hands, kids toss a Frisbee and some senior citizens savor ice cream cones. It's like a scene from a Frank Capra movie. Up the street, neighbors are out trimming their lawns, chatting over backyard fences. Home doesn't seem so far away.

One of the Midwest's most historic places, yes, but Marshall is also one of its most appealing small towns, a place that I could easily call home.

(*Clockwise, from opposite*) Antiques and glassware in a Marshall shop. Trompe l'oeil inside the exotic 1860 Honolulu House. An exterior view of the Honolulu House. Landmark Brooks Memorial Fountain in the town square. The National House, the state of Michigan's oldest continuously operating inn.

Somewhere in Time

A jet ferry spewing plumes of spray makes the crossing in just 20 minutes and magically transports everyone to the 19th century. As we near Mackinac Island, the postcard-perfect scene comes into focus once again.

You couldn't reinvent a place like the white-columned Grand Hotel, which spreads across a Mackinac (MACK-i-naw) Island bluff. This is an all-wood retreat on a remote northern island reachable only by ferry, where no motorized vehicles are allowed. (The town fathers outlawed the noisy automobile soon after it was introduced.) Half the year, it's an igloo on this outpost in the Straits of Mackinac between Michigan's two peninsulas, and even summer days can be brisk. There are no roller coasters or indoor water parks, much less slot machines or blackjack tables.

The Grand's most stirring moments are when middle-aged couples fox-trot to the sound of Cole Porter classics. Gentlemen must (repeat, *must*) wear jackets and ties, and women must wear dressy outfits for the five-course dinners served in the cruise-ship-size dining room.

Simply Grand

No tipping is allowed anywhere in the hotel, even though the tuxedoed waiters are unfailingly gracious in the face of a summerlong full house. Surely, this is one of America's, and certainly the Midwest's, most revered and successful summer resort hotels. Its 385 rooms already are mostly booked for tonight and throughout the prime vacation-season weeks ahead.

The hotel's statistics inspire awe: built in just 93 days in 1887; financed by two railroad companies and a steamship line; world's largest summer hotel; longest front porch in the world (660 feet) with 100 wooden rockers, plus 10 American flags fluttering from the columns; 1,600 geraniums potted in seven tons of soil filling 260 Chippendale-style planters; a staff of 600; two nine-hole golf courses as beautiful as the hotel itself.

Mackinac Island (about eight miles around) is home to some 600 horses in the summer, most of them hardworking draft breeds tended by one full-time veterinarian on the island and several others from off-island when necessary. In winter, the horses are ferried back to a farm on the mainland. Not a bad life.

During peak season, the Arnold Line alone ferries average 25 round-trips per day "from ice to ice" (mid-April to early January) from Mackinaw City, and another 23 trips per day from St. Ignace. The ferries bring a steady stream of visitors, guests and supplies, including fresh ingredients for the 4,000 meals served daily at the Grand.

Although closed to guests during the winter months, the hotel is still busy with crews doing the painting, decorating and maintenance work they can't get done in summer. Other small hotels and inns on the island are open, however, and the island becomes a haven for cross-country skiers, snowshoers and solitude seekers. Islanders snowmobile across the straits from St. Ignace, following an ice highway marked by Christmas trees. There's an airstrip on the island, plus police, fire and ambulance services. Although emergency vehicles are allowed here, I've never seen a single one on the streets.

In the movie department: Ever heard of *Somewhere in Time,* the 1980 movie starring Jane Seymour and the late Christopher Reeve? Or *This Time for Keeps,* a 1947 film with Esther Williams and Jimmy Durante? Both were filmed here. The Grand's guest book also includes five U.S. presidents and countless other celebrities.

For centuries, this island has been the strategic key to the straits linking Lake Huron to Lake Michigan and, eventually, Lake Superior. The whitewashed stone walls of restored 18th-century Fort Mackinac preside high above the quaint village where "fudgies" (that's tourists like me) roam the streets in search of souvenirs and confections to take home. Horses pull fringed surreys past dollhouselike Victorian summer homes that parade up hillsides. It's lilac time in June, and tree-size shrubs drip with fragrant lavender-color blooms at every turn.

The word Michilimackinac means Land of the Great Turtle to the Ojibwa, who always have considered the island sacred. Then came fur-trading voyageurs, fishermen and, relatively recently, resorts in the 1880s. At the fort, exhibits tell the

(Clockwise, from opposite) Lilacs, reportedly a legacy of early French missionaries, blooming on cue for the annual lilac festival on Mackinac Island. Arriving by horse-drawn carriage at Grand Hotel. Breakfast in the Grand's dining room. A view of the 1887 Grand Hotel from the sweeping front lawn.

(Clockwise, from left) Firing the cannon from the ramparts of Fort Mackinac. The ferry crossing to Mackinac Island. Mackinac's famous fudge.

story of the first battle of the War of 1812, which was fought here when the British surprised the American garrison. The restored officers' quarters offer a look at life on an 1800s military post, and we watch a court martial reenacted on the parade grounds. A boom rocks the compound when soldiers in 1880s dress fire a cannon from the ramparts.

Near the fort stands the white-frame mansion purchased in 1945 as the governor's summer residence. Not a bad perk of office. The mansion was offered first to the U.S. government as a summer White House. I would have grabbed it.

About that legendary Mackinac Island fudge: Murdick's is my choice (everyone who visits has a personal favorite). At the main shop in the village, aproned cooks deftly wield their paddles on 32-pound puddles of gooey chocolate, chocolate-walnut and chocolate-pecan, the most popular flavors here. In all, they'll fill their copper cooking kettles with enough chocolate, cream and sugar to make 700 pounds of fudge in one day. The secret, they say, lies in those marble slabs, which maintain just the right temperature for working the molten chocolate.

Old-Style Relaxation

Back to Grand Hotel for a few hours' relaxation before dinner. Recreation hasn't changed here much since the Victorian era. Guests choose pastimes such as croquet, golf, English tea, dancing to a live orchestra, strolling the grounds or swimming in that Esther Williams pool.

I settle into the long Grand Parlor with a hotel history book and soak up the almost startling mixture of colors and antiques. In 1977, the Grand commissioned celebrity designer Carleton Varney of New York's iconic Dorothy Draper design firm to spruce up the place. The result: a one-of-a-kind palette of lime green, pink, lilac, yellow, black and red that, improbable as it sounds, meshes beautifully.

All the rooms are different, including 31 themed suites. Some are named for First Ladies, others for royal figures or famous people of the day. Decorating ranges from chintz to the Hollywood Room, where my wife, Julie, and I once stayed, done in shades of bordello red—another side to this resort grande dame that made us laugh.

The whole idea is to make a memory here, staffers say. On that front, Michigan's totally enchanting Grand Hotel and Mackinac Island succeed like nowhere else.

Superior Country

Scenic, splendid, wild, unforgettable—my standard travel-writer's arsenal of adjectives doesn't do justice to Michigan's Upper Peninsula (UP), a 366-mile near-wilderness of woods, waterfalls and rushing streams.

Waterfall at Miners Beach within Pictured Rocks National Lakeshore

he wild country beyond the Straits of Mackinac doesn't seem to belong to the same state that produced Motown music, millions of automobiles and refined resorts the likes of Mackinac Island's Grand Hotel—and it almost didn't.

Michigan and Ohio came to blows back in 1835: the Toledo War. At issue was the boundary between the two states. For years, Michigan had claimed Toledo—actually, an area known as the Toledo Strip. No way, contended Ohio. Michigan's militia invaded, but no one was hurt—both state armies were hopelessly lost in swamps, as the story goes. Congress mediated the dispute and awarded Toledo to Ohio, and compensated Michigan with a wilderness tract that came to be called the Upper Peninsula.

Over the years, the fortunes of the UP waxed and waned with two industries: mining (iron ore, copper, silver) and logging. More recently, tourism has surged. Once, the UP was isolated by the straits—travelers often had to wait hours to board a car ferry. "Yoopers" and "Trolls" (their Lower Michigan cousins) alike cheered in 1957 when the Mackinac Bridge, a five-mile-long suspension marvel, opened.

Yet the peninsula remained remote enough to discourage developers. Those undaunted by distance backed off in the face of long, very snowy winters. Snow is measured in feet (or hundred of inches) in this north country, and the last patches might not melt completely until May or June. Summer has an almost frenetic quality, as if everyone is eager to squeeze in as much outdoor time as possible. We Mid-westerners love our seasons, and here they seem even more compelling and dramatic.

Thundering Falls

Late in the afternoon on State-123 near Paradise, a flatbed truck loaded with enormous logs rumbles past; the only other vehicle on the road, but what a vehicle! The giant passes our SUV with a whoosh. Nothing seems to be small here on the UP—not the forests, the views, or even the distances between towns.

One of the largest waterfalls between the Rockies and Niagara courses through the woods that cover much of this part of the eastern UP (about 70 miles north of St. Ignace). From the visitor parking area of Tahquamenon Falls State Park, an easy trail leads to the Upper Falls. Five smaller cataracts swirling around an island form the Lower Falls, about four miles downstream. Soon I hear it: a low roar, muffled by the dense pine-and-hardwood forest.

I get my first full view of the falls from an observation platform that reaches right out over the tumbling 200-foot-wide, 50-foot-high cascade. I'm mesmerized. The waterfall, one of more than 250 here on the UP, is crystal clear, with a striking amber-brown tint. The hue comes from tannins in the conifers growing in upstream swamps, which are drained by the 94-mile-long Tahquamenon River as it courses to Lake Superior. The suds at the base of the falls are natural, too, proof of the softness of the water.

Even with the surrounding state park and the clearly marked trail that leads to the falls, this place has a secret quality, and it feels like a discovery. For centuries, the Chippewa fished and hunted here. In "Song of Hiawatha," the poet Longfellow describes his immortal Indian brave building a canoe by the "rushing Tahquamenaw." Then in the late 1800s, lumberjacks felled millions of giant red and white

cious quality of this area, it was authorized in 1966 as the National Park system's first national lakeshore. Protected and hardly developed, the park remains relatively pristine, with few roads and mostly hike-in beaches and campgrounds.

Karen Gustin, the park superintendent, leads us down a raised wooden walkway to Miners Castle, one of the most spectacular formations and one of the only ones easily reachable by car. There's a chill in the air this morning, even though it's midsummer. Soon we reach the viewing platform and one of the region's most jaw-dropping panoramas. It's so incredibly beautiful here, and hushed—just the sound of the breeze and Lake Superior pounding against the rocky shore far below.

Karen's previous postings with the park service took her to places including Alaska and Iowa, as well as California's Death Valley, which was about as different from this place as possible. Except for one thing: Karen was amazed to discover the same colors (streaks of ochre, brown, and tan) in the UP rocks that she saw in California. The park's namesake "pictures"—as in the faraway desert—are the result of ages of mineral seepage. Across Trout Bay at Grand Island National Recreation Area, there's not a boat, car or another human being in sight. Just seagulls.

It's an easy hike to the beach below for a view of Miners Castle overhead. Even more awesome! "What's it like in winter here?" I wonder. About 250 inches of snow, Karen says, but that doesn't stop the campers, snowshoers and cross-country skiers. White-tailed deer, beavers, black bears, bald eagles and weasels are at home here year-round, as are a few moose. Hiking trails and old logging roads tunnel through the forests of sugar maple, spruce and fir, leading to small inland lakes and waterfalls (the lakeshore extends five miles inland).

The lakeshore defies every stereotype about Midwest scenery, with its dunes and cliffs painted a rainbow of colors . . .

pines. In those days, logs were floated downriver in timber drives to sawmills, plunging over the top of these falls like toothpicks into a bowl. Today, hardwoods and hemlocks, part of this area's 1,700-acre old-growth forest, tower overhead, along with a mature second-growth forest.

Still agape at the splendor, I ask a fellow falls-watcher where he's from. Houghton, he says, some 300 miles farther west on the UP. "Well, how was your winter last year?" I ask. "Not too bad. Only about 200 inches of snow."

"What's a bad winter?" I wonder.

"It's when you can't find the tops of the stop signs, more like 400 inches."

On the way back to my car, I imagine this 40,000-acre state park in January, when the falls freeze into gigantic icicles and snowmobilers, cross-country skiers

and snowshoers claim the area, in spring when the forest reawakens, and in autumn, when the foliage explodes with color. I decide I have to come back and watch those seasons unfold.

Dunes and Rock Castles

Pictured Rocks National Lakeshore stretches across 42 miles and 73,000 acres of the UP's Lake Superior shore, from Grand Marais to Munising. It defies every stereotype about Midwest scenery, with its majestic dunes, solitary beaches and cliffs painted a rainbow of colors by seeping minerals. There also are rock formations unlike anything you'll see elsewhere: the rocky prows of Battleship Row jutting into Superior, Rainbow Cave and the view I have to see again from the parapet of Miners Castle.

In recognition of the unique and pre-

(Clockwise, from top left) The observation platform overlooking Upper Tahquamenon Falls. Marquette Harbor Lighthouse. A wooded lane at Pictured Rocks National Lakeshore.

'Queen City of the North'

With a population of 22,000, plus more than 9,000 students at Northern Michigan University, Marquette is the Big Apple of the UP. But it's the city's setting on Lake Superior's shore that makes it unforgettable.

Mining made this city wealthy in its late-1800s heyday, and this booming town was dubbed the "Queen City of the North." From docks on a wide harbor, hundreds of ships sailed away with 40 percent of the world's iron ore. The harbor isn't as busy these days, but a hulking 1,000-foot-long ore dock still looms above the water, disgorging its taconite pellets into freighters bound for the Atlantic.

In the city, grand churches and homes built with mining fortunes line the streets. Downtown, imposing facades of native rose-color sandstone line up along hilly streets, crowned by St. Peter's Cathedral atop a hill. Several blocks away, I pass Marquette's claim to fame, in Hollywood at least: the imposing Marquette County Courthouse, setting for the 1959 Otto Preminger film *Anatomy of a Murder* starring Jimmy Stewart and Lee Remick. The Oscar-nominated trial classic was based on a best-selling crime story by Judge John D. Voelker, a native of nearby Ishpeming.

The freighters and their crews once lent a rough-and-rowdy quality to downtown. Today, galleries, boutiques and a coffee shop that mixes a perfect latté are taking over. An old ore dock is slated to be developed as condominiums.

Next to downtown, Lake Superior almost surrounds Presque Isle Park, teeming with so many bicyclists, walkers, joggers and picnickers that I wonder if a warm, sunny day constitutes an automatic holiday. Priceless views of the harbor, studded with dozens of rocky islands, stop me on the route around the perimeter. Sandy beaches filled with sunbathers and kids splashing in the shallows look inviting. Reportedly, the waters here are among Lake Superior's warmest; still, I'm certainly not jumping in.

I first visited Marquette in 1998, to present volunteers with a *Midwest Living*® award for their work in beautifying State-28/41 with petunias and marigolds. The plantings still look magnificent. On that memorable evening, my hosts took me for a twilight jaunt around the harbor in their cabin cruiser. When I curiously inquired when the last ice disappears from the harbor, they looked at each other and giggled: June, this year, they said. Sometimes not until August.

Beside the harbor, the old waterworks building houses the Marquette Maritime Museum, which now includes the nearby Marquette Harbor Lighthouse. A pilgrimage to a lighthouse is a must in Michigan and easy to accomplish with 116 of them along the state's shores—a quarter of those open to the public.

Marquette's distinctive red "schoolhouse-style" lighthouse, once occupied by U.S. Coast Guardsmen and now automated, was only recently acquired by the museum. Built in 1866 to caution ore and logging ships away from hazardous rocks, it stands on a sliver of a bluff jutting into the harbor, with steep steps climbing to the entrance and a catwalk leading to the shore. Marquette preservationists are at work on the exterior and soon will turn to restoring the now-vacant interior.

The museum holds a wide assortment of exhibits about ships and shipwrecks, including gigantic beehivelike Fresnel lenses that glowed for years at two area lighthouses. I never dreamed they were so colossal—10 feet tall each. What stories they could tell about raging storms, as well as the ships that once served the Queen City and the UP's Superior Country!

(From left) The overlook at Miners Castle.
Lake Superior and Miners Castle, an
outcrop in Pictured Rocks National
Lakeshore northeast of Munising.

Piece of Pie, UP-Style

A Muldoons pasty

Okay, for the uninitiated: It's pronounced "PAST-ee" or "PAH-stee." Never say "Pay-stee." Got that?

Now, exactly what is a pasty? Well, it's a hearty, stewlike concoction encased in a folded-over, D-shape piecrust—a bit larger than the palm of a man's hand—and filled with a mixture of veggies, ground meat and seasonings. Usually, they're eaten in hand like sandwiches.

On the UP, pasties originated long ago with the wives and mothers of the area's Cornish copper and coal miners. The bakers pulled the pies hot from their ovens in the morning and wrapped them in napkins, to be reheated later on shovels in the chilly, damp mines. Up here, they're considered essential—what chili is to a Texan and lobster rolls are to a New Englander. Pasty signs are everywhere.

At Muldoons, along State-28 on the northwestern side of Munising (another UP town with an impossibly scenic bayside setting), lanky Dale "Muldoon" Beckwith has been preparing pasties since 6 a.m. The cafe, a Victorian cottage with only 10 tables, serves 350 a day of what some say are the best pasties on the UP.

The classic UP recipe includes ground beef and pork mixed with onions, carrots, potatoes and rutabagas. You can order yours with or without rutabaga (it adds a pleasant bite and texture) or all-vegetarian or the chicken version. What really starts a debate among the Yoopers (those who hail from the UP) gathered for lunch, though, is just what to put ON a pasty. Ketchup? No, mayonnaise. No, go for butter. Mustard is best. Pickles. All of the above!

I find pasties in general to be a true comfort food. But, to be honest, mine is a bit on the dry side. Then one of my companions offers up a culinary insight: That's why God invented gravy. Of course! I order some of Muldoons' brown gravy on the side. Pure ambrosia. But now I have to eat my pasty with a fork. Muldoons Pasties & Gifts (906/387-5880).

Quick-and-Easy Pasties

These shortcut pasties are perfect when time is scarce and leftovers plentiful.

- ½ of a 15-ounce package (1 crust) rolled refrigerated unbaked piecrust
- ⅔ cup chopped cooked beef, pork, veal and/or lamb
- ⅔ cup chopped cooked potato, carrot, turnip and/or rutabaga; cooked corn or cooked peas
- ¼ cup chopped onion
- 1 tablespoon steak sauce
  Milk
  Ketchup, pizza sauce or dairy sour cream

Let piecrust stand at room temperature according to package directions. On a lightly floured surface, unroll piecrust. Cut piecrust into fourths.

For filling: In a small bowl, combine meat, potato, vegetables, onion and steak sauce; toss lightly to coat.

Spoon about ⅓ cup of the filling onto half of each piece of piecrust. Lightly moisten piecrust edges with a little milk. Fold other half of piecrust over filling. Seal edges by crimping with tines of fork. Cut slits in the top of the pasties. Brush with a little additional milk. Place on a large, ungreased baking sheet.

Bake in a 375° oven for 15 to 20 minutes or until crust is golden brown. Cool slightly on wire racks. Makes 4 servings.

BACK TO SCHOOL

Lansing is the capital of the Midwest's most populous state. It's also a comfortable city of 120,000. The streets of downtown radiate from the 1872 limestone capitol. The monumental Michigan Library and Michigan Historical Center stand nearby. The capitol building, with its handsome dome of Michigan limestone, has been splendidly restored—down to the hand-painted walls and ceilings and extensive pine paneling that resembles mahogany. The historical center includes a re-created 19th-century copper mine and an Ypsilanti-built World War II bomber.

To the east across the Grand River spreads the Michigan State University (MSU) campus. With more than 45,000 students, it's one of the largest universities in the nation. I can only imagine the absolute mayhem when the Spartans play against the rival Michigan Wolverines in 72,027-seat Spartan Stadium.

Laid-back campus-town cafes and shops line streets that surround the parklike 5,200-plus-acre campus and its extensive botanical and horticultural gardens. First stop: the 4-H Children's Garden, which I scouted for a *Midwest Living®* story a few years back. I watch kids and parents explore this colorful world of plants.

A green awning above the entry to my other MSU favorite reads simply: Dairy Store. Nostalgic MSU alums, book-toting summer students and a family on a bicycling outing join me in line.

What to order? The new white chocolate with chocolate chips and raspberry hearts, or the coconut with chocolate-covered almonds? Chocolate cheese is the most famous product, but I can order that online from dairystore.msu.edu. Greater Lansing Convention & Visitors Bureau (888/ 252-6746, lansing.org).

More Favorites

CHARLEVOIX

Every May, residents plant 50,000 petunias along the main street of this historic northwestern Lower Peninsula resort community. Follow the blooms to the center of the town of 3,000 and the bascule (works with weights) bridge that spans the Pine River Channel linking Lake Michigan with Round Lake and Lake Charlevoix.

Mansionlike summer homes of families who've vacationed here for generations peek from the hills above the yacht basin in the heart of the business district. Boats of every description line the docks alongside a park where something always seems to be happening, from concerts to art fairs. Vacationers and summer residents browse shops and galleries along Bridge Street, the main thoroughfare.

West of Bridge Street, visitors drive through Boulder Park to see homes with mushroom-shaped rooflines, which local architect Earl Young designed. You can swim, sun and picnic at town beaches, and golf at some dozen area courses. Charlevoix is the departure point for planes (15-minute trips) and ferries (two-hour trips) to Beaver Island, the Great Lakes' most remote island, with its quaint village and miles of trails and empty beaches. More information: Charlevoix Area Chamber of Commerce (800/367-8557, charlevoix.org). Beaver Island Chamber of Commerce (231/448-2505, beaverisland.org).

DETROIT

Downtown unfurls from the Detroit River and gleaming towers of the Renaissance Center (General Motors world headquarters). Traveling northwest on busy Woodward Avenue, you pass the marquees of the reborn Theater District, the Tigers Comerica Park and the Lions neighboring new stadium, sports bars and restaurants.

Most of the city's great museums cluster in the Cultural Center area, including the Wright Museum of African American History, Detroit Historical Museum, New Detroit Science Center and Institute of Arts. Farther north, the Motown Museum traces the city's music legacy.

In suburban Farmington Hills, the new Holocaust Memorial Center features state-of-the-art exhibits, testimonials of area Holocaust survivors, a library and archives.

The Henry Ford Museum highlights Ford's hometown of Dearborn. Tours of Ford Motor Company's historic Rouge complex, including a truck plant, begin and end at the museum. More information: Detroit Metro Convention & Visitors Bureau (800/338-7648, visitdetroit.com).

SLEEPING BEAR DUNES NATIONAL LAKESHORE

In the northwestern reaches of Michigan's Lower Peninsula, glaciers and a millennium of wind and water sculpted a 35-mile strip of sand monoliths beside Lake Michigan. Today, this 70,000-acre preserve attracts all sorts of outdoor enthusiasts.

Park headquarters in Empire supplies details about ranger programs and maps of more than a dozen trails. The seven-mile Pierce Stocking Scenic Drive just north of Empire takes you to overlooks and paths through the mammoth shifting sand hills. Kids love the Dune Climb. More information: Sleeping Bear Dunes National Lakeshore (231/326-5134, nps.gov/slbe).

Travel Journal

AN 'ALMOST' CAPITAL

One of the Midwest's most historic towns lost out to Lansing as the center of state government, but its citizens have preserved a treasure trove of 19th-century architectural styles. Marshall Chamber of Commerce (800/877-5163, marshallmi.org).

Featured Stops

Honolulu House An improbably designed Victorian treasure modeled after structures the owner saw as ambassador to the Sandwich Islands (now Hawaii), preserved as a historic site and open for tours (269/781-8544).

National House Inn Michigan's oldest continuously operating inn, a onetime stagecoach stop, now beautifully restored and renovated. $$$–$$$$ (269/781-7374).

Schuler's An amalgamation of several historic buildings, founded in 1909 as a cigar store and lunch counter, now operated by grandson Hans Schuler. Known for a lavish Sunday brunch, featuring hand-carved roast beef and hickory-smoked ham, eggs Benedict and house-made pastries. Also a special-occasion restaurant with a diverse menu including New England braised pot roast and Schuler's classic prime rib (269/781-0600).

SOMEWHERE IN TIME

Since the early 1800s, vacationers have visited Mackinac Island in summer to exchange the heat of the cities for fresh lake breezes. More recently, travelers have discovered the beauty of Mackinac in winter, enjoying the solitude and stillness that have characterized the island for hundreds of years. Mackinac Island Tourism Bureau (800/454-5227, www.mackinacisland.org).

Featured Stops

Fort Mackinac One of five Mackinaw State Historic Parks. (Others include Historic Downtown Mackinac Island, and Historic Mill Creek, Colonial Michilimackinac and Old Mackinac Point Lighthouse in lively Mackinaw City at the Lower Peninsula's northern tip.) Fort Mackinac exhibits tell the story of the first battle of the War of 1812, which was fought here, and the island's development as a resort destination. You can see officers' quarters, cannon and rifle demonstrations and reenactments by costumed interpreters. Hands-on activities for kids. Lunch in the Tea Room at outdoor tables overlooking the island and straits. Admission charged (906/847-3328).

Grand Hotel A century-old landmark with 385 individually decorated rooms, from cozy chintz to themed suites, plus the world's longest front porch. Huge lunch buffet is a good way for non-guests to experience the hotel. Proper dress required. $$$$, including dinner and breakfast (906/847-3331).

Murdick's Fudge Creamy delight from all-natural ingredients in nearly 20 flavors (906/847-3530).

Transportation Ferry service to and from the island from Mackinaw City and St. Ignace: Arnold Line (906/847-3351). Shepler's Ferry (231/436-5023). Star Line Ferry (906/643-7635). Great Lakes Air (906/643-7165).

More Great Stops

Bike Tour With Doc Crain, three hours of local legends and lore, including island landmarks such as Arch Rock, Skull Cave, Sugarloaf, British Landing and Devil's Kitchen. Rentals available. June through September (906/847-6337).

Carriage Tours Gough's Livery (906/847-3435). Jack's Livery (906/847-3391). Mackinac Island Carriage Tours (906/847-3307).

Wings of Mackinac Showcasing free-flying butterflies in a lush, green garden conservatory (906/847-9464).

Lodging

Chippewa Hotel Waterfront Affordable lodgings in a renovated landmark. Spacious waterfront suites with balconies, whirlpools and a view of the harbor and marina. $$$–$$$$ (800/241-3341).

Hotel Iroquois on the Beach A Queen Anne-style inn on Mackinac Island's shore, with bedrooms and suites decorated in romantic cottage style. $$$$ (906/847-3321).

Metivier Inn A charming historic family home near downtown, converted into a bed and breakfast offering rooms with private baths and flower-filled views, two wicker-furnished porches and a breakfast buffet. $$$ (866/847-6234).

Windermere Hotel Bed & Breakfast Along Main Street, with beautifully furnished rooms and a view of the harbor and Round Island Lighthouse. $$–$$$$ (906/847-3301).

Dining

Woods Bavarian charm in a casual-dining restaurant that Grand Hotel operates (906/847-3699).

Yankee Rebel Tavern Classic regional dishes in a lively pub setting in Historic Downtown (906/847-6249).

SUPERIOR COUNTRY

Some of the Midwest's wildest places and most spectacular scenery survive in the central area of the Upper Peninsula, including Tahquamenon Falls and Pictured Rocks National Lakeshore. The UP's largest city, Marquette, has a rich mining and maritime history. Alger County Chamber of Commerce (906/387-2138). Marquette Country Convention & Visitors Bureau (800/544-4321, marquettecountry.org). Upper Peninsula Travel & Recreation Association (800/562-7134, uptravel.com).

Featured Stops

Marquette Maritime Museum & Lighthouse Historic Marquette Lighthouse, plus Fresnel lenses, a small theater, ship models, original dugout canoes and more (906/226-2006).

Pictured Rocks National Lakeshore More than 40 miles of sand dunes and rock formations with trails, beaches, waterfalls, a historic lighthouse and primitive camping along Lake Superior. Maps and other information at the visitor center in Munising (906/387-3700).

Tahquamenon Falls State Park Michigan's second largest state park, surrounding one of the largest waterfalls between the Rocky Mountains and Niagara. Also, the smaller Lower Falls with more trails and canoe rentals (906/492-3415).

More Great Stops/Activities

Glass Bottom Shipwreck Tour Departing from Munising, a tour boat gliding over historic wrecks visible through a viewing window (906/387-4477).

Grand Island National Recreation Area A historic location reachable by passenger ferry from Munising. Known for primitive camping and hiking and scenic mountain biking trails (906/387-3700).

Marquette Mission Park and Museum of Ojibwa Culture In St. Ignace, a National Historic Landmark museum devoted to some of the UP's earliest residents. Also home to explorer Father Jacques Marquette's grave (906/643-9161).

Northern Waters Adventures Expert guides offering sea kayaking trips along Pictured Rocks National Lakeshore and Grand Island Recreational Area, plus kayak rentals, sales and instruction (906/387-2323).

Pictured Rocks Boat Cruises Two- to three-hour narrated tours along one of the most scenic areas of Pictured Rocks National Lakeshore, including sights such as Rainbow Cave, Miners Castle and Battleship Row (906/387-2379).

Sault Ste. Marie Historic shore city, site of the locks that link Lake Superior and Lake Huron, with observation areas where visitors can watch building-size freighters lock through, plus tours of the harbor and locks. Sault Convention & Visitors Bureau (800/647-2858, www.saultstemarie.com). Soo Locks Boat Tours for two-hour locks tours, dinner cruises and half-day lighthouse excursions (800/432-6301).

Seney National Wildlife Refuge A 96,000-acre preserve that's home to more than 200 bird species (45 miles east of Munising). Follow a driving-tour route and hiking and bike-refuge back roads (906/586-9851).

Rent mountain bikes at Northland Outfitters in Germfask (800/808-3386).

Skylane Pictured Rocks & Grand Island Air Tours Small plane taking up to three adults and one child on 30- or 50-minute air tours over the national lakeshore (906/387-5611).

Tahquamenon Falls Train and Riverboat Tour A 6½-hour train and boat trip through the wilderness to the falls (888/778-7246).

Shopping

Da Yoopers Tourist Trap West of Marquette near Ishpeming, hilariously offbeat outdoor exhibits in the tradition of the Da Yoopers comedy band (800/628-9978).

Lodging

Best Western of Munising A motel convenient to the national lakeshore visitors center. $ (906/387-4864)

Landmark Inn A renovated hotel between Lake Superior and historic downtown Marquette. $$ (888/752-6362).

Pinewood Lodge B&B In Au Train, near Munising, log home surrounded by tall Norway pines, with a sand beach on the shores of Lake Superior. Three suites and two guest rooms. Craft shop with handmade items. $$$ (906/892-8300).

Tahquamenon Hotel In Hulbert, with several meal and lodgings packages. Restaurant known for hearty breakfasts, steaks and desserts. $ (906/876-2388).

Dining

The Navigator In Munising, known for fish specials (906/387-1555).

Sweet Water Cafe and Bakery In Marquette, featuring natural foods, plus coffee, breads and desserts to go (906/226-7009).

Sydney's In Munising, steak sandwiches and whitefish served with an Australian touch (906/387-4067).

Tahquamenon Falls Brewery Near the entrance to the Upper Falls area in the state park, with beers brewed on site, root beer and bargain kids' menu. Also a large gift shop (906/492-3300). ∎

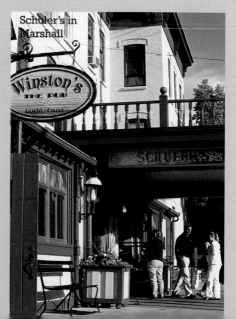

Schuler's in Marshall

Minnesota

■ Life is good in the North Star State, the Upper Midwest's burgeoning land of endless forests and prairies. The sprawling-yet-spotless Twin Cities and their very livable suburbs teem with attractions. From the tiniest Lake Wobegon village to the glass-and-steel downtown canyons of Minneapolis, Minnesotans are a hardy lot, tempered by brutal winters and that stoic Scandinavian outlook. Although they're proud of their growing diversity, the state's Nordic icons cannot be ignored: white-steepled Lutheran churches everywhere; lutefisk as soul food; phone-book listings of Andersons that seem to go on forever. No matter how sophisticated they become, I hope Minnesotans hold fast to their heritage, for all of us.

Madden's Golf Course in
the Brainerd Lakes area

Lakes and Legends

Central Minnesota's resort country is a land of tall tales: leviathan lumberjacks and wily whoppers, even golfers who lament the hole-in-one that got away. I've chosen Gull Lake, a personal favorite, for my story.

ear the geographic center of Minnesota, Brainerd is the heart of a vacation region spangled with almost 500 lakes and even more golf holes. Resorts seem to pop up at every turn. Heading into this north country (160 miles northwest of the Twin Cities) hardwoods gradually yield to dense stands of pine. Log structures are everywhere.

Once, this area was thick with virgin Norway and white-pine trees. In the late 1800s, lumberjacks felled those giants and floated them via the area's linked lakes and waterways to the not-yet-mighty Mississippi River at Brainerd (then a railroad and lumbermill town, with the maiden name of the wife of a railroad president). Many of the Midwest's homes were built with those Minnesota boards more than a century ago. Today's second-growth forests seem just as spectacular—including Pillsbury State Forest, eight miles west of Brainerd.

With 13,000 people in town and 66,000 in the surrounding area, once-backwater Brainerd, like many Midwest resort meccas, has boomed. New condos, chain motels and discount stores crowd retail strips at the edges of town. During the summer, 25,000 seasonal residents return to vacation homes ringing the nearby lakes—a few of them still jury-rigged cabins, more and more of them substantial year-round retreats.

Seven miles long and 80 feet at its deepest, Gull ranks as the area's best-known lake. But vacationers also are devoted to the Whitefish chain and Pelican Lake, as well as dozens of others.

In my book, Gull Lake is just about perfect. It's not remote, but not too crowded, either (although the old-timers I talk to seem to think it's becoming so). The shore is rimmed with woods and beaches, yet it's handy to golf, shopping and dining options. What more could you want?

Perfect Retreats

On Gull Lake's northeastern shore, a pine-canopied lane leads to the historic 1919 main building at Grand View Lodge. This historic retreat qualifies as the quintessential Minnesota resort. U.S., Minnesota and Canadian flags flutter above the entry, and flowers overflow from beds and pots. White trim outlines the dark-stained log exterior. Inside, the vintage lobby is all Indian blankets, found-antler light fixtures, leather furnishings and a big stone fireplace.

There's a more contemporary side to this property, too: four housing clusters on 700 acres, where you can rent lodgings from a single room to a 5,500-square-foot "cabin" with eight bedrooms and eight baths. Down by the lake, a big, angular log facility houses an indoor water park with a huge slide, plus an up-to-date fitness center. A handsome new Arts and Crafts-style bungalow serves as Grand View's Glacial Waters Spa, the place to go for services from relaxing facials and pedicures to the signature "Thermal Waters" massage.

As with most resorts in the area, Grand View takes great pride in its three golf courses, including the Arnold Palmer-designed Deacon's Lodge links. There's also bicycling, waterskiing, fishing and horseback riding—unless you prefer to just loll on the sandy beach with a good book.

Part of my mission here is fishing—serious fishing. Over the years, I've impaled my share of nightcrawlers on hooks, but the fine points of the sport have eluded me. Waiting by the shore to help is bearded, sun-bronzed sport-fishing pro Ron Lindner, 72, who along with his brother, Al, 61, heads a fishing-oriented family media empire. I gingerly board Ron's 20-foot, $40,000 bass boat. Soon, we're zipping across Gull Lake at almost 70 dizzying miles per hour.

Ron cuts the motor near some docks. Soon, he's reeling in a largemouth every two or three minutes. This goes on for about 10 minutes (Ron returns all the fish he catches to the water). "How did you do that?" I ask, incredulously. "Skip and sink." He shows me the technique. Somehow, it doesn't work quite as well for me.

The 130 resorts in the Brainerd area range from top-rated golf retreats such as Grand View to modest housekeeping cabins. Kavanaugh's, along neighboring Sylvan Lake, falls somewhere in between. Founded in 1969 by the late Sherm and Mae Kavanaugh, it has grown from nine

(Clockwise, from opposite) At Paul Bunyan Land in Brainerd. Gull Lake. Fishing with Ron Lindner. Grand View Lodge. Kavanaugh's chef/co-owner Tom Kavanaugh and his Walleye Amandine.

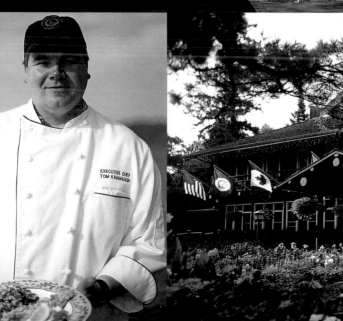

(*From left*) Nisswa shops.
Metal sculptor Jeff Kreitz.

cabins and a residence to 52 units and a lakeside restaurant operated by four of the six Kavanaugh sons who grew up here.

When I visited a few years ago for a story about resort dining, Tom Kavanaugh, the friendly, linebacker-solid executive chef, showed me secrets for cooking walleye, the Holy Grail of Minnesota fish. He's still in top form. Wearing his trademark baseball cap and chef's jacket, Tom rules the kitchen, where he learned to cook as a kid at his mother's side. He serves more than 200 pounds of walleye each week during the season. For me, he prepares a special walleye amandine, with his signature artichoke tartar sauce on the side. Mae Kavanaugh would be proud.

Woodsy Resort Towns

Nearby communities that started as logging camps now cater to vacationers who aren't necessarily interested in roughing it. The rail line that once linked these communities has been converted into the 100-mile Paul Bunyan Trail for bicycling and hiking. It's one of the longest rail trails in the nation, passing by 21 lakes.

Just north of Gull Lake at Nisswa (population 1,900), a big sign modestly touts: "Pretty Good Shopping." That's a typical Minnesota-nice understatement. Upscale furniture, accessories, antiques, crafts, toys, gourmet treats, books, jewelry and more pack the village's shops.

Nisswa's other hallmark is the Wednesday afternoon turtle races. Some 3,000 people show up to watch the low-key competitors go for the gold (all are handled very humanely). Left your racing turtle at home? You can rent one.

A few more miles north, a fishing-bobber water tower crowns Pequot Lakes (population 1,800). More shops and eateries tempt visitors, including Silver Creek Traders, a north-woods wonderland of style—much of it fabricated by Minnesota artisans. Next door, Sibley Station, the most popular restaurant in town, serves a trademark Hungarian mushroom soup.

Around the corner, the Plaid Duck sells all sorts of coffees. I doubt whether Paul Bunyan really would order his namesake drink: a mocha with caramel, praline and macadamia-nut flavorings. Inventive proprietor Linda Ulland is a longtime friend of mine and Julie's who decided a decade ago to quit the corporate world for life at the lake. I take a break on a bench near the re-created train depot that serves as the local tourism information office and watch bicyclists parade past on the trail.

Several years ago, Julie and I were exploring this area on a getaway with several other couples, when a metal sculptor's studio caught our eye. I never forgot him or his creations. He's Jeff Kreitz, and his roadside studio is in nearby Crosslake, a part of the Whitefish chain. High-energy Jeff, now 43, spent most of his growing-up years here, part of an artistic family. Then, he headed off to the Twin Cities and wound up working as a welder there.

Now he's back home in the north woods, raising two children with his wife, Julie, and applying those welding skills in a remarkable way. His unique combination of technical skills and creativity shines in the sculptures, home accessories and furnishings he fabricates. Jeff shows me a life-sized moose, a huge eagle and a stylized fish. The textures and tones he pulls out of copper, brass and other metals are amazing.

Why did he come back? "It's very inspiring. I get lots of ideas from the wildlife, the water and the landscape, the sun coming up over the lakes." That's exactly how I feel about this land of woods and water.

Magnificent Obsessions

Darwin's Twine Ball

I'd never thought of Minnesota's reserved Scandinavians getting passionate about anything. But I came across the stories of two men who zealously pursued very different dreams with fervor that counters the stereotype.

Dream Ship It's generally accepted that the Vikings beat Christopher Columbus to the New World (Canada) by a few hundred years. Back in 1971, Robert Asp, a Moorhead junior high school guidance counselor, was recovering from a back injury when a big idea grabbed him.

The father of seven decided to build and sail a replica Viking ship. Soon, Asp, his brother, Bjarne, and other family and friends were felling white-oak trees (chosen for their pliability) on a Red River Valley farm. The boards were air-dried for two years, then hand-cut for the ship they called the *Hjemkomst* (YEM-komst, "homecoming" in Norwegian). The men estimated they'd need 15 trees and two years to complete the project. Ultimately, it required 100 trees and eight years. Asp and his crew of family and friends toiled through weekends and vacations until the ship was trucked to Duluth for a test voyage on Lake Superior.

Then tragedy struck. Asp, who had been diagnosed with leukemia in 1974, died in December 1980, but not before seeing his ship—and his dream—successfully launched. His passing only steeled the resolve of his associates, who sailed in 1982 from Duluth to New York City via the Great Lakes, Erie Canal and Hudson River. From there, they braved the stormy Atlantic to sail to Bergen, Norway.

With only a tent on deck for shelter and a pail for their loo, the crew navigated their doughty 76½-foot-long, 17½-foot-wide craft. The ship now rests at the *Hjemkomst* Interpretive Center in Moorhead, just across the Red River from downtown Fargo, North Dakota. The tentlike center with its pole supports and white fabric roof was intended to evoke a sailing ship. Etched in a glass panel beside a bust of Asp is a quote attributed to him: "A dream is only a dream until it becomes reality." Heritage *Hjemkomst* Interpretive Center (218/299-5511, hjemkomst-center.com).

Wrapped Up in Twine One March day in 1950, 46-year-old Francis A. Johnson, a Swedish American bachelor in south-central Minnesota, picked up a discarded piece of thick sisal twine used to assemble bales of hay and straw. He fidgeted with it between his fingers, then started rolling it into a ball. Twenty-nine years later, when he called it quits, that ball of twine weighed 17,400 pounds and measured 40 feet wide and 11 feet tall. It's the pride of his hometown, Darwin (about 55 miles west of the Twin Cities, population 276).

By all accounts a quiet man, Francis was a frugal, self-employed carpenter. As time passed and his fiber Frankenstein grew and grew, he ingeniously employed massive railroad jacks (designed to lift boxcars) to help maintain its round shape. He improvised a shelter from the metal top of a silo and chained his prized possession to a tree to discourage potential twine-ball rustlers.

Francis died in 1989 at age 85. His creation was transported by forklift to Darwin—a milestone that even drew reporters from the Twin Cities. Today, the ball of twine reposes in splendor in a modern, Plexiglass-enclosed gazebo beneath Darwin's water tower, and the townsfolk celebrate with "Twine Ball Days" the second weekend in August each year. Clearly, Johnson's obsession gave this tiny farming community a mission and an identity. Twine Ball Museum (320/693-2199).

Hjemkomst Viking ship

Tale of Two Cities

Together, Minneapolis and St. Paul form a vibrant metropolis that I consider America's most eminently livable urban environment. But they're not identical. These "twins" are very different siblings.

First, the basics: 3 million people in an area that engulfs much of east-central Minnesota. It's the Midwest's third largest metropolis (after Chicago and Detroit), and the 15th largest in the nation. Smaller and older St. Paul (population 287,000) spreads mostly north and east of the winding Mississippi River. To the west, the river divides larger and younger Minneapolis (population 383,000). Each city has its own nest of suburbs, knit together by webs of freeways that often are discretely walled off from residential neighborhoods.

The Mississippi brought explorers, soldiers and settlers to St. Paul beginning in the early 1800s, and the river's St. Anthony Falls powered the lumber and flour mills that fueled Minneapolis' mid-1800s boom. Soon, the cities became the processing and transportation hub for the state's vast timber, mining and agricultural riches. Water also helps explain the cities' cachet as a place to live: Minneapolis alone has more than 22 lakes.

Venerable St. Paul

Prosperous, sophisticated, highly educated and proud of its heavily Scandinavian-influenced heritage—Minnesota's gorgeous twins are a world of their own. But don't assume that St. Paul and Minneapolis are interchangeable. These are fraternal, not identical, twins. On this trip, I want to track down differences, not similarities. I'll

start with the wonderful museums and historic attractions in St. Paul's blossoming downtown district. "If Minneapolis is glass and steel, then St. Paul is bricks and mortar." That's how one of my contacts summarizes the distinction.

But there's more. St. Paul has been an ethnic melting pot over the decades: It was settled by Irish, German and French immigrants, and later by Hispanics and Italians and now Hmongs from Southeast Asia. There still are plenty of Scandinavians here, but they don't dominate the way Swedes do in Minneapolis.

It's hillier. The regal state capitol and nearby Cathedral of Saint Paul give an almost European air to the compact downtown. St. Paul, despite its blue-collar image, is quite a college town. In proportion to its population, the city has the nation's highest ratio of institutions of higher learning after Boston.

I pull my SUV into the busy circular driveway of the esteemed 1910 Saint Paul Hotel, across the street from Rice Park in the heart of downtown. The hotel is a masterpiece of traditional elegance, originally designed for local tycoon Lucius P. Ordway by the firm that designed New York's fabulous Grand Central Terminal.

The hotel's always-busy St. Paul Grill is my favorite dining spot in the Twin Cities. I love the clubby atmosphere, the dark wood booths, the white tablecloths and the

bustling waitstaff dressed in white shirts and black ties. The food is excellent: walleye, chicken pot pie, salmon and beef.

Outside the window, through the pouring rain, I see the variety of structures that surround the tiny park: the chateaulike Landmark Center, a former federal courthouse, now an events center; the 2000 Xcel Energy Center, home of the Minnesota Wild NHL hockey club, as well as a venue for productions from rock concerts to circuses; the Ordway Center, where the St. Paul Chamber Orchestra and the Minnesota Opera perform; the St. Paul Central Public Library.

I can also make out the life-size bronze statue of novelist F. Scott Fitzgerald, who grew up just west of here along St. Paul's mansion-lined Summit Avenue. The edifices outside my window represent a range of architectural styles, which is another of the reasons I love St. Paul. The city looks like it's been around awhile, and it wears its age very gracefully. A few of St. Paul's five miles of downtown skywalks also are visible.

Next morning, my first stop is the awesome Cathedral of Saint Paul. The layout, scale and even the serpentine design of the black-and-gold Portoro marble columns of the altar canopy are similar to the Vatican's. Dedicated on Palm Sunday, 1915, this architectural wonder was the vision of Archbishop John Ireland (1838–1918), a

(Clockwise, from opposite) Inside the capitol dome. Cathedral of Saint Paul from the capitol near the quadriga. The St. Paul Grill. F. Scott Fitzgerald statue in Rice Park.

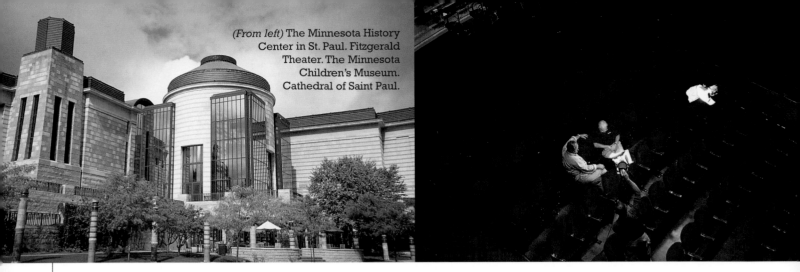

charismatic immigrant and Civil War chaplain. He who commissioned a Frenchman, Emmanuel Masqueray, to design his cathedral in the Renaissance and Beaux Arts styles. Alan Spillers of the cathedral staff tells me there are 780,000 Catholics in the Archdiocese of St. Paul and Minneapolis, many of them German, Italian, Ukrainian and Hispanic. This hushed sanctuary is rich in history. Alan points out the dark-oak pew where President John F. Kennedy worshiped the week before the Cuban Missile Crisis in 1962.

On our tour, I'm fascinated by one particular stone embedded here (among many historic artifacts from around the world). It's from the castle where Joan of Arc was held prisoner in 1431. Every time I look up at the soaring, 186-foot dome and the glimmering stained-glass rose window, I'm awed anew by the grandeur. Upkeep here is a lot more than a matter of changing light bulbs and polishing floors. Just recently, the cathedral underwent a $32 million exterior restoration, including tuck-pointing of 42 miles of Minnesota granite.

A block southeast along fabled Summit Avenue, America's richest collection of grand Victorian homes stands along a single street. Also lining the boulevard are 14 churches and four colleges. The huge red-sandstone Richardsonian Romanesque 1891 James J. Hill House is a tribute to what a railroad tycoon could do with his spare cash—pre-federal income tax.

Hill (1838–1916) was boss of the Great Northern Railway, one of the reasons St. Paul boomed in the late 1860s. Although the house hasn't been completely refurnished inside (too many original pieces are unaccounted for), it's still impressive, containing an art gallery and meeting facilities. I study the elaborate carved oak woodwork and stained-glass windows. The original owner glares down at me from a portrait. Obviously, he was a man who could make sure people got things done his way.

Downtown Family Fun

St. Paul is a dream getaway for families these days, because so much worth seeing is concentrated in a small area. The Minnesota History Center, Minnesota Children's Museum and the Science Museum of Minnesota all have moved to impressive new downtown facilities.

The Minnesota History Center, near the state capitol, is one of the Midwest's largest. I'm most intrigued by the gallery devoted to the state's weather, including a replica of a home basement where visitors wait out a re-creation of the tornado that ripped through a Twin Cities suburb on May 6, 1965. Over a period of six minutes, I experience the darkening skies, the loss of power, the deafening roar overhead and the subsequent devastation. A Nebraska tornado killed my great-grandmother on Easter Sunday in 1916. My mother and grandparents survived that murderous dreadnought. Now, I have a better understanding of the terror they felt.

Another weather exhibit deals with Minnesota winters and the paraphernalia required to withstand one: snowshoes, snow shovels, snow blowers, snow skis, snow boots, snow-everythings. Recent immigrants from warmer climes such as Venezuela and Somalia recount their first encounters with Minnesota winters. Still another weather exhibit deals with summer in Minnesota, notably good times at the lake. Things do seem to even out here over the course of a year.

Back down the hill along Seventh Street, the Minnesota Children's Museum focuses on hands-on fun. Parents, grandparents

and—oh, yes, kids—swarm all over a colorful collection of exhibits. I become an ant in a giant anthill, crawling through simulated tunnels. Then, I poke around other areas, including a toy warehouse "staffed" by visiting kids, a shadow theater where you can explore the properties of light and a paper factory that teaches about recycling and even lets you make some paper yourself. Finally, I linger at a for-fun market and restaurant that uses food to teach kids about respecting different cultures.

At the Science Museum of Minnesota, the big front entry is grand enough, but the real drama unfolds on the terrace out back, where you can gaze down the steep hillside to the busy Mississippi and the new park, condos, restaurants and retail shops. A dry-docked towboat gives me a chance to play river pilot. Back inside, large exhibit areas focus on the Mississippi, the human body and dinosaurs. I love the mellow tones of the seismophone, something like a giant wind chime. It's activated by earthquake activity anywhere in the world. I also enjoy the "collectors'" collection, with everything from the eggs of various species to Mexican textiles. There's a Minneapolis man's hoard of questionable medical devices.

Finally, what really intrigues me is a rough-sawn timber Hmong house, exactly as it would have been constructed in Southeast Asia, complete with furnishings and Hmong artwork on the walls. These hill people from Laos supported the U.S. during the Vietnam War. Then, they paid the price for that loyalty. Thousands of immigrants wound up in this area. Today, some 25,000 Hmong live in St. Paul, the largest community outside of California.

Progress and Prosperity

Next on my must-see list is Minnesota's 1905 state capitol, which presides over the Capitol Heights district overlooking downtown St. Paul. It appears almost snow-white, built of Georgian marble rather than Minnesota granite at the insistence of gifted Minnesota-raised architect Cass Gilbert. It's overcast but, as if on cue, a shaft of sunlight pierces the clouds to illuminate the gilded, recently restored quadriga (meaning a chariot pulled by four horses abreast, like the one over the Brandenburg Gate in Berlin) atop the south entrance. That sculpture is exactly what I want to see up close. On our way up to the roof, Carolyn Kompelien, capitol historic

site manager, points out the extensive detailing inside this landmark: paintings, murals, sculptures and lots of "M's" (for Minnesota) and gophers (for the Gopher State) embedded everywhere.

Designed in brass and marble directly beneath the huge capitol dome is the state's motto: *L'Etoile du Nord*, the North Star. We climb the stairs beside the dome. It's really windy now—but the view! Downtown office buildings on one side, that enormous cathedral dome just blocks away. The quadriga was created by Daniel Chester French, who did the Lincoln Memorial in Washington, D.C. Copper-covered, with 24-karat gold leaf and titled *The Progress of the State*, it features female figures named "Agriculture" and "Industry," with four horses representing earth, wind, fire and water. The charioteer is a handsome fellow named "Prosperity."

My next two stops deal with a side of Minnesotans that I haven't quite figured out. Maybe these visits will help. Some of the Midwest's most worldly urbanites live right here in the Twin Cities. Many of them reflect the reserved, cool Scandinavian personality traits you see in the brooding dramas of Ibsen and Strindberg. Yet when it comes to folk myths and humor, nobody in the Midwest surpasses Garrison Keillor's "Lake Wobegon" tales and the Ole and Lena stories Minnesotans love to tell.

When Keillor and Minnesota Public Radio needed a permanent home for his *Prairie Home Companion* live radio broadcasts in 1986, the theater in downtown St. Paul built as the Schubert in 1910 got a new lease on life. Then in 1994 came the new name (for F. Scott Fitzgerald). Almost 40 Saturday nights a year, 1,000-plus seats in the rich red interior are packed with Twin Citians and others from the Upper Midwest. They alternately laugh and cry during sketches, music and, of course, Keillor's classic monologues about life and ordinary people in fictional Lake Wobegon, the quintessential Minnesota small town.

prior to performances with fun like dancing the Ole and Lena *macarena*. Pam says the pair is like your lovable, but not overly bright, aunt and uncle. Almost everyone, Norwegian or not, knows an Ole and Lena.

Clean, Green Minneapolis

Minneapolis was named America's most fun city in a national report sponsored last year by a game manufacturer. It was based on such rankings as numbers of sports teams, restaurants, dance performances, toy stores and the share of the city budget devoted to recreation. The city also out-funned the other 49 in the survey, because it has more theater seats per capita than any city outside of New York, more parks than Rocky Mountain-high Denver and more golfers than any other community anywhere. After the party's

pin' town, a local tourism representative tells me. One way that's readily apparent is the $500 million spent on new and updated cultural attractions—from a new venue for the city's renowned Guthrie Theater to doubling the size of the contemporary Walker Art Center and expanding the Minneapolis Institute of Arts and the adjoining Children's Theater.

Pro sports are big here, too. The NFL Vikings and Major League Baseball Twins share the 64,000-seat, Teflon-coated, white-fabric-roofed Hubert H. Humphrey Metrodome downtown. Indoor sports facilities obviously make sense in this climate. The NBA Timberwolves take to the boards at the Target Center on First Avenue.

Twin Cities sports fans are interesting. They're relatively reserved, unlike the boisterous crowds in some cities. They certainly wouldn't do anything as rude as hiss or throw chairs at the players. However, you may recall Twins fans getting so whipped up a few seasons ago that they wantonly waved their white "homer hankies." Very civilized.

The dining scene has advanced well beyond the stereotypical lutefisk and Swedish meatballs. These days, just in the downtown area, you can taste Latin, Russian, Thai, Ethiopian, Somali and Greek fare. At night, downtown's Warehouse District jumps with live jazz and rock.

These are fraternal, not identical, twins . . .
Modern Minneapolis is glass and steel,
and gracious St. Paul is bricks and mortar.

More clues about Minnesotans' quirky funny bones come in the suburb of North Saint Paul. In a modest former Masonic temple, I stop by the Oops! Interactive Dinner Theater. Pam Docken is the Garrison Keillor of this mini phenomenon. A former state employee with a knack for comedy, she's now the writer, producer and star of Ole and Lena productions. I'm referring to blockbusters like "An Ole and Lena Christmas" and "Ole and Lena Go to New York in Search of the Big Apple."

Twin Citians are so into Pam's productions that many patrons show up wearing Ole and Lena attire: flannel, boots, aprons and camouflage hunting gear. Lena, I mean Pam, likes the audience to warm up

over, another study (this one sponsored by a national hotel chain) declared Minneapolis America's best city for a good night's sleep.

Corporate America must feel at home here: Nine of the Fortune 500 companies roost in Minneapolis (all told, there are 19 from the list in the Twin Cities). Among the Minneapolis corporate all-stars: General Mills and Pillsbury (this is America's original flour-power capital), Best Buy and Target. The city also is a magnet for advertising creative types. The first words that come to mind when I think of Minneapolis—with its Scandinavian eco-ethic and endless parks—are "clean and green."

But there's more. Minneapolis is a hop-

Lots of outlying neighborhoods beckon urban explorers as well, including Uptown in the lakes district, with its funky boutiques, and Dinkytown, near the University of Minnesota campus, with bookstores and coffeehouses. The city has what I consider one of America's most dazzling skylines, packed with muscular skyscrapers that now dwarf the Foshay Tower, for decades the region's tallest building.

It's a beautiful, sunny day after several recent downpours. The glassy skyscrapers with their futuristic shapes and angles seem to dance with light and shadows. On the fringes of downtown, especially along the Mississippi, a new influx of pioneers is transforming once-shabby warehouses into condos and lofts.

More than 40,000 people live in downtown Minneapolis. That's more than in Dallas, Houston, Denver and a few other cities combined! The blue, yellow and white cars (recalling the colors of the Swedish flag, perhaps?) of the new light-rail transit (LRT) system glide for 12 miles through the city, including a line that extends south to the airport and the enormous Mall of America.

A quick stroll along the main downtown pedestrian artery, Nicollet Mall, helps me get reoriented. Some of the scenes look vaguely familiar, especially inside the vast lobby of the 50-story IDS Center. Then, I eye a statue in front of Marshall Field's (formerly Dayton's) at the corner of Eighth and Nicollet. It's a bronze of the '70s TV megastar tossing that famous beret up in the air, just as she did playing Minneapolis TV producer Mary Richards every week in the *Mary Tyler Moore Show.*

Some of the city's seven miles of skywalks span downtown streets—more of these passages than you'll find anywhere else. But that doesn't mean Twin Citians hole up indoors in winter. There are dozens of places to go ice-surfing, -fishing and -skating, as well as cross-country skiing. One contact tells me: "You're not a gerbil in a tunnel here in winter. This city is built for winter."

Despite its affinity for the outdoors, Minneapolis also celebrates history and the arts. Near the river along South Second Street downtown, I learn about flour—specifically, how the white stuff launched this metropolis. From the breezy ninth-floor observation area at the new state-of-the-art Mill City Museum, an impressive view unfolds: the river, parks, dams, bridges and

(Clockwise, from top left) Le Meridien Minneapolis. The Mary Tyler Moore statue. A Lakes District bike trail. The castlelike American Swedish Institute.

(From left) View from the Mill City Museum near the Mississippi. *Spoonbridge and Cherry* at Minneapolis Sculpture Garden.

rehabbed industrial buildings repurposed as condos and lofts. It's a far cry from a century ago, when this neighborhood was packed with working flour mills.

Laura Salveson is a transplanted Chicagoan of Scotch-Irish descent, married to a Minnesota Norwegian. The museum she helps manage was rebuilt within the ruins of the huge 1880 Washburn A Flour Mill. Its goal is to tell the stories of the people and industries that built Minneapolis.

As early as 1821, the once-thundering St. Anthony Falls provided power for lumber and grain mills. Just after the Civil War, the railroads arrived, making it possible to ship endless boxcars of Red River Valley hard red spring wheat, perfect for baking flour. From about 1880 to 1930, Minneapolis ruled the industry with dozens of mills. These days, most of the milling in America is done in Los Angeles (go figure). The last mill on the Minneapolis riverfront closed in 2003.

I also find that the mills spawned their own mini industries: barrel making, bag making and, brutally, artificial limbs (due to the dangerous working conditions). Arch rivals Washburn-Crosby (the forerunner of General Mills) and Pillsbury squared off on opposite sides of the Mississippi. Various exhibits, including a ride on the informative Flour Tower multimedia elevator, show me how wheat was transported, milled and marketed.

Sophisticated Swedes

Another aspect of Minneapolis history I have to explore is the American Swedish Institute, housed in a turreted mansion built in 1908 by Swan Turnblad, who made a fortune publishing America's largest Swedish-language newspaper. Turnblad's fanciful 33-room French chateau-style home is packed with treasures: paintings, textiles, glass and crystal.

It's also a repository of historical and genealogical records about Sweden and the Swedes who migrated here from the late 1800s through about 1930 (today, one in ten Minnesotans claims Swedish lineage). Communications Manager Jan McElfish (her grandmother was Swedish) responds with a joke when I ask her to characterize the Swedish personality: "Did you hear the one about the Swede who loved his wife so much he almost told her?"

They may be standoffish, but Swedes appreciate artistic expression. This place is packed with beautiful Swedish furnishings, porcelain stoves, ceiling plasterwork, stained glass and elaborate wood-carvings (done by 18 carvers over two years).

The Minneapolis Institute of Arts and the neighboring Children's Theatre Company are two pillars of the local cultural scene that share a beautiful courtyard. Both are undergoing expansions that are part of the city's current arts-facility building binge. The institute's exhibits span 5,000

years of treasures, notably a Chinese collection that's considered the best in the nation.

I point the SUV southwest and take a quick breather on a park bench overlooking Lake Calhoun, part of a chain that flows through neighborhoods of beautiful old homes on the city's west side. Alongside the lake is a segment of the 53-mile Grand Rounds National Scenic Byway, the only such trail located entirely inside a city. Even though it's minutes from downtown, this area is a recreation paradise. Droves of sun-lovers roller blade, walk, bike and just lounge on and beside the paved byway. On the lake, sailboats and windsurfers glide by.

The Walker Art Institute nearby is another of those arts facilities getting a facelift, but across the street is the attraction I want to see: the Minneapolis Sculpture Garden, which showcases important works including Claes Oldenburg and Cossje van Bruggen's *Spoonbridge and Cherry*, which has become a sort of com-

munity symbol. Fittingly, the sculpture stands before a backdrop of that ever-changing Emerald City-like skyline.

For dinner, I head back downtown to the ultra-hip, 21-story Le Meridien Hotel and Cosmos, its fourth-floor restaurant. Wow. I'm feeling sort of like a Lake Wobegon James Bond entering the domain of nefarious Goldfinger. Outside, this enclave (which also includes Target Center, a Hard Rock Cafe and, of course, Starbucks) glows with so much neon that it looks like Las Vegas. Inside, it's sleek and contemporary.

Lots of celebrities and NBA stars stay here when they're playing or performing in the arena located on the other side of the skywalk. Curiously, everyone seems to be wearing black, except me. I head to the bar. Wow again. This is as slick a big-city hotel as any in New York or Los Angeles.

After screwing up my courage with a martini, I follow a black-garbed staffer to the hotel's Concert Suite that Cher recently

occupied. Your local Motel 6, this isn't: two 42-inch plasma TVs, a baby grand piano, a dining room table that seats eight, etched glass, blonde wood and stainless steel. In the bath: a Jacuzzi tub, marble floors, a sculptural sink and another TV.

Back in the dining room, my waiter is from France and, of course, is wearing all black. But he's a great guy, and dinner is fantastic—the emphasis is on exquisite presentation rather than quantity. A delicious French onion soup. An appetizer of scallops, cilantro, cashews and jicama. A salad with lobster and orange slices. Seared tuna entrée. All perfect. More beautiful people are streaming in—all wearing black.

I love it! And I love the Twin Cities. Minneapolis and St. Paul are the Upper Midwest's terrific twofer. They may seem similar at first glance, perhaps, but they're actually not at all alike. Each is packed with enough experiences to please even the pickiest Midwest traveler (me).

Enchanted Valley

The magical Root River Valley seems to cast a spell over everyone who visits. It's easy to see why. If the area's rugged bluffs, forests and quaint towns don't win you over, the pie-shop menu in tiny Whalan surely will.

Norwegian bonding

Southeast of Rochester, the view becomes more vertical: oak, maple, hickory and walnut trees clinging to soaring limestone bluffs. Geologists call this area—which encompasses adjoining corners of Minnesota, Iowa, Wisconsin and Illinois—the Driftless Region. The bluffs are the weathered, eroded remnants of ancient mountains that somehow escaped the glaciers that bulldozed much of the Midwest.

These ridges cradle the Root River and a handful of storybook towns on its banks. For visitors, it's a playground of bicycle trails, canoe liveries, restaurants and homey cafes, theaters, shops and inns.

Ask anyone who's been here—their eyes light up. I pick up the 42-mile Root River State Trail, which parallels State-16, on its western end at tiny Fountain (28 miles southeast of Rochester). Legions of

fans, including myself, probably never would have discovered this Shangri-la if it weren't for this path. In 1973, the old Milwaukee Railroad abandoned its tracks along the river. Visionaries convinced the state to transform that rail bed into this paved trail.

Now, a parade of bicyclists, hikers and in-line skaters follow the trail in summer, and cross-country skiers and snowshoers use it in winter. Threading its way east through dense woods and towering bluffs to Houston, the route crosses 48 old railroad bridges, some 500 feet long.

I spot a big yellow sign flapping in the breeze in front of the little Lutheran church in Fountain: Lutefisk and Meatball Supper! Can it be? Will I actually encounter the legendary Nordic soul food on this trip? Somehow, in my 18 years as editor-in-chief of *Midwest Living* maga-

zine, I've never experienced this Minnesota culinary rite of passage—preserved codfish drenched in a buttery white sauce that I've heard described as resembling Pine Sol-flavored Jell-O. I pull into the parking lot and step inside the church.

Clearly, I'm not in a city: The main doors are unlocked, and there's nobody about. I admire the beautiful royal blue-and-white sanctuary and note a few details about the upcoming fund-raiser posted on a bulletin board. Lutefisk and meatballs star, but Norwegian cooks also will be preparing *lefse*, *rommegrot*, sweet soup, *krumkake* and rosettes, along with more standard fare such as mashed potatoes and gravy, candied carrots and cole slaw. The dinner is several weeks away.

I call the phone number listed for the event chairperson, just to see if there's any

Near the Root River Valley

way I can sample a preview of the feast while I'm here, or perhaps pick up some frozen leftovers on a return visit.

A very nice lady at the other end of the line patiently explains that lutefisk isn't something that, well . . . keeps. Besides, it takes a day to soak out the lye. Hmmm . . . Maybe I can wait after all.

The supper in Fountain isn't the only clue to this area's Norwegian heritage. In Lanesboro, there's the Sons of Norway Lodge No. 376. In nearby Rushford, I spot a sign for the Nordic Lanes and Lounge. Considering the rugged terrain and snowy winters, it's no wonder those Norwegians felt at home.

Bicycle Heaven

Descending the steep-sided valley into Lanesboro (population 788), I'm dazzled. It's like a scene painted by a children's-book illustrator: church steeples, looping river, stone dam, narrow iron railway bridge (now part of the bike trail) and a wide main street lined with shops and eateries.

There's a big park with two trout-fishing ponds, and residential neighborhoods with grand old mansions, more than a dozen now converted into bed-and-breakfast inns. At a lazy bend in the river, this village has hosted travelers for centuries, starting with Native Americans who used the gorge as part of a trail to the Black Hills (some imaginative souls say you still can see their ghosts walking along the route).

The first Europeans (Norwegians and Irish) arrived in the 1860s. When the railroad came to the valley in 1868, eastern entrepreneurs had big plans for Lanesboro: a resort community in this perfect, healthful setting. Investors created that historic stone dam to impound a long-gone lake.

Pretty as it was, Lanesboro proved to be too much of a hike for 1800s fun-seekers from the East Coast. The limestone

Phoenix Hotel did get built, but it burned in 1885. The town eventually flourished as a grain-milling center and staging area for immigrants on their way to North Dakota and South Dakota.

The population peaked at about 2,000. When the immigrant influx slowed and several mills burned, once-busy Lanesboro became just another forgotten farm town with lots of vacant buildings—until that bike trail came along in the 1970s. Ironically, the original investors' tourism dreams have come true more than a century later.

Today, there are 110 guest rooms in the village, 61 of them in bed and breakfasts, with even more sprinkled elsewhere around the valley. Driving past a few of them on the south side of town, I pull over to chat with a happy-looking, middle-aged couple sipping red wine on the big porch of the 1897 Habberstad House, a fancifully painted Queen Anne mansion.

It's the couple's tenth year to return to Lanesboro (they're from Forest Lake, near Minneapolis). The gentleman tells me he's an avid canoeist who discovered Lanesboro on a weekend outing. "I hopped off here and fell in love with the town." Next time, he brought his wife along. She caught the bug, too. "It's so unspoiled and beautiful, like stepping back in time."

Former software engineer Jon Pieper, who owns the Old Village Hall Restaurant & Pub with his wife, Sarah, came upon Lanesboro while on a bicycling trip. Housed in a vintage 1886 limestone building with a bell tower, the restaurant exceeds all our expectations for a dinner in small-town Minnesota. They serve dishes such as five-mushroom soup (wild mushrooms thrive around here), halibut with lentils, penne pasta with shrimp and vodka sauce and—oh, my—seared duck breast with blackberry butter.

By the time we've finished, it's too late to

(From top) A bike trail bridge over the Root River near Lanesboro. Shops in downtown Lanesboro.

(From left) Bicycling through Lanesboro. The Preston Apple & Berry Farm.

take in a performance of *The Complete Works of William Shakespeare (Abridged)* playing at the nonprofit, professional Commonweal Theatre in a renovated former silent-movie house downtown.

The next day, I start bright and early with coffee and blueberry scones at the Lanesboro Pastry Shoppe. Most of the historic downtown's two- and three-story brick and limestone storefronts are well-kept, but not all are perfectly restored. That just makes them more real and inviting to me.

Little shops stock gifts and crafts. Das Wurst Haus is renowned for its homemade sausages, pumpernickel, sauerkraut, root beer and mustards—and live polka music. The Cornucopia Art Center showcases the works of more than 60 regional artists.

Then, there are the three bicycling concessions, which also offer canoes kayaks and more. The cyclists come in all shapes and sizes, but nobody seems to feel the least bit self-conscious in their stretch shorts and helmets. Families, teens, couples—people of all ages are having a great time, as they take to the trail. Bicycles rule in Lanesboro. There are so few cars and the trail is so well-marked that even novices feel comfortable.

Local businessperson Cheryl Lamon tells me: "We really like the bicyclists here. They're nice people; very courteous and respectful of nature." The feeling is mutual. I meet a group of 24 cyclists from the Twin Cities Biking Trail Club, here for a weekend. They're staying at various bed and breakfasts in the area. "It's always fun here, and you can feel secure nobody is going to steal your bike," one of them tells me. "The food is great. Don't miss the pie in Whalan!" I wouldn't dream of it.

On the Trail

The valley's other towns are smaller, but they have a magic of their own. At the hilltop Preston Apple & Berry Farm, one of many orchards in the area, owner Joe Gosi is pulling apple turnovers from the oven in the orchard salesroom. Smiling, ruddy-cheeked Joe fled his native Hungary, wound up in Minnesota and started his business here in 1985. In addition to apples ripening on 1,000 trees, Joe and his family grow strawberries, raspberries and vegetables. "I found my dream," Joe tells me.

There are more people lining up for pie (as well as soups and sandwiches) at the Gustavson family's cottagelike Aroma Pie Shoppe in Whalan than the entire population of the town (64). The sign outside reads "World Famous Pies," and that's no exaggeration. People all over have touted this landmark to me.

Inside, I scan the glass display case. Today's selections include raspberry, lemon supreme, chocolate brownie, raspberry-rhubarb, Georgia peach, cherry, apple-cream cheese, caramel apple and cherry streusel. They're all made with lard crusts, by the way—these folks are purists. None of the bicyclists seems to have any qualms about scarfing down a piece or two.

I sample slivers of an obscene eight. My vote goes to delectable peach, but each rates a "10." Looking out from the screened-porch eating area, I watch the world go by on the busy trail just outside. I even see a couple who brought their pet poodle along in a pull-behind kid seat.

To the east, you can't miss Rushford (population 1,500). Just watch for the huge letters that spell out the town's name on the side of 440-foot Magelssen Bluff (envision Tinseltown's hillside "Hollywood" sign). A winding back road takes me to the top of that overlook, where I drink in a sunset-tinted vista of the town, the valley and yet more bluffs. It's hard to say goodbye to Minnesota's Root River Valley—but I know I'll be coming back.

Taste of Minnesota

Walleye Amandine
Kavanaugh's Resort, Sylvan Lake

    4 8- to 10-ounce skinless walleye,
         trout, red snapper or catfish
         fillets, ¾ to 1 inch thick
    1 tablespoon butter, melted
         Salt and ground black pepper
    ⅓ cup slivered almonds
    ¼ cup butter
    2 tablespoons lemon juice (optional)
         Lemon wedges (optional)

Rinse fish; pat dry. Line a large baking pan with foil. Place fish in the pan; brush with half of the melted butter. Sprinkle with salt and pepper. Turn fillets, repeat. Tuck any thin portions under to make fillets a uniform thickness.

Broil 4 inches from the heat for 5 minutes. Turn and broil 4 to 5 minutes longer or until fish flakes easily when tested with a fork.

In a medium skillet cook almonds in butter until golden. Remove from heat. If you like, stir in 2 tablespoons lemon juice.

To serve, place fish on a platter and spoon almond mixture over. If you like, serve with lemon wedges. Makes 4 servings.

Artichoke Tartar Sauce

    2 cups mayonnaise
    1 13¾-ounce can artichoke hearts,
         drained and finely chopped
    3 tablespoons finely chopped onion
    2 tablespoons snipped fresh flat-leaf
         parsley (optional)
    ⅛ teaspoon cayenne pepper

In a medium bowl, stir together all ingredients. Cover and chill for at least 2 hours before serving. Serve with seafood or fish. (Cover and chill any leftovers for up to 1 week.) Makes about 2½ cups.

More Favorites

DULUTH

Downtown and waterfront revitalization have reenergized this vibrant northeastern Minnesota port city, which extends 26 miles along Lake Superior's shore. Ocean-going freighters dock near historic Canal Park, a lively dining, shopping and entertainment district.

The natural harbor still nurtures this city of 85,000, the Great Lakes' busiest port. Along Skyline Drive, which follows a ridge that rims Duluth, climb the tower at Enger Park for a sweeping view. Mansions that lumber and iron ore barons built dot the hills and streets. You can tour Glensheen, a lakeside estate.

Streets plunge from the hills into downtown past the 1890s depot that houses four museums and the North Shore Scenic Railroad. The train makes daily round-trips to destinations along Lake Superior. The Lakewalk, a 4.2-mile concrete ribbon, parallels the water. More information: Duluth Convention & Visitors Bureau (800/438-5884, visitduluth.com).

ELY

Clinging to ridges between forests and lakes at the southwestern edge of the Boundary Waters Canoe Area, this one-time mining settlement has become a base for northeastern Minnesota vacationers. More than a dozen outfitters operate in and around the town of 4,000 (110 miles north of Duluth).

From nearby entry points, visitors canoe, camp and fish among the Boundary Waters' million acres. Hundreds of miles of mountain-biking and hiking trails also attract outdoor enthusiasts. From the International Wolf Center at the edge of town, interpreters lead "howling" expeditions into the woods, where wolves again roam. Resorts including River Point Resort and Burntside Lodge sprinkle Ely and the shores of surrounding lakes. More information: Ely Chamber of Commerce (800/777-7281, ely.org).

NORTH SHORE DRIVE

Minnesota's North Shore is the edge of a wilderness that sprawls across the state's northeastern corner. Stretching 150 miles between Duluth and Canada, State-61 provides almost the only link to harbor towns and state parks beside Lake Superior, as well as to the north woods and Sawtooth Mountains inland.

At seven state parks, activities range from camping and mountain biking to kayaking and fishing. Several trail systems feed into the 130-mile Superior Hiking Trail. Kayakers paddle the Lake Superior Water Trail between Gooseberry Falls and Two Harbors. At Split Rock Lighthouse State Park, you can climb the lighthouse tower and visit the restored light-keeper's residence.

Save time for shore towns. Part artists' colony and part staging point for treks into the woods, harborside Grand Marais brims with galleries, restaurants and shops. You'll find resorts, cabins and motels all along the shore, including Cove Point Lodge, Stone Hearth Inn bed and breakfast and historic Naniboujou Lodge. More information: Minnesota Office of Tourism (800/657-3700, exploreminnesota.com).

Travel Journal

LAKES AND LEGENDS

Family vacationers return year after year to the scores of lakes around Brainerd in central Minnesota (160 miles northwest of the Twin Cities). More information: Brainerd Chamber of Commerce (800/450-2838, explorebrainerdlakes.com).

Featured Stops

Creative Steel Works Studio Sculpture artist Jeff Kreitz uses stainless steel, bronze, copper and aluminum to create 3-D sculptures, furniture and wall murals. In Crosslake (25 miles northeast of Brainerd) (218/692-3669).

Grand View Lodge Historic first-class resort on the shore of Gull Lake (12 miles north of Brainerd). Ask about packages that include meals. $$$$ (800/432-3788).

Kavanaugh's Resort & Restaurant Cabins, log homes and townhouses on spring-fed Sylvan Lake (10 miles northwest of Brainerd). Open May–October. $$$–$$$$ (800/562-7061). Reservations recommended for Kavanaugh's Restaurant (218/829-5226).

Nisswa Near Gull Lake, specialty shops, boutiques and restaurants (12 miles north of Brainerd). Nisswa Chamber of Commerce (800/950-9610, nisswa.com).

Paul Bunyan State Trail All-season, 69½-mile paved trail (800/657-3700).

Plaid Duck In Pequot Lakes, coffee, wine, fruit smoothies and specialty beverages, plus breakfast and sandwiches (218/568-7440).

Silver Creek Traders In Pequot Lakes, selling gifts, furniture and handcrafted jewelry in a two-story log lodge (888/568-5144).

More Great Stops

Paul Bunyan Land at This Old Farm Pioneer Village Eighteen-foot-tall, 2½-ton talking statue of mythical giant lumberman Paul Bunyan, plus his blue ox, Babe and amusement park rides (seven miles east of Brainerd). Open daily Memorial Day through Labor Day. Admission charged (218/764-2524).

Reed's Sporting Goods/Minnesota Fishing Hall of Fame In the hall of fame, displays, videos and memorabilia of Minnesota fishing legends, such as brothers Ron and Al Lindner (218/824-7500). Adjoining Reeds Sporting Goods, a large, well-known outdoors store with all sorts of gear for fishing, hiking, camping and hunting. Also

Silver Creek
Traders,
Pequot Lakes

an eight-acre kids pond stocked with fish (218/824-7333).

TALE OF TWO CITIES

Twin Cities Minneapolis and St. Paul grew up along the Mississippi's northernmost navigable stretch, maturing from rough-and-ready river ports into a savvy metropolis. More information: Greater Minneapolis Convention & Visitors Association (888/676-6757, minneapolis.org). St. Paul Convention & Visitors Bureau (800/627-6101, visitstpaul.com).

Featured Stops

American Swedish Institute In a 1904 castle, with photographs, diaries and artifacts tracing the experiences of Minnesota's Swedish American community (612/871-4907).

Cathedral of Saint Paul Built in 1915 and inspired by St. Peter's Basilica in Rome, with 186-foot-high interior dome and 307-foot-high exterior dome (651/228-1766).

Fitzgerald Theater In downtown St. Paul, restored historic venue known for its main production, Garrison Keillor's *A Prairie Home Companion*. Also, concerts, lectures and other productions (651/290-1200).

James J. Hill House A five-story, 36,000-square-foot mansion. Reservations recommended. Admission charged; children age 5 and younger free (651/297-2555).

Le Meridien Minneapolis An elegant, modern hotel in the heart of downtown. $$$$ (612/677-1100). Cosmos bar (612/312-1168).

Mill City Museum Chronicling the flour-milling industry that fueled the growth of Minneapolis for 50 years and highlighting the lives of people who worked in the milling and lumber industries. Located inside the limestone ruins of an old mill, with a rooftop observation deck. Admission charged (612/341-7555).

The Saint Paul Hotel

Minneapolis Institute of Arts Housed in a 1915 neoclassical building, with a wide-ranging collection spanning 5,000 years of diverse cultures (612/870-3131).

Minneapolis Sculpture Garden Just south of downtown, the nation's largest urban sculpture park with more than 40 contemporary and modern works. Claes Oldenburg and Coosje van Bruggen's giant *Spoonbridge and Cherry* has become a Twin Cities landmark. The garden is part of the Walker Art Center, one of the world's premier contemporary art museums (reopening in April 2005 after a major expansion). Sculpture Garden free; admission charged to museum (612/375-7622).

Minnesota Children's Museum Seven galleries packed with hands-on exhibits. Admission charged (651/225-6000).

Minnesota History Center In St. Paul, chronicling significant state events, from the Ice Age to the Twins' 1991 World Series victory (800/657-3773).

Minnesota State Capitol Opened in 1905, just north of downtown St. Paul. Guided tours on the hour (651/296-2881).

Oops! Interactive Dinner Theatre In North St. Paul, home of the popular "Ole and Lena" productions, featuring folksy Norwegian humor (651/777-4150).

Saint Paul Hotel Historic landmark luxury hotel in downtown St. Paul. $$$$ (800/292-9292). St. Paul Grill, reservations recommended (651/224-7455).

More Great Stops

Mall of America In Bloomington, a southern suburb, the nation's largest mall, with more than 520 stores and 50 eating establishments, plus nightclubs, movie theaters and attractions for kids. Camp Snoopy, the mall's indoor theme park, includes a 74-foot Ferris wheel among its 28 rides. Ticket charges. Underwater Adventures, on the mall's lower level, is Minnesota's largest indoor aquarium. Admission charged (952/883-8800).

Dining

Brit's Pub and Eating Establishment Classic English pub food, including shepherd's pie, bangers and mash (sausages and mashed potatoes) and Cornish pasty, in authentic atmosphere with dark wood, cozy fireplace and high-backed British lounge chairs. Along Nicollet Mall in downtown Minneapolis (612/332-3908).

ENCHANTED VALLEY

The Root River Valley in southeastern Minnesota stretches west from the Mississippi River to the community of Wabasha in the north and the town of Harmony 90 miles south. Lanesboro is a great stop along the Root River. More information: Southeastern Minnesota Historic Bluff Country (800/428-2030, bluffcountry.com). Lanesboro Visitors Center (800/944-2670, lanesboro.com).

Featured Stops

Aroma Pie Shoppe In Whalan, for homemade pies, soups and sandwiches, plus other home-baked treats, such as raspberry cream and chocolate brownies. Open April through October, closed Tuesdays and Wednesdays (507/467-2623).

Commonweal Theatre Company In Lanesboro, a 126-seat theater with live productions Thursday–Sunday nights. Ticket charge (800/657-7025).

Lanesboro Pastry Shoppe In Lanesboro, for European-style breads, puff pastries, quiche and homemade soups (507/467-2867).

Lanesboro Tours and Treasures One-hour narrated trolley tour of the Lanesboro area. Admission charged (866/349-4466).

Old Village Hall Restaurant & Pub In Lanesboro, fine dining in an 1886 stone building with a spacious deck overlooking the Root River Bike Trail. (507/467-2962).

Preston Apple and Berry Farm East of Preston, 15-acre orchard; fall horse-drawn carriage rides (507/765-4486).

More Great Stops

The Cornucopia Art Center In Lanesboro, selling the works of more than 60 artists from throughout the region (507/467-2446).

Das Wurst Haus German Village and Deli In Lanesboro, old-fashioned sandwich shop serving from-scratch sausage, Reubens and braunschweigers, plus frothy homemade root beer. With live polka music. Open April through October (507/467-2902).

Great River Bluffs State Park Located high on the bluffs overlooking the Mississippi River, with hiking, cross-country skiing, camping and picnicking (17 miles southeast of Winona). Trails lead to scenic overlooks (507/643-6849).

Lodging

Berwood Hill Inn A luxurious bed and breakfast in an elegant 1878 home, with spa services, extensive gardens and a restaurant (four miles south of Lanesboro) $$$–$$$$ (800/803-6748).

Meadows Inn Bed & Breakfast In Rushford, a European-style home featuring luxury linens and toiletries in five spacious guest rooms with private baths. $$–$$$ (507/864-2378).

Mrs. B's Historic Inn In Lanesboro, 10 elegantly furnished rooms in an 1872 limestone building. Restaurant serves four-course dinner Wednesdays–Sundays. $$–$$$ (800/657-4710).

Oakenwald Terrace Bed & Breakfast In Chatfield, six guest rooms packed with antiques and collectibles. $$–$$$$ (507/867-3806). ∎

Missouri

■ This border state melds Northern and Southern traditions with a diverse blend of Ozark folksiness and big-city sophistication. Two distinctly different metropolises—St. Louis on the eastern edge and Kansas City on the western border—anchor the state. A land of rivers, Missouri is known for transporting the Heartland's early explorers and settlers. The mighty Mississippi River carves out the eastern boundary, and the muddy Missouri River bisects the state from the northwestern corner to its confluence with the Mississippi near St. Louis. From rich history, tantalizing barbecue and wineries making noteworthy vintages to world-class museums and major league ballparks, you'll find it in Missouri.

The Gateway Arch, centerpiece of the Jefferson National Expansion Memorial

Gateway City

The Gateway Arch commemorates St. Louis' role in opening the West. Back then, the city bustled with pioneers and adventurers. That energy is surging again in the revitalized downtown and renovated Forest Park.

t. Louisans spend a lot of time apologizing for themselves and their historic city. The litany: We're too traditional, too conservative and too stay-put. Which local high school we attended tends to lock us into our social circle for eternity. We're the last staid "eastern" city before that upstart intrastate rival, Kansas City, 250 miles west. And we have a quirky regional accent that emerges every so often, such as when we make "four" sound indistinguishable from "far."

So what's the problem with all that? Nice people, serene residential neighborhoods, lots of history and local color. Besides, when it comes to innovation, this is a cradle of the aviation industry and a transplant-pioneering medical research center. In 1965, this city had the chutzpah to unveil the soaring Gateway Arch—perhaps America's single most recognizable monument—to commemorate its role as the springboard for America's westward expansion. Now, thanks to a multimillion-dollar renovation of sprawling Forest Park west of downtown, I'm more in love than ever with this very Midwestern, sort-of-Southern, Mississippi River metropolis.

Dream Come True

The Gateway Arch perfectly depicts the soaring spirit of frontier exploration and settlement. Flying over or arriving in St. Louis any time of day or night, in all seasons of the year, you'll see the simple span of gleaming stainless steel shining through clouds, fog, snow and rain, glistening in the midday sunshine and glowing in orange sunsets. It seems magical. The span rises above the Mississippi River bank where St. Louis was founded, and where Lewis and Clark outfitted for their epic journey up the Mississippi to the Missouri River two centuries ago.

It's hard to imagine this now-sprawling city as a predominantly French settlement on the edge of the frontier. The city's simple stone Old Cathedral and Old Courthouse, both still standing, must have seemed as imposing then as the Arch does today.

In the two centuries since the Corps of Discovery departed from this site, the city has flourished. Steamboats clogged the river landings, loading and unloading goods. Covered wagons rumbled through. The railroads arrived. Then began a long, slow decline. Eclipsed only by Chicago as the Midwest's largest metropolis, the downtown area of St. Louis faded for a time.

During the mid-1900s, a farsighted civic booster suggested a national landmark to commemorate St. Louis' role in westward expansion. After Congress endorsed the idea, a design competition was held. Finnish American architect Eero Saarinen won the award. Construction began in February 1963, and the glorious Arch was completed in October 1965.

The two sleek legs had to be built simultaneously and joined on-site. The city held its breath when they stood farther apart than the ⅟₆₄-inch tolerance, minutely askew due to heat expansion. For hours, the St. Louis fire department hosed down the metal to make the connection possible.

Saarinen's vision actually is a catenary curve, equivalent to a flexible chain hanging upside down. The span rises 630 feet, with the two legs planted 630 feet apart. It's 75 feet taller than the Washington Monument and twice as tall as the Statue of Liberty; it weighs 17,246 tons. The structure, which can withstand winds of 150 miles per hour, sways up to 18 inches. The monument cost $13.4 million to build, plus another $1.9 million for the trams that take up to 40 passengers at a time on four-minute trips through the hollow legs to the top.

Beneath the Arch and the surrounding park in the underground Museum of Westward Expansion, animated figures depicting people such as William Clark tell stories about their roles in opening the West. Huge panoramic photos portray landscapes and landmarks that Lewis and Clark encountered, along with quotes from their journals.

Those 1960s visionaries would be pleased with the Arch and what's happened downtown since then. The park surrounding the monument, which replaced 40 city blocks of deteriorating buildings, has matured into a beautiful public space. People are moving downtown again as it becomes a safe environment with plenty of

(Clockwise, from opposite) At the top of the Arch. The view looking west. A summer night at The Muny in Forest Park. The statue of St. Louis in front of the Saint Louis Art Museum in Forest Park.

activities for everyone. Beyond the Arch-crowned riverfront, St. Louis is framed by 93 municipalities to the west. With 2.6 million residents, the metro area population ranks 18th nationally.

Party of the Century

From the 11th-floor rooftop of the Chase Park Plaza Hotel in St. Louis' trendy Central West End neighborhood, I look downtown toward the gleaming Arch. This is the same hotel I stayed in on my first business trip 30 years ago, and I was awed then, too. The Chase also has experienced a rebirth and once again exudes class.

Forest Park spreads to the west. In 1904, when it was the fourth largest city in the country and the most populous city west of the Mississippi, St. Louis threw a huge party in this park: the Louisiana Purchase Exposition—also known as the World's Fair—an extravaganza of architecture, food and art that included the United States' first Olympic Games.

Some 500 acres larger than New York's Central Park, the green space took its name from thousands of trees that once covered its 1,371 acres, many of which were cut down to make way for the fair.

Only 80 acres of the original forest remain. Huge old trees planted after the fair shade much of the area. From my bird's-eye vantage point, I can see Washington University on Skinker Boulevard, with its trademark castle tower, anchoring the opposite end of the park. Grand mansions, built for fair officials, line Lindell Boulevard to the north. Busy US-64 runs along the southern edge of this ocean of greenery.

Incredibly ornate Beaux Arts-style temporary fair buildings constructed of staff (lime, plaster, fiber and cement) drew an astounding 20 million visitors. Scores of nations, states and territories showcased their cultures and products. The Philippine Exhibit alone comprised 47 acres and 100 buildings. Visitors were dazzled by the huge illuminated Palace of Electricity, the 112-foot Floral Clock, the Colonnade of States and a giant Ferris wheel with a capacity of 2,160 passengers. The Saint Louis Art Museum, the only permanent structure remaining from the fair, is a memorable symbol of the glorious event.

On an atypical St. Louis day (for July), I enjoy mostly clear skies and 70-degree temperatures on the park tour, where I share space with joggers and walkers, golfers on the four nine-hole courses, tennis players, pedal- and rowboaters and people settling on the grass to sit and reflect.

My first stop is the new visitors center, in a former trolley station. Lee Anna Good, vice president of the Forest Park Forever preservation organization, provides some historical background. In 1876, the park was developed on farmland two miles outside the St. Louis city limits. At that time, some residents feared that families without access to horse-and-carriage transportation would find the park inaccessible. Today, the location is one of the park's biggest assets—12 million people visit annually.

With the park's popularity, citizens were eager to pitch in when updating and renovating were called for. During the mid-1990s, St. Louis developed a master plan to return Forest Park to its former beauty in time to celebrate the World's Fair centennial, as well as the bicentennials of the Lewis and Clark expedition and the Louisiana Purchase. Ninety-four million dollars were raised in half-public, half-private funds. Threadbare Forest Park was granted a new lease on life with extensive landscaping, including 7,500 new trees, a boathouse, an expanded and refurbished

(From left) Cypress Swamp exhibit in the 1904 Flight Cage at the St. Louis Zoo. Lindbergh plane replica at the Missouri History Museum. The Saint Louis Art Museum and fountains in the Grand Basin. Lakeside dining at The Boat House.

Grand Basin pool, fountains and other waterways, as well as a new golf course, clubhouse and visitors center.

Regal Legacy

The Grand Basin is reminiscent of the grounds of a European palace: eight fountains at the foot of a hill that's crowned by a bronze statue of the community's patron saint, Louis IX, which was presented to the city by the fair organization to commemorate the exposition. Behind the statue, atop Art Hill (an understandably favored wintertime sledding site) stands the regal Saint Louis Art Museum.

The art museum was known during the fair as the Palace of Fine Arts. Now, it's one of America's busiest and finest art museums, with more than a half million visitors annually. It presents a rich smorgasbord of works from pre-Columbian American art to the largest collection of 20th-century German art in the world. Works by Missouri's own masters, George Caleb Bingham and Thomas Hart Benton, as well as Old World masters including Degas and El Greco, fill the galleries.

And it's all free. That's a staunch St. Louis tradition, Kay Porter of the museum staff explains. Almost all the major cultural attractions in Forest Park and elsewhere in St. Louis are open at no cost, except for special exhibits. Just try to tamper with that philosophy, Kay says, pointing to the message carved above the museum portico: "Dedicated to Art and Free to All."

The park also encompasses a zoo, a science center, the Missouri History Museum, the Municipal Opera (known simply as The Muny, billing itself as the country's oldest and largest outdoor theater), an Art Deco greenhouse and a skating rink. At the re-created wood-shingled Boat House, modeled after the 1927 original, there are boat rentals, an outdoor restaurant and a beer garden. From a rocking chair near the dock, I watch boaters setting out for voyages on the park's linked waterways.

At the history museum, staff member Donn Johnson notes that the building was constructed in 1913 as a memorial to Thomas Jefferson, champion of the Lewis and Clark expedition. In 2000, the building was modernized and expanded. Suspended from the ceiling inside is the replica of the *Spirit of St. Louis* used by Jimmy Stewart in the movie that celebrated Lindbergh's pioneering 1927 transatlantic solo flight that

was sponsored by a group of St. Louis businessmen. Other exhibits cover events from the early days of St. Louis from Lewis and Clark to the fair.

Donn, an affable former local broadcast newsman, explains just how dear this park and the memories it enfolds are to people here. He says most longtime St. Louis families have a story about the fair.

At twilight, a parade of cars heads for The Muny. The stars who've played at this amphitheater since 1919 constitute a mini Hollywood walk of fame: Bob Hope, Gene Kelly, Betty Grable, Ethel Merman, Douglas Fairbanks and a young British fellow named Archie Leach (later known as Cary Grant). The amphitheater seats 12,000 (with 1,000 seats reserved for free admission every night).

On this delightful summer evening, the theater is packed. On stage, Professor Harold Hill woos Marian the librarian in that quintessentially Midwestern musical, *The Music Man*. Treetops and stars form a canopy for the stage far below my hillside seat. As with Forest Park in general, I'm told every St. Louisan has a Muny memory. Now, I have mine. It's a perfect way to end a day in the Gateway City.

Taste of Missouri

St. Louis Toasted Ravioli

Charlie E. Gitto, Jr., of Charlie Gitto's restaurant in St. Louis' Hill neighborhood, shares the eatery's fabled recipe.

1 beaten egg
2 tablespoons milk
⅔ to 1 cup seasoned fine dry bread crumbs
1 16-ounce package frozen ravioli, thawed (for the recipe for Charlie's homemade ravioli, log on to midwestliving.com)
Shortening or cooking oil for frying
1 cup spaghetti sauce or pizza sauce
Grated Parmesan cheese

In a shallow dish, combine egg and milk. Place bread crumbs in another shallow dish. Dip ravioli in egg mixture; roll in bread crumbs, coating evenly.

In a 3-quart heavy saucepan, heat 2 inches of shortening or cooking oil over medium heat for 15 to 20 minutes (oil should be 350°F). Add 4 or 5 ravioli. Fry about 1 minute or until golden. Turn carefully. Fry about 1 minute more or until crisp and golden. Drain on paper towels. Keep warm in a 300° oven while frying the remaining ravioli.

In a small saucepan, heat spaghetti sauce. To serve, sprinkle ravioli with Parmesan cheese. Serve with warm sauce for dipping. Makes 12 to 14 appetizers.

MISSOURI Baking Co

(Clockwise, from top) "The" place for gooey butter cake. The Hill's icon and St. Ambrose Catholic Church. Toasted ravioli at Charlie Gitto's.

That's Italian!

In St. Louis, mention "The Hill" and people instantly envision two things: Italian American families and great food. This neat-as-a-pin, tight-knit district one mile south of Forest Park began as a German enclave, like most of St. Louis. After a devastating fire in the 1840s, much of the city was rebuilt—in brick and terra-cotta instead of wood. Italian immigrant laborers locally mined the clay that built much of St. Louis. The men came first, then sent for their wives, sweethearts and families.

This is a genuine neighborhood. You know when you're in it, and when you're leaving it. Italian red-green-and-white flags flutter everywhere—on fire hydrants, in shop windows. Narrow shotgun-style houses with basement kitchens (which were cooler when these compact homes were built) line the quiet streets. The Hill now is becoming a population mix with "only" 70 percent of the residents still Italian Americans whose families originated in areas from Sicily to Genoa.

For many in the neighborhood, life revolves around Mass and feast days at St. Ambrose, the imposing Lombardy-style parish church. Organized activities include a bocce club. These are the streets that gave the baseball world Yogi Berra and Joe Garagiola. Tommy Lasorda is a regular at local restaurants.

In front of red brick St. Ambrose, on the corner of Wilson and Marconi streets, is a 1971 bronze statue that sums up how Italian Americans feel about The Hill. It portrays a humble immigrant couple, holding an infant and looking hopeful but frightened. They're carrying everything they own in a single suitcase, risking all for a better life. For most residents, the gamble paid off, right here.

One of The Hill's specialties is a confection called gooey butter cake, a slightly undercooked, doughy batter with a thin crust on top that tastes much better than it sounds. I love it, and Missouri Baking Company along The Hill's Edwards Street makes some of the best. The bakery is packed, and everyone takes a number. Customers (mostly businesspeople and suburban types here on a mission) are smiling. They know what's in store. Display cases hold cannoli, custard-filled puffs, cheesecakes, mini pineapple upside-down cakes, tiramisu, baklava, all sorts of cookies and more. There's an enticingly yeasty, sweet smell permeating every corner of this place, which Chris Gambaro runs with his sister, Mimi Lordo.

Their grandfather founded the institution in 1926. Now Chris handles the baking, while Mimi manages the shop out front. Uncle Lino Gambaro still works at the bakery. He's 88. The scene reminds me of Cher's 1987 movie *Moonstruck*.

Mimi and Chris live with their respective families on The Hill, across the alley from each other and their parents. Sundays, the whole family walks to Mass at St. Ambrose. "I have three kids I'm raising here. They don't have a chance to get in trouble in this neighborhood," Mimi says.

According to Chris, gooey butter cake was created in the 1930s. Legend has it that a baker was making a batch of butter cakes with his crew when they goofed and put in only half the usual amount of flour. The batter and resulting cakes were mushy inside—and tasted incredibly good.

A few blocks away, Charlie Gitto's is one of 20 great Italian eateries on The Hill, and the reported source of another food tradition—toasted ravioli. Charlie Gitto, Jr., is the quintessential Italian male: intense, tough-acting type-A on the outside and (I learn later) softhearted on the inside, especially when he talks about his family. In 1947, when this place was called Angelo's, the chef accidentally dropped some fresh-made ravioli in bread crumbs and decided to deep-fry them. And so, yet another St. Louis dining legend was born. Charlie summons a waiter, and a plate of toasted ravioli appears. He showers the meat-stuffed pasta pockets with Parmesan. My first bite tells me that the long-ago kitchen accident was orchestrated by the gods.

Charlie's grandfather came to The Hill from Italy, and his parents worked here when it was Angelo's. He left The Hill, cooked in New York, Las Vegas, Texas and Chicago, then came back. Why? He says, "This is where I'm from."

Charlie Gitto's (314/772-8898). Missouri Baking Company (314/773-6566).

America's Hometown

Visiting Hannibal, Mark Twain's town, sets me on a quest. I want to learn about the real Tom Sawyer, Becky Thatcher and Huck Finn. Along the way, I reconnect with memories of my own boyhood.

The wonderful thing about the writings of Samuel Clemens, a.k.a. Mark Twain, is that his stories are based on growing-up escapades that so many of us can relate to more than a century after they were written. Standing in front of the simple two-story white clapboard home where Samuel Clemens lived as a boy, just a couple of blocks up Hill Street from the rolling Mississippi River, I recall my own early years in another Midwest river town.

My thoughts return to Council Bluffs, Iowa, on the Mississippi's principal tributary, the Missouri River. Summertime in the 1950s and '60s meant Schwinn bicycles, frogs, fistfights, clubhouses, playing hide-and-seek and camping out in a rickety tree house. Those days were filled with fishing in a muddy pond, all-day picnic hikes to the assuredly haunted cemetery across town and wearing bathing suits just to dance in the rain. I remember Monopoly marathons on the front porch, my ragtag gang of summer buddies, and swarming from yard to yard, adventure to adventure.

Storybook Boyhood

Mark Twain knew all about those sorts of good times. And he knew how to tell the stories. Samuel Clemens arrived in this world with Halley's Comet in 1835 and exited with that same comet, just as he predicted he would, in 1910. In the intervening years, he lived a most amazing life, with a storybook small-town boyhood and careers as a printer's apprentice, river pilot, adventurer, miner, newspaper correspondent, globe-trotting lecturer and renowned author and humorist. He was a friend of presidents and kings; he knew both abject poverty and great wealth. He had a beautiful family. Agonized, he witnessed as death robbed him of two daughters and his beloved wife, one at a time. He knew great joy and black despair. America and the world loved him through it all.

A century and a half after Sam Clemens lived in this Midwest town, he and the characters who populate the novels about his childhood—Tom Sawyer, Becky Thatcher, Huck Finn, Aunt Polly and all the rest—still seem to live here. Most were based on young Sam's friends and neighbors. A few were composites.

Becky Thatcher was Laura Hawkins (later Frazer), the curly-haired girl who lived across Hill Street and remained his friend for life. Other citizens of Hannibal also were unwittingly the source of Sam's creative

(Clockwise, from top) Richard Garey, a Samuel Clemens/Mark Twain reenactor. Downtown Hannibal. Tom Sawyer and Becky Thatcher lookalikes painting the fence. The *Mark Twain* plying the Mississippi at Hannibal.

genius. Tom Blankenship was the model for Huck Finn, whose character was the son of Hannibal's ne'er-do-well town drunk. Aunt Polly is mostly Sam's red-haired mother, Jane Lampton Clemens. (Before his mane turned its trademark white, Sam was a red-head.) By all accounts, Mrs. Clemens, who died in 1890, was a vivacious woman who endured much, including ongoing financial struggles. Through it all, she retained a zest for life that her son clearly inherited.

At the Mark Twain Boyhood Home and Museum, curator Henry Sweets supplies critical biographical details: Clemens was born in 1835 in nearby tiny Florida, Missouri. When he was 4 years old, the family moved to Hannibal. John Clemens, a justice of the peace, never got ahead money-wise, and died of pneumonia in 1847. Mrs. Clemens took in boarders. I love Henry's story about Mrs. Clemens' steadfast belief in alcohol-laced patent medicines, à la Aunt Polly. Sam lived here until 1853, when he left to seek his fortune on the river.

Millions of people have traipsed through this landmark since it opened for tours in 1912. After a 1991 renovation it's in remarkably good shape, owned by the city and operated by a foundation.

Of course, everyone wants to know about "the picket fence" that is the source of a whole chapter on enticing friends to tackle a job just for the fun of it. The real fence is long gone, if it ever existed, but there is a smaller version of Tom Sawyer's fictional whitewash boondoggle out front.

Back to the Future

When Sam Clemens moved to Hannibal with his family in 1839, the river village had only 750 inhabitants. By the time Sam left his hometown to fulfill his grand dream of becoming a riverboat pilot, Hannibal had grown to 4,000 residents. The population today is approximately 18,000.

An exuberant and mildly kitschy quality suits this place perfectly. Eateries, shops, historic sites and museums crowd the compact downtown: Becky's Old Fashioned Ice Cream Parlor; Mrs. Clemens' Shoppe and Emporium; Tom Sawyer Dioramas; Twainland Express Depot; Haunted House Wax Museum. I think Tom Sawyer (and Mark Twain) would have loved the unabashed entrepreneurship.

Banjo tunes and calliope music drift up from the riverfront. The *Mark Twain* riverboat, with its churning paddle wheel and flared stacks, powers up to the dock, returning video-camera-toting river travelers from a one-hour round-trip ride. I settle into a bench near the Center Street landing and study the river, as Sam Clemens must have done whenever he heard the cry, "Steamboat's a-comin'!"

In 1847 alone, records show a thousand steamboats docked at Hannibal. The pull of adventure grew so strong that Sam left home, eventually to become a river pilot. When the Civil War ended all commercial river traffic in 1861, Sam moved on—with a pseudonym: Mark Twain, the term used to indicate the river is at a navigable depth.

Mark Twain married a daughter of one of Elmira, New York's, wealthiest families, Olivia "Livy" Langdon, in 1870. He wrote several of his major works in a quirky octagonal study built for him on a hilltop at Quarry Farm, just outside Elmira.

I'm well-versed in Twain's Elmira years. My Nebraska-raised mother married my East Coast father there, and they had their small wedding reception at the Mark Twain Hotel in Elmira in 1943. When I was born a few years later, they lived across the street from Woodlawn Cemetery, where Twain and his family are buried in the Langdon family plot. It's part of the reason I feel such a special connection with Twain here in Hannibal today.

All That Jazz

It all comes together in this onetime cow town along the Missouri River—great architecture, African American heritage, a grand jazz tradition and some of the best barbecue anywhere.

When my wife, Julie, and I are in the mood for a close-to-home weekend getaway in the city, we head to Kansas City. This hilly, tree-blanketed metropolis means good times and great memories: barbecue and steaks, major-league sports, sublime jazz and elegant Country Club Plaza, our favorite shopping district anywhere.

We find more fountains splashing than in any city except Rome, broad European-style boulevards that rival those of Paris, grand parks, craggy limestone bluffs, wooded hills, and classical statues in every nook and cranny. How did this rowdy cow town—once nicknamed Possum Trot—happen to take on such highfalutin airs?

Perfect Location

To learn more about this area, I stayed close to its heartbeat in Kansas City, Missouri, just south of downtown's eclectic array of Art Deco and contemporary skyscrapers. This city's surprising story unfolds in these areas and their landmarks: Country Club Plaza, Union Station, Crown Center and the African American historic district surrounding 18th and Vine.

Bill Worley, a local historian and educator, explains that Kansas City's story starts with those three words chanted by real estate agents everywhere: Location, location, location. The valley where the Missouri meets the Kansas River (or the Kaw, to locals) first attracted the Osage nation

and fur traders in canoes. Then came steamboats, railroads and airlines.

Settlement brought grain and livestock markets, meat-packing and other food processing, banking, auto assembly plants and hundreds of commercial suppliers to serve this rich agricultural region. Thanks to Hallmark, Kansas City is as synonymous with sentiment as it is with steaks. Local entrepreneurs also launched Russell Stover Candies and H&R Block Tax Accountants. Among the many notables who've called this area home over the years: Jean Harlow, William Powell, Walter Cronkite, Walt Disney and Count Basie.

Just a mile or so from my hotel, ragtime and Dixieland jazz draw Kansas Citians to bars in historic Westport, which once outfitted wagon trains bound for the Santa Fe and Oregon trails. At one time or another, Jesse James, Wyatt Earp, Wild Bill Hickok, Doc Holliday and Bat Masterson rubbed elbows with cardsharps, cowboys and madams in Kansas City saloons. Then came slaveholding farmers from southern border states, followed by 20th-century Italian immigrants and, more recently, Latinos. Those cultures, mixed with the long-established African American community, make K.C. about as ethnically diverse as it gets in the Heartland.

Kansas City, Missouri, has a population of about 450,000. Add that to Kansas City, Kansas, plus the many fast-growing sub-

urban communities on both sides of the state line (most notably thriving Overland Park, Kansas, which has surpassed Kansas City, Kansas, with a population of 175,000), and the metro population is just under 2 million.

I recall reading a survey that indicated workers here are among America's happiest. Maybe it's because it's so easy to get to and from work on the metro area's extensive freeway system. Or maybe it's because housing is so affordable. I'm told there's $2 billion in construction under way in the downtown area, including an expanded convention center and a new civic arena. As that prophetic cowboy sings in the Broadway musical *Oklahoma!*, "Ev'rythin's up-to-date in Kansas City."

Old Kansas City

Genteel "old money" residential neighborhoods with stately homes preside south of the plaza. In the spring, redbud and magnolia trees bloom prolifically, and in autumn, huge maples and oaks are ablaze with color. This area is a virtual catalog of 20th-century residential styles, such as Arts and Crafts, Tudor, Beaux Arts and Colonial Revival.

Shady thoroughfares including Ward Parkway, Brookside Boulevard and State Line Road lead to secluded residential streets on both sides of the state line. Native limestone, a distinctive feature of

(Clockwise, from opposite) Live music in the American Jazz Museum. Country Club Plaza. J. C. Nichols Memorial Fountain at the plaza. Claes Oldenburg and Coosje van Bruggen's "*Shuttlecocks*" at the Nelson-Atkins Museum of Art. The Kaleidoscope children's area at Hallmark's Crown Center.

many modest and grand Kansas City homes, was used to build fences and exteriors.

I wonder whether Kansas City has always been this beautiful. "No!" Bill Worley replies, with a chuckle. Built on muddy river flats that flooded regularly, the original settlement crept up into ravines and atop bluffs scarred by huge cuts that were excavated to accommodate development on higher ground. Kansas City in the mid-1800s was, in fact, quite ugly.

The City Beautiful movement that was then sweeping the nation inspired publisher William Rockhill Nelson, founder of the *Kansas City Star*, who envisioned a network of parks and boulevards. Nelson's dreams became reality thanks to a tax fund designated specifically for beautification,

the Plaza—among dozens of fountains and statues—are the huge, mythologically inspired J. C. Nichols Fountain and the Giralda Tower, modeled after the cathedral tower in Seville. Nichols spent $1 million in the 1920s to buy the land, then from the 1920s to his death in 1949, outfitted his village with art, statuary and those misty fountains. Iron grillwork, red tile roofs and decorative tiles enhance the theme. During the winter holidays, hundreds of thousands of twinkling lights illuminate the district.

As we stroll along the plaza, we see all kinds of people: a band of Hare Krishnas; stylish matrons clutching their designer-label shopping bags; couples holding hands; casual middle-agers in shorts and flip-flops walking their dogs. Nobody

cocks" sculpture and a major collection of Henry Moore artworks. A $200 million expansion will be completed in several years.

Crowning Achievements

About three miles north, the sight of Kansas City's colossal Union Station brings back a wave of memories. When I was a boy, my parents and I visited family in K.C. every summer, arriving in this classically proportioned station, now the home of restaurants, gift shops and Science City. This is one of those rare places that looked huge to me as a child and still does. Once again, I crane my neck upward at the elaborately decorated ceiling, with its huge suspended timepiece. Generations of Kansas Citians rendezvoused "under the clock."

Station tours are led by guides dressed in attire that resembles the famous Harvey Girls' outfits. "First decent food and first decent girls in the West," restaurateur Fred Harvey claimed in 1882, when he deployed the first of thousands of waitresses at his train-depot eateries along the legendary Atchison, Topeka and Santa Fe line.

What I most want to see at the station is just outside one of the main entrances. I check carefully. Yes, they're still there!—the bullet holes my Uncle Woody pointed out to me when I was a kid, listening wide-eyed to his tales of Kansas City's gangster past. On June 17, 1933, one federal agent, two Kansas City police detectives, an Oklahoma police chief and their charge, mobster Frank Nash, were mowed down by a spray of bullets as they left the station.

This was the nation's third largest terminal during the early 1900s. Traffic peaked at 230 trains arriving and departing daily. When train travel gave way to automobiles, the station fell into almost two decades of neglect until it was restored and reopened in 1999. Once again the station is a busy place, with more than a million people

> Union Station brings back memories . . .
> It's one of those rare places that looked
> huge to me as a child and still does.

and the collaboration of landscape gardener George Kessler and park board president A. R. Meyer. Kansas City grew into one of America's most carefully planned parklike communities.

By the turn of the 20th century, Jesse Clyde (J. C.) Nichols—a charismatic Phi Beta Kappa graduate of Kansas University and Harvard who had traveled throughout Europe after college—mapped out the nation's first planned suburban shopping district, complete with filling stations and curbside parking for automobiles. By 1922, what had once been a swampy hog farm and brickyard became Country Club Plaza.

Cassie Lane of Highwoods Properties, which owns the 14-block Spanish-inspired plaza, explains that Nichols was particularly taken by what he had seen in Seville, Spain. Today, the dominant landmarks in

seems in too much of a hurry.

The shopping includes Hall's department store, Tiffany & Company and Armani Exchange, as well as small shops that offer merchandise from books and toys to fine fabrics and kitchenware. Eateries range from chains such as Cheesecake Factory and P. F. Chang's to the locally owned Plaza III The Steakhouse.

Statues decorate many corners: an organ grinder and monkey; a Santa Fe Trail wagon master; Winston Churchill with his wife, Clementine; Benjamin Franklin; and mythical figures such as Mercury. The area doubles as an outdoor museum.

About a block east across Main Street from the templelike J. C. Nichols Fountain is the art museum, which crowns a huge lawn with the oversize whimsical Claes Oldenburg/Coosje van Bruggen "Shuttle-

visiting annually. Across the street, the huge hilltop stone shaft, Kansas City's World War I Memorial, is being expanded with an underground museum.

A skywalk extends from the station to a modern-era landmark: the 85-acre Crown Center, launched in the 1970s by greeting card magnate Joyce C. Hall. Now this "city within a city" encompasses offices, shops, restaurants, stage shows, movie theaters, an ice-skating rink, apartments and two hotels.

The Hallmark Visitors Center displays original works by Winston Churchill, Grandma Moses and other famous artists who've worked with Hallmark over the years. Among Christmas ornaments of all shapes and sizes and a bow-making machine, an exhibit of official White House holiday greeting cards catches my eye. Clips from Hallmark Hall of Fame television programs and the company's TV commercials play on monitors.

The man behind the legend, Joyce C. Hall, came to Kansas City as an 18-year-old from his native Nebraska in 1910. Hall realized he'd be able to travel just about anywhere from this rail hub, peddling his two shoeboxes of postcards. The company he founded, Hallmark Cards, Inc., now employs 18,000 people around the globe, 5,000 of them in Kansas City. The inventory has grown to 23,000 new and re-designed products annually. Joyce Hall died in 1982, but his son, Don, and grandson, Don, Jr., still run the company.

Homegrown Legends

My next stop of the day is a trip to the area of 18th and Vine for a memorable tour of the adjoining American Jazz Museum and the Negro Leagues Baseball Museum. In the 1930s, this strip was the place to be for Kansas City's 30,000 African Americans. On Saturdays, residents dressed in their finest gathered at some of the numerous

(Clockwise) The Blue Room at the American Jazz Museum. The landmark clock at Union Station. Barbecue at Gates & Sons Bar-B-Q. The American Jazz Museum's Blue Room in the 18th & Vine Historic District.

THE MAN FROM INDEPENDENCE

President Harry S. Truman's formidable mother-in-law, Madge Gates Wallace, died in 1952. Then, and only then, did 219 North Delaware in Independence, now a Kansas City suburb, finally become the Truman home. Now, it's the Harry S. Truman National Historic Site.

This 1867 stark white Victorian is no painted lady. Adorned only by gingerbread trim and a single stained-glass window, it's preserved as it was when Bess Truman died in 1982 at age 97, 10 years after her husband's passing at age 88. Bess wanted nothing altered, and her wishes have been respected.

It's clear the Trumans were frugal and unpretentious: The large, high-ceilinged rooms don't look "decorated." A 1960s console color TV contrasts with a Victorian settee beside it. Oil portraits of Harry, Bess and their daughter, Margaret, hang on otherwise plain walls.

Harry Truman clearly loved Bess, whom he affectionately called "The Boss." He wrote her some 1,300 letters. Bess saved them all. And Truman always showed respect for his mother-in-law. That's the kind of man he was. Truman Presidential Museum & Library (800/833-1225, trumanlibrary.org).

Niel Johnson, a Truman reenactor at the Truman Presidential Museum & Library

jazz clubs or socialized streetside. Often, the next morning meant church services, followed by an afternoon Monarchs baseball game. Inside the Negro Leagues Museum, photos and exhibits give details about the teams and players of this pre-Jackie Robinson sports phenomenon.

Across the courtyard, sounds of homegrown legends such as pianist Mary Lou Williams, saxophonist Charlie Parker and bandleader Count Basie, as well as other jazz greats including Ella Fitzgerald, Duke Ellington and Louis Armstrong, fill the neon-bright American Jazz Museum. Exhibits trace the history of jazz as well as the African American experience.

Next door at the Blue Room, the Darryl White Quintet plays mellow jazz before an appreciative audience. Darryl, the trim, buttoned-down lead musician, teaches trumpet at the University of Nebraska–Lincoln and visits here regularly. He says he loves this place on two levels: People come to hear the music, not just to have a backdrop for conversation. And jazz is an original art form that evolved from his own ancestors' African American culture.

Food for the Soul

Kansas City is, without question, the top barbecue town in America, and I never visit here without wolfing down my fill. Various establishments cater to every barbecue predilection you can imagine. There's K.C. Masterpiece (upscale suburban families); Jack's Stack downtown (the business crowd) and the original Jack's Stack in suburban Martin City (a hole-in-the-wall that locals swear by); and Arthur Bryant's (down and dirty, but a fave of the literary crowd ever since *New Yorker* writer and K.C. native Calvin Trillin proclaimed it America's best way back in the 1960s). The list goes on: Rosedale, Oklahoma Joe's, Smokin' Guns, Danny Edwards, L.C.'s.

Today, I'll get a fix of my slow-cooked, hickory-smoked ambrosia at Gates & Sons Bar-B-Q on the southwestern edge of downtown. George W. Gates founded the chain in 1946. His son, Ollie, now operates six locations, plus two stands at Royals Stadium. I'm meeting the founder's granddaughter, Arzelia Gates, for lunch.

As I step in the door, the cashier up front shouts across the dining room: "HI! MAY I HELP YOU?" That enthusiastic greeting, the dining-car ambience, the tuxedoed-man icon and the red roof outside all are trademarks at the "original" Gates location.

Someone enters behind me and "HI! MAY I HELP YOU?" rips down the aisle again. This greeting has been part of the experience for 30 years. Why? Arzelia, tall and elegant, tells me it's all about personal and fast service. ("She's not yelling, she's *projecting*.") Besides pork ribs and beef, one of the best-sellers is mutton. I've never had barbecued mutton, so I order all three. The feast appears, served with pickles and sauce on white bread (all the better to soak up the drippings). Everything is wonderful, but the mutton ribs hook me at first bite.

I ask Arzelia why Kansas City barbecue is so special. Her take: It's the location (once again). Kansas City became a barbecue melting pot combining recipes and methods from both the South and Southwest. Visitors often say they find K.C. barbecue a little sweet, but not too sweet. Hot, but not too hot. And K.C.'s famous stockyards have provided all the quality meat a serious barbecuer could ever want.

Enough talking. I'm finishing up my mutton ribs. More napkins, please! As I get up to leave, I check my shirt and slacks for sauce splatters. Yes, they're there, despite my best efforts. But it was worth it. Opening the door to leave as another customer enters, I know what to expect now: "HI! MAY I HELP YOU?"

The Little Town That Roared

In 1946, war-weary Britons voted Winston Churchill and his Conservative Party out of office. Not long after, Franc McCluer, the president of Westminster College, a small Presbyterian liberal arts school in Fulton (population 12,250), was looking for a speaker for a lecture series. And he knew that Westminster graduate Major General Harry Vaughn was an adviser to President Harry S. Truman. McCluer wrote a letter, and Vaughn asked Truman to add a personal endorsement. Truman consented, and agreed to introduce Churchill if he spoke.

So Winston Churchill and Harry Truman met in St. Louis, took a train to Jefferson City, then were driven to Fulton. It was March 5, 1946, a beautiful spring day. Throngs filled the streets. The speech, titled "The Sinews of Peace," was duly delivered before an overflow crowd in the college gymnasium. The primary message: "From Stettin in the Baltic to Trieste in the Adriatic, an iron curtain has descended across the continent." Feathers were ruffled as far away as Moscow and even in Churchill's London.

Leap forward almost half a century, most of it dominated by the Cold War. Mikhail Gorbachev, former president of the Soviet Union, came to Westminster with a theme of peace. On May 6, 1992, standing before a 322-foot-wide, 11-foot-high section of the now-defunct Berlin Wall, shipped from Germany to Fulton and reerected on the Westminster campus, Gorbachev referred to Churchill's 1946 speech. The Cold War was over; Westminster and Fulton again helped the world mark a turning point.

But the story wasn't done yet. On the 15th anniversary of the speech that put Westminster on the map, then-college president Larry Davidson decided that a chapel would be a fitting commemoration of Churchill's visit. Davidson had recently read a magazine article about London churches damaged during World War II, including St. Mary the Virgin Aldermanbury. In 1969, the church was rededicated on the Westminster campus, having been shipped stone by stone and reassembled. The chapel is serene, awash in sunlight this summer afternoon. On the balcony, an organist rehearses for a wedding. I ask her to play a favorite English hymn, Ralph Vaughan Williams' unmistakable "For All the Saints." In this place, the words resound . . .

> "And when the strife is fierce, the warfare long,
> Steals on the ear the distant triumph song,
> And hearts are brave, again, and arms are strong.
> Alleluia, Alleluia!"

Winston Churchill Memorial and Library, admission charged (573/592-5234, www.wcmo.edu). Area information: Chamber of Commerce (800/257-3554, callawaychamber.com).

(From top) St. Mary the Virgin Aldermanbury. Remnants of the Berlin Wall.

Taste of Wine Country

My wife, Julie, and I have visited wineries in Napa Valley and elsewhere. But the one that captured our hearts is right here in the Midwest: Stone Hill Winery, on a bluff overlooking Hermann in the Missouri River Valley.

Hardworking Germans established Missouri's oldest winery in 1847. They chose the bluffs along the Missouri River about 90 miles west of St. Louis because the area reminded them of their homeland's Rhine River Valley. By the turn of the last century, it had grown into the second largest wine region in the country, producing more than a million gallons annually.

Then along came Prohibition in 1920. Streets in Hermann ran red with wine dumped from the more than 60 wineries. Stone Hill Winery, on its regal hilltop perch high above Hermann, was ignominiously converted into a mushroom farm, the dark and damp conditions of its huge underground cellars being just right for the fungus to thrive. Prohibition got the ax in 1933, and the wine industry was reborn—

but not in time to rescue Stone Hill from decades of neglect.

In 1965, the then-owner had a notion. He sought out an up-and-coming young area farmer, Jim Held, who had been raising hogs and row crops, and talked to him about restoring Stone Hill as a winery. It seemed like an outlandish notion to Jim and his wife, Betty. You'll grow foliage but no fruit, the pessimists warned. But something made the Helds go ahead with the winery. Home wine making always has been a tradition in Jim's family, as it is for many in this area.

The Helds took out a $5,000 loan and moved into the space above the main winery building with their four young children. Today, three of those children have studied enology and viticulture—that's wine

making and grape growing—in college, and are active in the family business; the fourth is an attorney in Manhattan.

Vintage Success

Jim and Betty planted four acres and produced 1,500 gallons of wine (they now have seven vineyards covering 120 acres). They worked hard. Very hard. By 1967, they were producing 5,000 gallons per year. Now the figure is 200,000 gallons. All told, the Held family employs about 120 people at three Missouri locations.

The setting that drew those first winemakers to Hermann, now a prospering community of 2,700, hasn't changed much. I somewhat nervously drive across the narrow iron bridge over the murky Missouri coursing far below. I watch for the

(Clockwise, from top) **A sampling of Stone Hill's wines. Sunset view of the Missouri River near Hermann. Among Stone Hill's vines.**

signs as I wind along hillside roads to the Stone Hill entrance, just as Julie and I did together on a perfect September afternoon during our first visit years ago.

I meet founder Jim Held in the sunny conservatory located off the cupola-topped main building, built in 1869. Years of toil have taken their physical toll on soft-spoken Jim, whose full gray beard and red suspenders give him a jolly Santa Claus air. He's a very thoughtful, kind man. Jim tells me his family's No. 1 business tenet is to make what the customer wants.

His most celebrated wine is a delicate, semidry Steinberg white. Stone Hill bottles 19 varieties and three grape juices, and prides itself on being the Midwest's most awarded winery (253 medals in 2003 alone). Jim's favorite is Chardonel, a dry, barrel-aged white. It's mine, too. I leave with four bottles, along with a Riesling-like Vignoles. Stone Hill's other best-sellers are Norton, a dry red made from a Virginia grape reintroduced after Prohibition, and a red Steinberg.

Do his customers prefer white or red? Jim says the ratio has remained steady: 70 percent white, 30 percent red. These are non-snobbish wines, Jim says, made only from Missouri grapes. He's proud of that. I am, too.

More Favorites

ST. CHARLES

About 20 miles northwest of St. Louis, near where the Missouri merges with the Mississippi, a new larger-than-life statue depicting William Clark and Meriwether Lewis and their lumbering Newfoundland dog, Seaman, towers near the river in St. Charles. This fast-growing suburb was the starting point of the Corps of Discovery in May 1804.

Its long, rich history sets apart this city, settled in the 1760s by French Canadian, Spanish and German immigrants. Daniel Boone arrived in 1799 and died at home in Charette Village (now Defiance) in 1820. Along Main Street, 12 blocks of vintage buildings hold dozens of specialty, crafts and collectibles shops, bakeries and candy stores. The adjoining Frenchtown district is an enclave of antiques stores.

In addition to the oversize bronze statue, St. Charles has established a new museum nearby, the Lewis & Clark Boathouse and Nature Center. Greater St. Charles Convention & Visitors Bureau (800/366-2427, historicstcharles.com).

STE. GENEVIEVE

In 1735, decades before the U.S. was born, French farmers and traders founded Ste. Genevieve (60 miles south of St. Louis). It's the state's oldest community and the oldest permanent settlement west of the Mississippi. In this town of 4,400, the business district centers on the courthouse square. You can shop for goods from antiques and lace to paintings and quilts. Then, have lunch at the historic Anvil Restaurant and Saloon.

The spire of Ste. Genevieve Catholic Church rises above the square, and The Southern Hotel, resembling a plantation house, presides nearby. The Old Brick House restaurant occupies the oldest brick building west of the Mississippi.

Among some 30 buildings from the late 1700s and early 1800s, you'll see sturdy brick German structures as well as French Colonial-style houses with wide porches. Innkeepers have transformed several venerable buildings into bed and breakfasts, including the Inn St. Gemme Beauvais and The Steiger Haus. Ste. Genevieve Interpretive Center (800/373-7007, ste-genevieve.com).

BRANSON

Twisting, two-lane roads through southwestern Missouri's Ozark Mountains take you to the bright lights of Branson (35 miles south of Springfield). Between Table Rock and Taneycomo lakes, Branson really is two communities in one. Shops, restaurants and lodgings line the streets in historic downtown Branson.

Visitors can take walking tours of 20 historic sites and board glass-domed railcars at the landmark depot for rides into the hills. Along or near "the strip" (State-76 west of downtown), variety and music shows, from country to gospel and 1950s rock, take place day and night at 46 live performance theaters. You'll also find every kind of lodging, restaurant and attraction. Celebration City, a 20th-century theme park, brings nights to life with rides, a re-created Victorian street and Route 66, and a laser light show. Branson Lakes Area Convention & Visitors Bureau (800/214-3661, explorebranson.com).

Travel Journal

GATEWAY CITY

Although the Gateway Arch may be St. Louis' most famous symbol, other world-class attractions also distinguish this city on the banks of the Mississippi River. St. Louis Convention & Visitors Commission (800/916-0040, explorestlouis.com).

Featured Stops

Charlie Gitto's For some of The Hill's best Italian cuisine (314/772-8898).

Chase Park Plaza First-class, refurbished landmark hotel along the eastern edge of Forest Park. $$$$ (877/587-2427).

Forest Park Landmark green space (314/367-7275) with attractions including Missouri History Museum (314/746-4599), St. Louis Science Center (800/456-7572), St. Louis Zoo (314/781-0900), The Muny (314/361-1900), and Saint Louis Art Museum (314/721-0072).

Gateway Arch Charge for tram rides to the top (877/982-1410).

Missouri Baking Company Specializing in gooey butter cake (314/773-6566).

More Great Stops

Grant's Farm Southwest suburban estate, once the property of the beer-making Busch family with a cabin that belonged to Ulysses S. Grant. Tram rides through a wildlife preserve and to

historic stables, home of the Anheuser-Busch Clydesdales. Open mid-April through October. Free admission; parking $6 (314/843-1700).

Missouri Botanical Garden Southeast of Forest Park, nearly 80 acres of indoor displays and outdoor gardens. Historic home of founder Henry Shaw, glass-domed Climatron rain forest conservatory, home demonstration garden and Japanese garden with footbridges, lake and teahouse. Admission charged (800/642-8842).

Shopping

St. Louis Union Station More than 100 shops and restaurants in the renovated 19th-century downtown train depot (314/421-6655).

Saint Louis Galleria About 15 minutes west of downtown, mall with more than 165 stores, including well-known retailers such as Kenneth Cole New York, plus full-service restaurants and a movie theater (314/863-6633).

Lodging

Drury Inn Union Station Elegant decor in a renovated historic building downtown, with an indoor pool. $$$ (800/378-7946).

A creamy, icy "concrete," a St. Louis legend.

Omni Majestic Hotel Downtown, renovated 1913 landmark within walking distance of Union Station. $$$ (800/843-6664).

Renaissance Grand Hotel St. Louis 1917 building restored to reflect the Roaring Twenties. $$–$$$$ (800/397-1282)

Dining

The Boat House in Forest Park Family-friendly restaurant along a lake in Forest Park (314/367-2224, ext. 2).

Meriwether's Overlooking Forest Park, a serene cafe in the Missouri History Museum (314/361-7313).

Ted Drewes Frozen Custard A landmark along old Route 66, famous for an ultra-thick shake known as a "concrete." (314/481-2652).

Tony's Restaurant An elegant downtown institution serving delicious food, from classic steaks to inventive pastas (314/231-7007).

AMERICA'S HOMETOWN

Mark Twain's characters come alive in an 11-block historic district. Hannibal Convention & Visitors Bureau (866/263-4825, visithannibal.com).

Featured Stops

Mark Twain Boyhood Home and Museum White frame house with period furnishings. Original Norman Rockwell paintings, displays inspired by scenes from Twain's books and a replica of a steamboat pilothouse. Admission charged (573/221-9010).

Becky Thatcher Home and Bookshop Former home of Laura Hawkins, Twain's inspiration for Becky Thatcher (573/221-9010).

Mark Twain Mississippi Riverboat Tours aboard a replica of an old-time craft. Admission charged (573/221-3222).

More Great Stops

Mark Twain Cave One-hour tour featuring points of interest mentioned in Twain's books

The Chase Park
Plaza Hotel, St. Louis

(one mile south of Hannibal). Admission charged (573/221-1656).

Lodging

Best Western Hotel Clemens Refurbished inn downtown, with river views. $–$$ (800/359-4827).

Holiday Inn Express Whirlpool suites and an indoor pool. $–$$ (800/465-4329).

Garth Woodside Mansion Bed and breakfast in 1871 Victorian mansion. $$$–$$$$ (888/427-8409).

Dining

Riverview Café at Sawyer's Creek A wide-ranging homey menu and a great view of the river (573/221-8292).

Mark Twain Dinette A child-friendly eatery featuring fried chicken, homemade root beer and other treats (573/221-5511).

ALL THAT JAZZ

As the frontier pushed west, cattle drives and railroads converged along the Missouri River, making Kansas City one of the largest and rowdiest cow towns. From this beginning grew a sophisticated, sprawling metropolis, with renowned attractions, splendid shopping and great restaurants. Convention & Visitors Bureau of Greater Kansas City (800/767-7700, visitkc.com).

Featured Stops

American Jazz Museum First museum in the world devoted entirely to jazz (two miles east of downtown). At the museum's Blue Room nightclub, local and national jazz musicians performing four nights a week. Admission charged to Friday and Saturday shows (816/474-8463).

Country Club Plaza Landmark shopping district, resembling a colorful Spanish marketplace (816/753-0100).

Crown Center Downtown, three-level entertainment center with more than 50 stores, 20 dining spots, two live-show theaters, a movie theater and Hyatt Regency and Westin Crown Center hotels (816/274-8444).

Gates & Sons Bar-B-Q A Kansas City institution with six locations (816/923-0900).

Hallmark Visitors Center At Crown Center, the history of Hallmark Cards (816/274-3613).

Negro Leagues Baseball Museum Celebrating the leagues that lasted from just after the Civil War into the early 1960s. Admission charged (816/221-1920).

The Nelson-Atkins Museum of Art Prestigious collection spanning more than 5,000 years (816/751-1278).

Union Station Downtown, renovated 1914 train depot containing restaurants, theaters and shops, plus Science City, with more than 50 interactive exhibits (816/460-2020).

More Great Stops

Kansas City Zoo In Swope Park on the city's eastern edge, the nation's 10th largest zoo. Admission charged (816/513-5700).

Westport North of Country Club Plaza, a reborn historic district with cafes, nightclubs, galleries and boutiques (816/531-4370).

Shopping

Pryde's Old Westport In Westport, three floors packed with home accessories and kitchen gadgets, plus local and regional artisans' works (800/531-5588).

Town Center Plaza In the southern suburb of Leawood, 90-store open-air center touted as "The Plaza of the South" (913/498-1111).

Lodging

Fairmont Kansas City at the Plaza Luxurious contemporary hotel with 366 rooms and pool and deck overlooking Country Club Plaza. $–$$$$ (800/257-7544).

Southmoreland on the Plaza Posh 12-room inn on the northeastern edge of Country Club Plaza. $$$ (816/531-7979).

Westin Crown Center Downtown, full-service hotel that's part of the Crown Center complex of shops, restaurants and theaters. $$$$ (816/474-4400).

Dining

Classic Cup Café On the Plaza, bistro serving contemporary cuisine, including crabmeat-stuffed salmon and goat cheese ravioli. Sidewalk seating (816/753-1840).

Kansas City barbecue Popular barbecue spots including Arthur Bryant's (816/231-1123), Fiorella's Jack's Stack Barbecue (816/472-7427), and K.C. Masterpiece Barbecue & Grill (816/531-3332).

Lidia's Kansas City Just north of Union Station, upscale Northern Italian fare in a converted railway freight house (816/221-3722).

PeachTree Restaurant East of downtown, specializing in healthful soul food, including sweet potato-cornbread muffins, fried chicken, slow-cooked collard greens, Okra and tomatoes, and sweet potato pie for dessert (816/472-8733).

Pierpont's at Union Station Seafood and steaks amid dark-wood paneling, stone and sparkling glass (816/221-5111).

Plaza III The Steakhouse On Country Club Plaza, for prime beef and famous steak soup in a clublike atmosphere (816/753-0000).

TASTE OF WINE COUNTRY

More than 150 years ago, German immigrants planted vineyards and founded tidy villages such as Hermann (90 miles west of St. Louis). Now, this village is the heart of Missouri wine country. Hermann Visitor Information Center (800/932-8687, hermanmo.com).

Featured Stop

Stone Hill Winery Missouri's largest vineyard with tours, tastings and the acclaimed Vintage Restaurant (800/909-9463). ∎

Nebraska

■ In population, Nebraska is one of the most lopsided Midwest states: More than half its citizens live in the east in a 60-mile corridor that includes the largest city, Omaha, and the capital, Lincoln. Still more Nebraskans cluster in farming and ranching communities along the broad, well-traveled Platte River Valley that runs east-west through this 450-mile-long state. Beyond those corridors, the abundance of wide-open spaces—notably the ecologically unique Sandhills country— seems to have instilled an independent-minded streak in Nebraskans. That's true, except when it comes to cheering unanimously for the University of Nebraska Cornhuskers football team, tantamount to a state religion.

A lonesome lane in the
Nebraska Sandhills

Noble Capital

To many I-80 travelers, Lincoln means "Big Red," the University of Nebraska football team. But how many fans, I wonder, stop to explore the Midwest's most inspiring capitol?

Lincoln sprawls between the Corn Belt and the Great Plains. A collection of small towns that eventually became today's city, the state's capital and home to the University of Nebraska, Lincoln (metro population 250,000) always has struck me as the model community: wide streets, lots of open, green spaces and enough fresh air to fill your lungs for a lifetime. It's also been rated one of the least stressful places in America to raise children.

Designation as the capital came when Nebraska achieved statehood in 1867. Famous Lincolnites include silver-tongued populist orator, three-time Democratic presidential candidate and U.S. secretary of state William Jennings Bryan. You can tour Fairview, his 1903 Queen-Anne/Classical Revival-style home. Late-night TV host Dick Cavett hails from Lincoln, too. Johnny Carson went to college here. Those are some big-time talkers. Most folks here strike me as thoughtful listeners, however.

Just 45 minutes southwest of Omaha (metro population 750,000), Lincoln is quite distinct from its larger sibling. The two urban areas, which together account for well more than half of Nebraska's 1.7 million population, seem to be steadily sprawling along the I-80 corridor toward a future merger near "the mile-wide, inch-deep" Platte River.

One of my favorite places in Lincoln is the Historic Haymarket downtown. Its restored brick warehouses, some of which once stored furs and hides, now house shops, restaurants, coffee shops and brew-pubs, where customers linger at sidewalk tables. On summer Saturdays, farmers market vendors crowd the plaza in front of Lincoln's former Burlington railway depot.

Big Red

A few blocks north, you can't miss fortress-like Memorial Stadium—Nebraska's third largest "city" on football weekends. Here's where some 78,000 normally sane, easy-going Nebraskans go bonkers rooting for the home team. Every game has been a sellout since 1962, the longest such record in the NCAA.

I feel as if I'm being brainwashed as I near the 1923-vintage stadium. Everywhere I turn, huge red "N" signs, pennants and flags flutter. Despite painful setbacks in recent seasons, Nebraska football has been a national force since shortly after the late and legendary Coach Bob Devaney arrived in 1962. The equally beloved Tom Osborne, who's a Nebraska native, followed. Osborne now represents Nebraska in the U.S. House. The two coaches led the team to five national championships.

"Not the victory but the action." "Not the goal, but the game." "In the deed the glory." These lofty inscriptions are etched above the stadium's main entrance. Because the stadium is almost empty on this summer morning, I act out a few schoolboy fantasies. First, I claim a broadcaster's choice seat in the press box on the 50-yard line. Then, I'm on the field, sprinting to a game-winning 100-yard touchdown.

Every autumn, tailgaters in red caps, sweaters, blankets and jackets claim their prized seats. In between the cheers, they'll consume upwards of 10,000 Runzas. Huh?

That's right—Runzas. Runza "hand-warmers" are yeasty, baked buns filled with ground beef, onions, cabbage and spices and served in more than 70 Runza restaurants across the state. They're an evolution of the cabbage rolls cooked by early settlers. The Runza chain began in Lincoln, and is spreading through the Midwest. On my stop, I devour two Runzas. Mine are original, but the huts serve several variations. I'm one of many Runza addicts. One fellow even launched a campaign to have a Runza emblazoned on the Nebraska quarter.

Capitol Inspirations

Now, I'm ready for some food for the soul. Nebraska's is my favorite Midwest capitol—and one of my favorite buildings anywhere. I consider this 400-foot-tall downtown marvel an architectural masterpiece. The structure was finished in 1932, with a budget of $10 million. The final price tag? $9.8 million. Try that today.

Roxanne Smith knows more about the

building than most people know about their own homes. She should. For 17 years she's led tours through its ornate interior.

I feel as if I'm entering the nave of a huge, hushed cathedral as we walk down the columned, vaulted foyer. Roxanne explains that the design of this building, which I loosely would call Art Deco, actually is a melting pot of Greek, Roman, Assyrian, Gothic, Byzantine, Renaissance and Beaux Arts styles, with Egyptian influences. New York architect Bertram Goodhue equated the Nebraska prairies with Middle Eastern deserts. So, he designed a building that looks like an ancient monument, in some respects.

Goodhue wanted geometry. Geometry he got. While the "cross within a square" floor plan of horizontal low-rise floors containing four courtyards symbolizes Nebraska's vast prairies, the tower in the center portrays the soaring hopes of its people. Crowning it all is a heroic 19-foot bronze statue titled *The Sower*.

Ambitious? Yes, and gloriously so. Outside, images of historical figures from the philosopher Socrates to lawgiver Hammurabi and emancipator Abraham Lincoln tell the story of the 3,000-year development of democracy.

Inside, an amazing collection of mosaics and murals speaks directly to Nebraskans. Bronze busts in the Hall of Fame depict the state's luminaries, among them author Willa Cather, showman Buffalo Bill Cody and Boys Town founder Father Flanagan.

Roxanne and I walk down more high-ceilinged hallways, alive with bold contemporary works, as well as the original 1930s art. The intent is to underscore the noble purposes of government, inspiring visitors to become better citizens. If I were a Nebraskan, I'd make a pilgrimage to this shrine every year.

(Clockwise, from opposite) *The Sower*. Capitol interior. Memorial Stadium. The Historic Haymarket.

Trails West

Nebraska's story is as much about the people who've traveled through the state as it is about those who settled here. My stops underscore the significance of the Platte River Valley as America's highway to the West.

riving west from Lincoln, the land becomes flat and I-80 straightens. Some travelers expect this of Nebraska. I know better, however, based on many journeys around this state, from forested Pine Ridge buttes in the northwest to tumbling Missouri River bluffs in the southeast.

At Grand Island, I-80 enters the Platte River Valley. My grandparents and great-grandparents farmed in this valley, and my mother was born near the Platte.

The Platte (French for "flat water") sometimes appears laughably shallow. It's comprised of myriad braided mini channels—not the kind of waterway that steamboats and barges ply. For eons, though, the river has offered a wide swath of water, trees, food and shelter to migrating birds and animals. I've been here in the spring to see some of the celebrated transients: the four-foot-tall Sandhill cranes that rest here by the thousands while winging their way from Mexico and Texas to Canada, Alaska and Siberia. It's an incredible sight!

Since ancient times, the Platte Valley also has been the highway west for people. Plains tribes and fur traders trekked here, followed by gold-seekers and pioneers on the Oregon, Mormon and California trails.

Celebrating the Trail

About two hours west of Lincoln, my first destination looms. An interstate road sign admonishes: "No stopping or photo-graphs!" But it's hard not to gawk. Two eight-story-tall, log-stockade towers flank the highway, crowned by a pair of 12-ton stylized aluminum sculptures. In between, a huge, tunnellike span arches over the interstate, housing The Great Platte River Road Archway Monument. Dedicated in 2000, it was visionary former Governor Frank Morrison's dream fulfilled.

Some 12,000 vehicles whiz underneath each day (you can track their speed from viewing windows 30 feet above the highway). Inside, Nebraska's longest escalator ascends to two levels of engaging interactive exhibits. A huge motion-picture screen depicts covered wagons traveling west. Headset in place, I linger at my first stop: a clamorous thunder-and-lightning storm at nearby Fort Kearny.

Not far from here, you can visit the real Fort Kearny, where at times 2,000 trail immigrants and 10,000 oxen rested daily. Elsewhere in the arch, a simulated steam engine clatters high atop a wooden trestle. I meet reenactors portraying Platte Valley settler Ellen O'Brien, a villain named Black Bart and buckskin-clad Meek the Mountain Man. They're among the real and fictitious characters who represent 350,000 Americans who traveled along the Platte from 1841 to 1866. Another stop tells about the old Lincoln Highway, which was America's first transcontinental roadway, tracing the immigrant trail.

As I exit the exhibit area, a Woody Guthrie folk song resonates over the sound

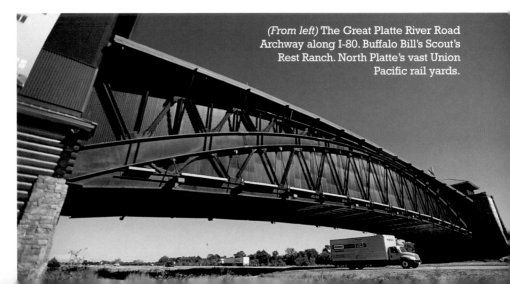

(From left) The Great Platte River Road Archway along I-80. Buffalo Bill's Scout's Rest Ranch. North Platte's vast Union Pacific rail yards.

system. The Depression/Dust Bowl-era singer gave voice to the dreams and frustrations of dispossessed Great Plains farmers. A verse from Guthrie's classic "This Land Is Your Land" conveys what the archway monument is all about:

"As I was walking,
That ribbon of highway,
I saw above me
That endless skyway,
I saw below me
That golden valley.
This land was made for you and me."

Train Town

Back on I-80 and heading west, the sky dominates the landscape. I gradually become aware there's a constant stream of freight trains passing on dual tracks just north of the interstate. I recall my own childhood fascination with trains. A railroading uncle used to give me a Union Pacific (U.P.) photo calendar each year, featuring those gargantuan, bright-yellow U.P. locomotives tugging mile-long trains through the spectacular mountains and canyons of the American West.

At North Platte (population 25,000), the north (from Wyoming) and south (from Colorado) branches of the Platte meet. Buffalo Bill Cody lent the town a measure of fame when he lived here at Scout's Rest Ranch, which you now can tour. Mostly, though, this is a quintessential railroad town, with 2,600 employees at the Western Hemisphere's largest rail nexus, the Union Pacific's Bailey Yards.

Retired U.P. railroader Deloyt Young takes me on a tour of the yards. Our first stop is at something like an airport control tower. On the orderly ranks of track below, cars loaded with goods ranging from coal to lumber and vegetable oil are assembled into freight trains heading east and west. Deloyt rattles off remarkable statistics: The yard is eight miles long with 300 total miles of track, up to 192 tracks wide; more than 160 freight trains—some 10,000 cars—pass through North Platte daily. Before leaving, we stop at the huge diesel repair shop where the hulking locomotives are maintained, cleaned and repaired.

Only large groups can tour the yard. The local dream is a nine-story public observation tower. For now, you can explore a vintage small-town depot at Cody Park, then pretend you're at the throttle of one of several huge locomotives that repose here.

At the Lincoln County Museum, I learn about the railroad's and North Platte's finest hour: the North Platte Canteen. During World War II, more than six million men and women, or half of those who served in America's armed forces, traveled through North Platte on troop trains. Each of those men and women received 15 to 20 minutes of tender loving care—perhaps the last they'd experience—during their stop in North Platte.

Troops were treated to sandwiches and fruit, coffee, milk, cookies, fried chicken, hard-boiled and deviled eggs. Soldiers celebrating birthdays received birthday cakes. Volunteers even sewed buttons on uniforms and offered first aid to weary and ill travelers. For four years, the food was paid for, prepared and served entirely by women volunteers from the North Platte area. A half-century later, the town still receives thank-you notes from veterans.

I ask myself: How on earth did they do it? When you think about it, nearly every family in America is connected in some way to this big-hearted Great Plains community and its amazing role in America's transportation story.

Wide-Open Spaces

Nebraska's Sandhills are like no other place I've been: 20,000 square miles of pure, undulating solitude. I'm fascinated by this country, and by one family's way of life, raising quarter horses.

O n some of these lonesome highways in western Nebraska, you don't see strip malls, fast-food places or gas stations for 50 miles or more. Trees and telephone poles seem like an intrusion. I'm driving from Ogallala north to Arthur County, where the entire population is 444 and the county seat (and only town) is Arthur (population 145). There are no bridges to drive over in the 720-square-mile county, because there are no streams. No railroad lines or stoplights. Just cattle grazing on grass-covered dunes.

Today is a vivid, blue-sky summer day. Black-eyed Susans decorate the roadside. Occasionally, I spot spiky yucca plants with stalks of white blossoms; otherwise, the only color comes from subtle brown shades of the grama, needle grass, bluestem and switchgrass that thrive in the semiarid land.

Only a thin layer of prairie grass stabilizes America's largest expanse of sand dunes. The rare trees I see are cottonwoods, mainly in marshy wetlands that cover 1.3 million acres of the Sandhills and provide a priceless habitat for migrating wildfowl. In this spartan realm, up to 15 acres of land is required to support one cow-calf pair. Still, cattle far outnumber people.

On the occasions when I do encounter a pickup truck on this lightly traveled highway, I get the universal greeting in these polite but reserved parts: The driver ever so slightly lifts his index finger from the steering wheel and nods.

My companions are Beldora Haythorn and her daughter, Sally Haythorn-Mayden. Not the no-frills ranch women I expected, but elegantly coifed redheads wearing tailored Western outfits and exquisite silver jewelry.

Sally, a speech and language pathologist for schools in four counties, travels nearly 4,000 miles a month from one small school district to another. Both women live in Ogallala. Beldora's son—and Sally's brother—Craig and his family run the Haythorn Land and Cattle Company ranch north of town. Theirs is considered a mid-size ranch by local standards: about 90,000 acres, or 140 square miles.

Beldora is the widow of Waldo Haythorn, a legendary rodeo cowboy, quarter-horse expert and rancher. She raised two children on the ranch before phones and electricity arrived. What was it like, I ask? "You have to be self-sufficient and content with yourself," she says.

The Haythorn ranch was founded by Harry Haythornwaite, an English farm boy who in the 1870s emigrated as a teenage stowaway on a ship sailing for Texas. Harry became a drover on cattle drives, then ran a livery in Ogallala prior to starting his ranch, which the family has retained and expanded for five generations.

Now, the Haythorns are America's largest breeders of quarter horses, a breed renowned for intelligence, hardiness and versatility. A single gelding can fetch as much as $20,000. The Haythorns pride themselves on selling horses that are trained, or "broke," by cowboys working approximately 4,000 head of cattle. In all, the Haythorns graze more than 500 horses.

The busiest time of year on the ranch is branding season when, during three weeks in June at six campsites, calves are marked with the distinctive Haythorn "Figure 4" brand. It's a return to the old days for the Haythorns and their cowboys—eating out of a chuck wagon, sleeping under the stars and working and roping cattle all day long.

Bouncing along a narrow lane, Beldora, Sally and I reach the ranch complex: a large bunkhouse and dining hall, barn, house and outbuildings. During the summer, about 20 cowboys and college students work here, and tour groups of seniors and students visit regularly.

I hook up with Denley Norman, a ruddy-faced, mustachioed cowboy. He sets me up to ride a very tame quarter horse named Scat. It's been a really long time since I rode a horse. I'm uneasy. But Denley patiently helps me with the basics. I'm thinking he's the quiet type, until he starts talking about his life here: "I like the quiet, the sound of coyotes howling at night, and crickets chirping and frogs croaking," he says. "You can really see the stars out there. You're closer to nature."

(Clockwise, from opposite)
Arthur's 1928 Haybale Church.
Quarter horses at Haythorn
Ranch. Roping and riding.

More Favorites

NEBRASKA CITY

This Missouri River town (45 miles south of Omaha, population 7,200) holds on to a rich pioneer past and the legacy of an early conservationist. The onetime frontier riverboat stop and trading post now boasts some 300 buildings on the National Register of Historic Places.

The Otoe County Courthouse, Nebraska's oldest public building, towers above the manicured square downtown. Nearby, you can browse antiques stores and the Pendleton Woolen Mills outlet. For more bargains, drive south to the outlet mall.

Visitors tour several historic homes, including the elaborate Wildwood House. The Old Freighters Museum documents the town's past. Mayhew Cabin and Historical Village includes a cabin that hid slaves traveling the Underground Railroad.

J. Sterling Morton, a frontier journalist who established Arbor Day, nurtured the town's devotion to trees and green spaces. Lawns and gardens surround Arbor Lodge, Morton's 52-room mansion in a state historical park. Morton's legacy also lives on at the National Arbor Day Foundation's Lied Lodge Conference Center.

Hungry? Stop at Ulbrick's Cafe for legendary family-style, pan-fried chicken.

More information: Nebraska City Tourism & Events (800/514-9113, nebraskacity.com).

OMAHA/COUNCIL BLUFFS

On opposite sides of the Missouri River, sprawling Omaha, Nebraska, and smaller Council Bluffs, Iowa, built fortunes as outfitting centers for pioneers heading West.

With its downtown of tall, sleek buildings, Omaha pushes west for miles from the river. Near the revitalized riverfront, trendy restaurants, nightspots and shops fill the Old Market, 12 square blocks of 19th-century warehouses.

The Western Heritage Museum in renovated Union Pacific Railroad Station chronicles the city's rough-and-tumble past. Templelike Joslyn Art Museum showcases Western art, as well as 19th- and 20-century art from Europe and America. Visitors at Boys Town stroll the gardens and browse the Hall of History museum. Top-notch Henry Doorly Zoo boasts the world's largest indoor rain forest.

El Museo Latino, along with neighborhood restaurants serving Mexican fare, attracts visitors to the stockyards district on Omaha's south side. You can get a great steak at Gorat's or The Drover.

Save time to look for bargains at Borsheim's, among the nation's largest jewelry stores, and Nebraska Furniture Mart, North America's busiest furnishings store.

Across the river, Council Bluffs has more of a small-town feeling. At the Kanesville Tabernacle, learn the saga of Brigham Young and his followers. You also can explore the past at the Union Pacific Railroad Museum, the Western Historic Trails Center and the Victorian home of General Grenville Dodge. Return to the contemporary world at riverfront casinos.

More information: Omaha Convention & Visitors Bureau (866/937-6624, www.visit-omaha.com). Council Bluffs Convention & Visitors Bureau (800/228-6878, www.councilbluffsiowa.com).

Chicken-Mushroom Strata

A favorite tailgating recipe from Nancy Osborne, wife of former Nebraska head football coach Tom Osborne.

1 8-ounce loaf French bread, cut into 1-inch cubes (8 cups)
2 cups chopped cooked chicken
1 8-ounce can drained, chopped water chestnuts
¼ cup sliced green onions
1 8-ounce package sliced mushrooms
½ cup chopped green sweet pepper
1 tablespoon butter or margarine
2 cups shredded Monterey Jack cheese
3 eggs
1½ cups milk
1 10¾-ounce can condensed cream of chicken soup
2 tablespoons coarse-grain mustard
¼ teaspoon ground black pepper
⅔ cup fine dry bread crumbs
¼ cup butter or margarine, melted

Place bread cubes in a greased 13x9x2-inch baking dish. Layer chicken, water chestnuts and green onions over bread. In a skillet, cook mushrooms and sweet pepper in butter until tender. Layer mixture over green onions; sprinkle with cheese.

Whisk together eggs, milk, soup, mustard and pepper. Pour over layers in dish and press mixture lightly with a spoon. Cover and chill for 4 to 24 hours.

Bake in a 325° oven for 30 minutes. In a small bowl, combine bread crumbs and ¼ cup melted butter. Sprinkle over casserole. Bake about 10 minutes more or until a knife inserted near the center comes out clean. Let stand 10 minutes before serving. Makes 10 to 12 servings.

NOBLE CAPITAL

Nebraska's state capital also is home of the University of Nebraska–Lincoln. More information: Lincoln Convention & Visitors Bureau (800/423-8212, www.lincoln.org).

Featured Stops

Historic Haymarket District Antiques and specialty shops, galleries and restaurants in six blocks of restored 19th-century buildings downtown (402/435-7496).

Nebraska Memorial Stadium On the campus, home to the legendary Cornhuskers football team (402/472-1132).

Nebraska State Capitol 400-foot, gold-domed limestone tower with elaborate mosaics, murals and sculptures inside. Panoramic views from the tower observation deck. Guided tours (402/471-0448).

Runza Restaurants throughout Nebraska featuring stuffed sandwiches. (402/423-2394).

More Great Stops

Folsom Children's Zoo and Botanical Gardens More than 300 animals, including red pandas

An original Runza sandwich

and a two-toed sloth. Train and pony rides, and a 14-acre garden featuring some 4,000 plant species. Admission charged (402/475-6741).

Sheldon Memorial Art Gallery and Sculpture Garden On the NU–Lincoln campus, housing Modern American works (402/472-2461).

University of Nebraska State Museum On campus, featuring the world's largest mounted fossil elephant and a planetarium. Admission charged (402/472-2642).

Dining

Billy's Named after William Jennings Bryan, Nebraska beef served in an 1887 house a block from the capitol (402/474-0084).

Misty's Famous for its thick slabs of prime rib and Cornhusker football memorabilia (402/466-8424).

Valentino's Legendary pizza parlor, with restaurants across the state (402/467-3611).

Lodging

Rogers House Bed & Breakfast Ivy-covered 1914 brick mansion. $$$ (877/220-8419).

TRAILS WEST

Kearney was founded across the Platte River from famous Fort Kearny. The rodeo was born in North Platte in 1882, when residents asked Buffalo Bill Cody to organize a Western-style show. More information: Kearney Visitors Bureau (800/652-9435, kearneycoc.net). Lincoln County/North Platte Convention & Visitors Bureau (800/955-4528, visitnorthplatte.com).

Featured Stops

Great Platte River Road Archway Monument, Kearney Spanning I-80, chronicling the Platte River Valley's rich history (877/511-2724).

Cody Park, North Platte Life-sized bronze of Buffalo Bill and a railroad museum featuring one of the largest steam locomotives ever built (800/955-4528).

Buffalo Bill Ranch State Historical Park, North Platte Tour the ranch and an 18-room Victorian mansion filled with Cody memorabilia. The surrounding recreation area offers camping along the Platte River (308/535-8035).

Lincoln County Historical Museum and World War II Canteen, North Platte Tools, weapons and other artifacts in a restored Old West town. Admission charged (800/955-4528)

Union Pacific Bailey Railroad Yards, North Platte View the world's largest rail yards from an observation deck (800/955-4528).

Dining

Depot Grill & Pub, North Platte American and Mexican favorites (308/534-7844).

Lodging

Quality Inn & Suites Sandhills Convention Center, North Platte Remodeled hotel with a restaurant, indoor pool. $$ (800/760-3333).

WIDE-OPEN SPACES

Ranching and Old West traditions thrive in the Sandhills. More information: Nebraska Division of Travel & Tourism (877/632-7275, visitnebraska.org).

Featured Stops

Haythorn Land and Cattle Company A 90,000-acre working quarter-horse ranch near Arthur. Packages available (888/918-5444).

More Great Stops

Haybale Church In Arthur, built in 1928 with walls of baled rye straw plastered over and whitewashed (308/764-2391). ∎

North Dakota

■ One of the nicest surprises of my journey is seeing more of friendly North Dakota. Thoroughly up-to-date Fargo anchors the incredibly fertile Red River Valley in the east. In the heart of the state, the Missouri River led Lewis and Clark and their party to a winter haven among the hospitable Mandan Indians. The name of vast, man-made Lake Sakakawea honors the brave teenage translator and guide who joined their journey here. Out west, young Teddy Roosevelt lived a bully life ranching among the prairies and canyons. To me, off-the-beaten-path North Dakota is one of the Midwest's undiscovered travel treasures.

A rural church surrounded by wheat fields near Stanton.

The Explorers' Trail

Unless you knew better, you probably wouldn't expect to find much in central North Dakota. Well, surprise! Your heart will sing on these open prairies. In my SUV, I'm retracing the route Lewis and Clark paddled.

ne of the first things I notice driving northward, roughly parallel to the Missouri River, is fields of yellow sunflowers exploding across the gently rolling plains. North Dakota is the nation's No. 1 producer (the same goes for spring and durum wheat, barley, flaxseed, pinto beans, canola and honey). All told, the state ranks third in the nation in total cropland.

Development is spread thin in this rural state. Gargantuan bales of hay, white-spired country churches and occasional farmsteads with neatly planted windbreaks pop up here and there. The farther north I drive, the more the land looks like someone dropped an enormous velvet cloth over the terrain and artfully added creases. The only incongruities are the enormous electric plants that turn this region's vast lignite coal resources into power for Minnesota's Twin Cities suburbs.

At every stop, people are genuinely warm and friendly—even the state trooper who hands me that $60 speeding ticket (I bear no grudge). North Dakotans are no strangers to hardship. Many hopeful newcomers settled here, then left, dispirited by blizzards, droughts and prairie fires. The descendants of those who remained clearly spring from hardy stock.

The state's population isn't growing, the result of a rural exodus from its farms and small towns. In fact, there are fewer North Dakotans now (634,000) than in 1920. But what doomsayers miss is that many North Dakotans have relocated to the state's larger cities, including Fargo and Grand Forks—gateways to the Red River Valley east of here—and to Bismarck, the capital.

Prairie Capital

After several hours of not encountering a large town or city, the Bismarck/Mandan area (population 72,000) comes into view along I-94. North Dakota's state capital is a tidy town. Handsome new homes and condominiums line the banks of the Missouri River, where the clear waters beckon boaters and anglers. Agribusiness and state government dominate, where riverboats once picked up freight at the end of the railroad line. A rather incongruous, 19-story office-tower capitol soars in the center of town. Thank Germany's 19th-century "Iron Chancellor" (Otto von Bismarck) for the city's oft-misspelled name. The idea was to attract German investment in the railroad, and it worked.

Although the 1929 capitol itself is no-frills, the 14-acre grounds are lush. Next door, I stop briefly at North Dakota's impressive state historical center and prowl the varied exhibits. Three distinctive black iron crosses represent the grave markers you see in cemeteries wherever Germans from Russia settled in North Dakota. In the 18th century, Catherine the Great wooed German farmers to the underpopulated steppes of southern Russia, promising to leave them alone. A century later, the Russians reneged on that promise. A mass exodus beginning in the late 1800s led many German-Russians to the Great Plains.

That immigrant legacy lives on here in several ways: I still can detect traces of the unmistakably nasal Lawrence Welk accent in many North Dakotans' speech. Then, there are the German-Russian food specialties. I drop into sleek and shiny Kroll's Diner in Mandan for a sampling. Along with generic diner fare (cheeseburgers, fries, malts), Kroll's serves dishes such as *fleischkuechle* (a seasoned hamburger patty wrapped in pastry dough and deep-fried).

Just across the Missouri from Bismarck and seven miles south of Mandan, I visit reconstructed Fort Abraham Lincoln on the west bank of the Missouri. It's been restored to its appearance in 1876, the year General George Armstrong Custer unwittingly led 263 doomed Seventh Cavalry soldiers and personnel to battle with as many as 5,000 Sioux braves at the Little Bighorn massacre in Montana. The site includes a replica of the grand house that Custer built for his wife, Elizabeth; barracks, a commissary and other structures; a parade grounds; and a view of the Missouri where it meets the Heart River.

Next door, On-A-Slant Indian Village gives me my first peek at the domed earth-lodges built by the Mandans. Four lodges

(Clockwise, from opposite top) Fields of sunflowers, a common sight across the state. View from near the Missouri River Lodge. Earthlodge at Knife River Indian Villages. Interpreter at Fort Abraham Lincoln.

(From left) Inside a BirdWoman tepee, Washburn. Rancher Orville Oster of the Missouri River Lodge. Near Knife River Indian Villages.

have been reconstructed, including a main council lodge you can enter. At one time, it's estimated that 1,000 Mandans lived in 85 lodges here, before many of them were wiped out by smallpox.

It's just after daybreak, and I'm standing atop a bluff looking out over a broad vista—the Missouri River channel, clumps of cottonwood trees and more bluffs on the other side. And it's all the more inspiring because I'm viewing almost the same landscape lawyer-turned-painter George Catlin rendered from this spot in 1831 (the original painting, now at the Smithsonian, is reproduced on a marker here).

Lewis and Clark Lore

Missouri River Lodge, owned by North Dakota natives Orville and Diane Oster, both in their 60s, nestles in the river valley at the foot of a butte north of Stanton. Coyotes serenade me as I rest in my comfortable room. The critters live behind the Osters' house and barn in caves that pock this area's striated badlands formations.

The Osters have operated their history-rich 2,000-acre ranch since 1969, raising 200 cow-calf pairs, fed with the alfalfa and corn the couple grows in their fertile river bottomlands. A few years ago, they opened their home to lucky guests like me.

It's one of my all-time favorite bed-and-breakfast experiences. A cheerful, well-organized ranch wife and innkeeper, Diane makes out-of-this-world gooey cinnamon rolls that I've dreamed about since my last visit. I've never seen ruddy-faced Orville not wearing a seed-corn cap. His gnarled hands reveal years of toil as a rancher. He's also an encyclopedia of Lewis and Clark lore, which suffuses this ranch. It's the perfect base for nosing around the Lewis and Clark sites in the area.

My first stop, the big, log-style Lewis & Clark Interpretive Center, overlooks the Missouri River northwest of Washburn. We've all heard the story: In 1803, President Thomas Jefferson acquired from France the 800,000-square-mile Louisiana Purchase, which someday would encom-

pass much of today's Midwest. He paid a bargain $15 million for the largest peacetime transfer of land in history. Jefferson appointed his personal secretary, 29-year-old Meriwether Lewis, to head an expedition to check out the territory and search for the elusive Northwest Passage (a water route to the Pacific that turned out to be nonexistent). Lewis in turn recruited his friend, William Clark, 33, who'd retired from the military to run a Virginia plantation.

They left the St. Louis area in May 1804, and arrived in this area in autumn, planning to winter among the friendly Mandan. Exhibits at the interpretive center detail their two-year, 8,000-mile journey. I hear music the explorers might have enjoyed, feel a woolly buffalo robe and see a cradle-board like the one used by their interpreter, Sakakawea (North Dakotans insist on this spelling, based upon the Hidatsa Indian words for bird and woman).

Out on the big deck in back of the center, I'm awestruck once again by the 180-degree panorama that surrounds me

on this cloudless day—the cottonwood-lined river, the buttes far in the distance. The only sound is the relentless wind.

Not far from where the explorers probably camped, the Yunker family's Bird-Woman Missouri Rim Canoe Adventures gives groups of up to 25 a taste of what the expedition experienced, paddling the river and sleeping in tepees on its banks. Doug Yunker relishes the story of a woman from New York who came with her children and their nanny just to sleep in a tepee.

It's a short drive to a wooded riverside park, site of a visitors center and Fort Mandan. This A-shaped reproduction fort was built in the 1930s from cottonwood logs like those the explorers would have used. Nobody knows the exact location of the original fort where the expedition spent the winter of 1804–05, but the site is thought to be nearby. The explorers diplomatically chose their location to be equidistant from Mandan and Hidatsa villages, although it was the friendly Mandan who helped them survive the brutal winter. Here, they mapped out the journey they resumed in spring.

I'm told the winter layover was a friendly, positive time. The adventurers studied Indian culture, hunted buffalo and traded for supplies. By April, they were ready to forge on, sending their keelboat back to St. Louis laden with journals and specimens for President Jefferson. I can't resist trying on a Bonaparte-type hat and raising a spyglass in the captains' joint quarters.

Mound Metropolis

North Dakota was a latecomer as a state, entering the Union in 1889, but Native Americans have lived here for 11,000 years. Mound-building Indians began settling in the 16th century. Unlike tribes of wandering hunters such as the Sioux, the Mandan and Hidatsa stayed put, growing crops and living in villages of earthen lodges along the Missouri and Knife rivers. The first French explorers arrived in central North Dakota in 1738. They might have been surprised to find a flourishing trading center populated by as many as 4,000 Indians. By the time Lewis and Clark arrived, smallpox had started to attack the Native American population.

Sakakawea once lived at my last stop, Knife River Villages National Historic Site. Mustachioed Terry O'Halloran, chief interpreter for the National Park Service, gets more and more animated as he points out saucerlike depressions left by 60 vanished earthlodges from three villages clustered in the area, housing perhaps 2,500 people. Entire families, plus their horses, dogs and belongings, occupied the 30- to 60-foot-diameter lodges.

We walk beside a steep bank that descends to the Knife River. This was a busy place at one time. Terry points out pieces of flint, bone and pottery—the soil is rich with artifacts. It's eerie, this empty, wind-blown place that once hummed with life.

A reconstructed lodge gives an inside view of Hidatsa life. It's a remarkably sturdy structure, built on a framework of four wooden posts covered with wood, then a layer of soil and grass. Inside, the lodge is surprisingly cool on this warm day. The indoor temperature remains comfortable year-round. I see where an extended family might have slept, kept their horses and cached their food. There are even children's balls, dolls and sleds.

As for Sakakawea, a Shoshone from what's now Idaho who'd been captured and adopted by a Hidatsa family, Terry tells me the only thing really known about her is that she wore buckskin with a blue, beaded belt and carried her child in a cradle on her back. She was invaluable to the expedition, with her language skills and knowledge of the route. The explorers dropped her and her family off here on their way home. What a celebrity she must have been—and is to this day! Yet, nobody knows with certainty when or where this woman we all owe so much died.

Prairie Panache

Does "Fargo" bring to mind the black comedy (actually set in Minnesota), or maybe a bleak arctic-tundra outpost? Both images are dead wrong. I wish I'd had more time to explore this thriving Red River Valley city.

The windswept, griddle-flat Red River Valley of North Dakota and Minnesota is one of the world's most fertile agricultural larders. Rich, black soil from a prehistoric lake bottom combined with the valley's reliably high water table sustains mile-square fields of sugar beets, potatoes, soybeans, barley, wheat and flaxseed. Normally shallow, the north-flowing Red River can turn into a 20-mile-wide lake when swollen by spring floods, as it did in 1997 after a record 117 inches of snow melted.

Weather is a big deal here. It's been as cold as minus 48 degrees and as hot as 114. The arrival of the Northern Pacific Railroad launched Fargo in 1875 during the great Dakota Territory settlement boom. Bonanzaville USA in West Fargo gives visitors a glimpse of the huge corpo-rate farms that ruled the prairies in those days, helping lure more settlers. The city is named for railroad director William G. Fargo, also associated with what became Wells Fargo and American Express. Fifty trains a day still roll through town, and two downtown passenger depots are preserved.

This is the unofficial capital of the Red River Valley, with a population of 93,000 in the city and 170,000 in the metro area. Health care, education and computer soft-ware services mean a thriving economy and low unemployment. The surveys that rank cities love Fargo—the weather cate-gory notwithstanding.

When it comes to local heroes, Fargo claims a baseball star my pals and I wor-shiped as boys: Roger Maris. Today, there's a Roger Maris museum in a local mall, and the home-run king is buried here in Holy Cross Cemetery beneath a gravestone shaped like a baseball diamond.

On Broadway

I leave my bags at the hotel, and walk a few blocks along Fargo's Broadway to Monte's Downtown to meet Cole and Laura Carley, lifelong Fargoans who happen to be my age (Cole is high school class of '67; Laura is '68). Fellow boomers. Instant bonding. Cole is with the area visitors bureau and Laura works for her family's construction firm.

Solicitous manager Monte Jones is dressed in Fargo-tropical summertime finery: yellow silk shirt, yellow linen slacks and ostrich-skin cowboy boots. Totally cool. He grew up on an area farm, pursued a career as a dancer in New York and

returned 30 years later to launch this bistro. "I finally made it to Broadway after I got back home to Fargo," Monte says, smiling.

My meal is out of this world: chilled cantaloupe/passion-fruit soup and herbed rack of lamb. Our conversation is equally satisfying. Laura is an active local volunteer and the ranking member of the Fargo school board. She tells me that Fargo is a community with a mission. For example, the local Lutheran Social Services organization has sponsored so many refugee groups that 56 languages and dialects are spoken in Fargo schools. We talk about the local cultural scene, which includes a symphony, community theater and two downtown venues: the Plains Art Museum and the Fargo Theatre.

Cole tells me that North Dakota's scant population (at 634,000, it's the least populated state in the Midwest and one of the least populated in the nation) means the state feels like one big small town. As if on cue, U.S. Senator Kent Conrad steps over to our table. "What's going on at the school board?" he asks Laura.

Besides the new restaurants, downtown is being revitalized by shops and even lofts and condominiums. There's also a new hotel, the Hotel Donaldson, that rivals any I've experienced in Chicago, Los Angeles or New York in comfort and sophistication.

It's a handsome three-story corner brick building built by the Fargo Odd Fellows lodge in 1894 and later converted into a workmen's hotel. In 2003, local entrepreneur Karen Burgum transformed the forlorn building into 17 luxurious rooms, and added the HoDo Lounge and Restaurant on the first floor. While the exterior is carefully preserved, the Hotel Donaldson is purely contemporary inside.

On the roof, there's a sleek, open-air Jacuzzi surrounded by heated tiles, so it's usable even during a Fargo winter. Modern lounge chairs, an artful rooftop landscape of native prairie grasses and great views all around make this spot irresistible. And there's an even loftier side to this little gem of a hotel. Burgum's goal is to spotlight Downtown Fargo's arts scene for her guests. To that end, each room is inspired by a different local artist (64 artists are represented throughout the hotel, 300 works all told). A cozy third floor library features books by regional authors. Burgum says "We want to make staying here a memorable experience by celebrating Fargo."

Two blocks away, the Plains Art Museum slips into the shell of a century-old former International Harvester showroom and warehouse. It's one of the best and most innovative repurposings of a historic structure I've encountered. Inside, I see lots of contemporary works by regional artists. Edward Pauley, the president/CEO here, came to Fargo just last year. I ask what strikes him most. "The land," he says. "The sheer flatness. Here, where your feet are planted, is where the sky begins."

Just blocks away, the 1926 landmark Art Deco Fargo Theatre reigns. National television cameras converged here on Oscar night in 1997, when *Fargo* (the movie) was nominated for seven Academy Awards. With its 870 seats, a grand Wurlitzer organ and its huge "Fargo" marquee, this movie palace now shows first-run independent films and art-house movies.

Before I leave town, I stop at the beautiful campus of North Dakota State University on Fargo's north side. With 12,000 students, this technology- and agriculture-oriented school is the largest of four community institutions of higher education. Looking around, I see the most courteous, well-groomed and all-around good-looking bunch of college students I've come across—yet another tribute to the Red River Valley's ability to grow good things.

(Clockwise, from opposite top) The Hotel Donaldson's "Sky Prairie on the Roof." The hotel's corner lounge. Finery at Bonanzaville USA. Monte's Downtown restaurant. Inside the historic Fargo Theatre.

Taste of North Dakota

Creamy Borscht
Kroll's Diner, Mandan

2 tablespoons butter or margarine
2 medium onions, coarsely chopped
1 tablespoon brown sugar
½ teaspoon salt
¼ teaspoon pepper
⅛ teaspoon ground cloves
2 15-ounce cans small, whole beets,
    drained and cubed
1 14-ounce can vegetable broth
1 cup whipping cream
2 tablespoons lemon juice
    Snipped fresh dill

In a saucepan, melt butter over medium heat. Add onions, brown sugar, salt, white pepper and cloves. Cover, cook for 10 to 12 minutes or until onions are tender, stirring occasionally. Transfer to a blender. Add 1 can of drained beets and ½ cup of the vegetable broth. Cover and blend or process until nearly smooth.

In the same pan, combine remaining can of drained beets, remaining broth, whipping cream and lemon juice. Stir in blended beet mixture; heat through (don't boil). Sprinkle with dill. Makes 4 servings.

A WUNNERFUL LIFE

Lawrence Welk's birthplace near Strasburg is like a scene from *Little House on the Prairie*—a modest whitewashed home with siding-covered turf walls, a granary, summer kitchen, blacksmith shop and barn filled with old-time implements. Oh yes, and the original, neat-as-a-pin outdoor privy. Polka music blares from a loudspeaker.

Welk's German-Russian parents, Ludwig and Christina, homesteaded here in 1903 and raised eight children. Lawrence was born that first year. After a long fourth-grade illness, he never went back to school, but he didn't want to be a farmer. At 17, the aspiring musician struck a deal with his father to lend him $400 for an accordion. In return, Welk would remain on the farm until the age of 21. It was only then that he began speaking English and wed South Dakotan Fern Renner. Married 51 years, they had a son and two daughters.

After years crisscrossing the Midwest and the nation, Welk launched his *Champagne Music Hour* on ABC in 1955. He died in 1992, but his music empire didn't. Public TV rebroadcasts Welk's shows. Entertainers from his "musical family" still perform in Branson, Missouri, and there's his resort village and museum in Escondido, California. Champagne music lives! Ludwig Welk Homestead. Admission charged (701/336-7777).

Favorites

MEDORA

"I never would have been President if it had not been for my experiences in North Dakota," Theodore Roosevelt once remarked. It's fitting then, that the centerpiece of the vacation area, which includes the Old West town of Medora, carries the president's name. Theodore Roosevelt National Park sweeps across 70,000 acres.

Spreading along the Little Missouri River north from I-94 and Medora, the park is divided into two big units (70 miles apart) and a smaller third unit encompassing the frontier Elkhorn Ranch. Buffalo graze and prairie dogs chatter beside roads that link one scenic turnout after another.

Hiking trails wind down hills. You also can follow a 36-mile paved loop. Along the way at Peaceful Valley Ranch, many visitors embark on guided horseback tours.

The park's gateway, Medora (24 miles east of the North Dakota/Montana state line) has fewer than 200 residents during the winter. Each summer, the town fills with visitors from around the world who come to see the national park (the visitors center is at the edge of town) and to soak up the charm of Medora's 10 blocks of museums, restaurants and galleries.

Take a tour in a horse-drawn buggy, and sample buffalo burgers at the rustic Rough Rider Hotel. Summer nights, the Burning Hills Amphitheatre on a bluff above town hosts the Medora Musical. Before the show, join the "pitchfork fondue" feed of steaks speared on pitchforks and seared in kettles of beef tallow. City of Historic Medora (701/623-4828, www.medorand. com). Theodore Roosevelt National Park (701/842-2333, www.nps.gov/thro/).

Travel Journal

THE EXPLORERS' TRAIL

Bismarck, North Dakota's capital, rises on the banks of the Missouri River, the heart of Lewis and Clark country. The famous explorers spent more time in North Dakota than in any other state. North of Bismarck and Mandan, historic sites mark the route the expedition followed. More information: Bismarck-Mandan Convention & Visitors Bureau (800/767-3555, bismarckmandancvb.com).

Featured Stops

Fort Abraham Lincoln State Park/On-A-Slant Indian Village Seven miles south of Bismarck, five reconstructed Mandan earthlodges on the site of the original village. Also, reconstructions of Fort Abraham Lincoln, General George Custer's last command post and Custer's home (701/663-4663).

Knife River Indian Villages National Historic Site Reconstructed, furnished Hidatsa earthlodge, plus 11 miles of trails and a visitors center with a museum (just north of Stanton). A trail leading from the lodge to the Knife River past the remains of the original lodges, where Lewis and Clark met Sakakawea (701/745-3300).

Lewis & Clark Interpretive Center/Fort Mandan Historic Site Across the river northwest of Washburn, telling the explorers' story from when they arrived in 1804 to when they returned in 1806 (877/462-8535).

Missouri River Lodge Bed and breakfast on a 2,000-acre working ranch north of Stanton. With trails along the river, boat dock and private sandy beach. $–$$ (877/480-3498).

North Dakota State Capitol Built in the early 1930s and known as the "Skyscraper on the Prairie." (701/328-2480).

More Great Stops

BirdWoman Missouri River Canoe Adventures Guided trips in a 26-foot replica voyageur canoe along part of the Lewis and Clark route on the Missouri River near Washburn (38 miles north of Bismarck) (701/462-3367).

Lake Sakakawea State Park North of Stanton, the largest man-made reservoir in the U.S. (180 miles long). Camping, marina, fishing, boating (701/487-3315).

Lewis and Clark Riverboat Daily Missouri River cruises on an old-fashioned stern-wheeler. Departs from the Port of Bismarck. Ticket charge (701/255-4233).

North Dakota Heritage Center In Bismarck, museum chronicling North Dakota's history from the age of dinosaurs to the present. Highlights: a Native American camp, homesteader's yard and a mosasaur, a prehistoric marine animal (701/328-2666).

PRAIRIE PANACHE

Fargo nestles in the rich Red River Valley, which outlines North Dakota's eastern reaches. Sister city Moorhead is just across the river in Minnesota. With 93,000 people, Fargo is North Dakota's largest city. Visitors will discover a historic downtown and other attractions. More information: Fargo-Moorhead Convention & Visitors Bureau (800/235-7654, fargomoorhead.com).

Featured Stops

Bonanzaville USA Fifteen-acre historic village depicting life in the Red River Valley at the turn of the last century (800/700-5317).

Hotel Donaldson In a historic building with rooftop garden and wine bar. Suites are designed around the work of regional artists. $$$ (701/478-1000).

Monte's Downtown Fine dining in stylish, upscale atmosphere (701/526-0149).

Plains Art Museum Collections of regional, American Indian, traditional folk and contemporary art in a renovated early-20th-century warehouse downtown. Admission charged; children free (701/232-3821).

More Great Stops

Heritage Hjemkomst Interpretive Center In Moorhead, with a 76-foot-long, 16-ton replica of a 9th-century Viking ship. Also, a replica of a 12th-century Norwegian church. Admission charged; children age 4 and younger free (218/299-5511).

Dining

HoDo Restaurant Gallery At the Hotel Donaldson, with a diverse, European-inspired menu using local produce (701/478-1000). ∎

Paddling the Missouri on a BirdWoman outing.

Ohio

■ For me, the Buckeye State encapsulates our entire region: To the north stretches an inviting Great Lakes shoreline (Lake Erie), with a few islands sprinkled offshore. The mighty Ohio River, replete with stern-wheelers and barges, defines the southern flank. In between spreads a patchwork of rural areas and great cities—Cleveland, Columbus and Cincinnati—where steel mills and auto plants mingle with tree-shaded small towns, forested foothills and the largest Amish community in the world (centered in Holmes County). Norman Rockwell would have loved Ohio. I know I do. That's why I made Ohio history, from a variety of eras and perspectives, the focus of the time I spent revisiting my favorite places here.

Holmes County, Amish Country

Villages That Time Forgot

Did you ever stumble upon an out-of-the-way place that seemed like some sort of Brigadoon? I felt that way the first time I visited two towns in east-central Ohio. Both cast their spells again when I returned.

I arrive in Roscoe Village at just the right time of day: Summer twilight gives a mellow amber glow to the brick and sandstone buildings along Whitewoman Street. As I stroll the wooden sidewalks and peer through windowpanes, it's easy to imagine myself as a traveler during the 1840s heyday of this hillside town and its historic canal.

Transportation plays a starring role in the story of the Midwest. We're the crossroads for everything and everyone, it seems. Travelers first crisscrossed the region in canoes and on footpaths. Then came wagons and stagecoaches, followed by trains, automobiles and airplanes. Along the way, canals have come and gone.

Growing up in the Missouri River Valley on the fringe of the Great Plains, I wasn't aware of the importance of these manmade waterways in the development of states such as Ohio, Michigan, Indiana and Illinois. In the early and mid-1800s, Ohio alone built almost 1,000 miles of canals. That's why single-street Roscoe Village, just outside Coshocton (60 miles south of Canton), made such an impression on my first visit more than a decade ago.

On this trip, the canals and Roscoe Village are just as striking as I remember them. In Lake Park, hulking Percheron draft horses pull the *Monticello III* canalboat replica that takes visitors on 45-minute trips. In the peak years, from the 1830s to 1870s, some 3,000 of these craft plied the Ohio River and Erie Canal, which linked Cleveland and Lake Erie with Portsmouth along the Ohio River.

Entire families lived on the 70- to 80-foot-long, 14-foot-wide boats that transported passengers and freight at a stately rate of four miles per hour. Ingeniously engineered locks and aqueducts carried the boats up, down and over the rolling hills of eastern Ohio.

That commerce made Roscoe Village a bustling inland port. Into the wilderness came civilization in the form of housewares, cloth, furnishings and building materials. Out went furs, grain and wool. The canals spiked Ohio's development as a state and helped outfit Civil War troops. By the end of the 19th century, however, railroad builders who, ironically, had helped supply the canal boats, had doomed the canals.

Then, in March 1913, the rampaging Walhonding River nearly wiped out Roscoe Village's famed triple canal locks. The village steadily declined, overshadowed by nearby Coshocton, until local businessman and benefactor Ed Montgomery launched a preservation campaign in 1969 that became the Montgomery Foundation. The organization now welcomes 250,000 visitors a year to restored Roscoe Village.

Back in the village on my twilight walk, I step into the cellar of what's now the Warehouse Restaurant, awed by the huge hand-carved sandstone foundation blocks that are like the ones lining the canal locks. I have to wonder: How did the builders do it without power equipment?

Drawn in by shop windows, I linger to explore the merchandise, notably the tempting candy counter, at the Roscoe General Store. In all the shops here, I see products that might have filled the shelves in the 1840s: leatherwork, baskets, quilts and pottery. In the cozy John Dredge Bookstore, I read up on canal-era history. The toll collector's cottage charms me with its finely filigreed Victorian porch arches.

This part of Ohio, with its wooded rolling hills, must be even more enchanting in the fall. I'm vowing to return with my wife, Julie, one autumn for the apple butter festival. I'll pick up more canal-days history—and more of that rich, thick Roscoe Village apple butter.

A Place of Refuge

As I turn off the interstate south of Canton and drive through an early evening cloudburst to Zoar, I see many new houses, businesses and even a fast-food drive-in. But the Cobbler Shop Bed and Breakfast, an antiques-filled 1828 retreat with a big, screened-in back porch, reassures me. Zoar remains just about as I remember it.

The town name is a biblical word for refuge, and it fits. Even so, I wonder how the Zoarites (and so many of our ancestors) found the courage to risk everything,

(*Clockwise, from opposite*) The Zoar star, a symbol used by the Utopians. Zoar's greenhouse and garden. An interpreter in period costume. An antique bed in a Zoar house. Furniture crafted by Zoarites.

betting on a new life in America. For the Zoarites, the motivation was lofty—the ideal of a communal Utopia.

Some 200 brave German separatists, who opposed the state Lutheran church, were aided in their journey to freedom by sympathetic Quakers in England and Philadelphia. In 1817, they followed their leader, Joseph Bimeler, to this then-wilderness valley of the Tuscarawas River (at that time simply known as a branch of the Muskingum River).

Penniless and led by women, because many of the men had been imprisoned in Germany, the Zoarites hand-dug a seven-

Monticello III canal boat near Roscoe Village

The town name is a biblical word for refuge, and it fits. I wonder how the Zoarites found the courage to risk everything . . .

mile stretch of the Ohio and Erie Canal near their village to pay for their 5,500 acres. Self-imposed celibacy yielded to marriages only after the first years of brutal toil. For many years, Zoar children were left to live in dormitories, rather than with their parents, so workers wouldn't be distracted. The community developed bountiful farms, thriving industries (baskets, straw hats, tin lanterns, wood-burning stoves) and a self-sufficient lifestyle.

The second day of my visit arrives dewy and misty, which only serves to fuel my imagination on a guided tour through the compact village, now protected on three sides by a giant levee. Green lawns and blooming gardens surround solidly built brick-and-timber homes that might have been occupied by one or several families during the commune's peak years. There's a central kitchen where families picked up their "to-go" meals, a bakery that made all

the village's bread and a dairy that supplied milk. Crafters are at work in the sewing and weaving houses and tinsmith shop.

On a hilltop overlooking the village, a handsome cupola still tops the Assembly House, where Zoarites gathered to receive their daily work assignments. I sit admiring the big, hand-painted organ pipes in a pew at the light-filled Meeting House. My footsteps echo in the halls of nearby Number One House, an early assisted-living experiment for elderly residents, who didn't go for the idea (Zoarites had a reputation for being stubborn). It became the home of several of the village trustees' families.

I love the romantic European architectural flourishes and embellishments on surviving furnishings: the cupolas, reddish tile roofs—even on log cabins, ornate headboards and hand-painted and -lettered wardrobes. The buildings themselves stand as monuments to the ingenuity of

their designers—refreshingly cool, even on a hot morning.

I'm surprised to learn Zoar was a tourist mecca as long ago as 1833, when the once-grand Zoar Hotel welcomed Ohioans who came via the Ohio and Erie Canal for the country air. Even President McKinley, a Cleveland resident, traveled to Zoar.

A white picket gate opens to the Garden of Happiness at the heart of the village. It fills the entire square with an allegorical arrangement of colorful flowers, trees and shrubs that radiate from the central Tree of Life, a huge Norway spruce planted when the garden was re-created in the 1920s. Beside the garden stands the Zoar greenhouse, which was so advanced in its day that wealthy Ohioans sent their houseplants via the canal to winter there.

The communal way of life ended when quibbling Zoarites disbanded in 1898, having amassed more than $1 million in assets. The Ohio Historical Society and preservation-minded residents rescued what remained. Only a few descendants of the original settlers are among today's 175 residents, but their legacy lives on just minutes—yet a world away—from that bustling interstate highway.

Amish Country Time Warp

After a half-hour of browsing, I find I'm getting lost in the labyrinth of interconnected buildings and aisles at Lehman's Hardware in the northeastern Ohio hamlet of Kidron (25 miles west of Canton). Maybe it's because I'm concentrating more on the merchandise than the layout. That's easy to do. Hand-operated wringer washing machines, gas-powered refrigerators, corn shuckers, wood-burning stoves, apple peelers—those are just some of the 10,000 items in stock.

The colorful oil lamps fill an entire display room of their own. Checking the guest book (customers are invited to sign in and leave comments), I note that this *über* department store for the self-reliant brings visitors from all over the world to tiny Kidron (population 630).

Jay Lehman founded the store in 1955 to serve the needs of the local Amish community, the world's largest. These self-described "plain people" grow and make what they need and live without modern conveniences such as cars and electricity. Over the years, Jay found he was selling fewer items to the Amish than they were selling to him. Now, thanks in part to the Internet and a thriving catalog-sales operation, Lehman's is known around the world as the place to shop if you live somewhere without electricity (by choice or by circumstance).

That means missionaries, military personnel and back-to-the-land survivalists in remote parts of the globe all count on Lehman's. So do moviemakers, who've discovered that Lehman's stocks period props for a movie such as, say, the 2003 Civil War tale *Cold Mountain*.

On this return trip, I find the store even bigger and busier than I recall. Jay's son, Galen, and daughter, Glenda Lehman Ervin, have helped him expand. With an old-fashioned bottle of soda in hand, I chat with Glenda and finally work up the courage to tell her I hadn't quite expected to meet someone here with a modern hairdo and wearing pink hoop earrings and a sundress. Glenda explains that she and her family are Mennonite, which means their religious roots are related to those of the Amish, but that their rules aren't as strict.

The people I keep bumping into in the busy aisles at Lehman's look a lot like me: city slickers used to their dishwashers, microwave ovens, power mowers and VCRs—and simply awed and delighted that so many of these low-tech products still exist.

Anyone out there looking for a butane clothes iron or treadle sewing machine?

Lehman's Hardware (330/857-5757). More information: Wayne County Convention & Visitors Bureau (800/362-6474, wooster-wayne.com).

Totally Cool Cleveland

Cleveland has come a long way in recent years. I came to see all the progress and ended up reconnecting with my past—first at the Rock and Roll Hall of Fame, then at an old-time soda fountain in a here-to-stay small town.

While many Midwest cities struggled, Cleveland faced even greater challenges than most. Remember when the Cuyahoga River, which runs through downtown, caught fire in 1969 and the media called Cleveland "The Mistake on the Lake"?

A monumental turnaround already was in full swing when I visited in 1995. Restaurants and clubs thrived in onetime industrial areas along the river, as did a vibrant theater district and new sports venues. This city was on its way to symbolizing the rebirth of the Midwest.

Of everything going up and going on, what really captivated me was a place that seemed to belong to me, or at least to that wannabe surfer boy within. As the kid from landlocked Iowa who grew up listening to the Beach Boys and Jan and Dean, I couldn't wait to tour the Rock and Roll Hall of Fame and Museum on that first visit. But when I saw the I. M. Pei glass pyramid towering above an expansive plaza beside Lake Erie, I was worried. It didn't look like a place where an Iowa kid at heart could reconnect with his musical roots. Now I know better.

On this trip, the fun starts as soon as I step inside. Jerry Lee Lewis' "Great Balls of Fire" blasts from the sound system, and cars that U2 used as stage props on tour hang from the ceiling. Oh, yeah, it's all about the music all right.

Once again, I can't just stand there and listen. That's not the point here. I head straight for the lower level, don a headset and click to *my* music. First, I play The Beach Boys' "California Girls," then some Beatles and Four Seasons.

This place was a musical heaven as soon as it opened. Now there's even more to see—and hear. I'm standing next to (but not touching!) Beatle George Harrison's 1964 Gibson guitar, which he played on almost every Beatle album, and Beach Boy Dennis Wilson's drum kit. Zowie!

In addition to one-of-a-kind memorabilia (I had to check out John Lennon's report card and a flaming orange tuxedo jacket that James Brown wore), there's the Jimi Hendrix Theater, along with "And the Beat Goes On," an exhibit that traces popular music styles. Part of the hall of fame's mission is to educate its half million annual visitors about pop music and culture. I learn what groups influenced my favorite performers. I didn't know, for example, that Paul McCartney gave credit to Little Richard for helping pave the way for the Beatles' music.

Almost as compelling as the music are the stories about the thousands of pieces of memorabilia. Take George Harrison's Gibson, for instance. Curatorial Director Howard Kramer loves telling that story: "After Harrison essentially was done with this guitar, he gave it to Pete Hamm of the group Badfinger . . . . It then was played on

a number of hits for Badfinger . . . . It was rumored to have been sold . . . . But, in fact, it sat in Hamm's brother's house in Wales for nearly 20 years, until it was loaned to us." With his goatee and glasses, Howard looks too much like a professor to know all this cool stuff, but know it he does.

"Why Cleveland?" I wonder. Howard explains that a lot of sounds from both black and white American musicians have melded in clubs here over the years. Besides, a pioneering radio deejay named Alan Freed actually coined the term "rock and roll" in Cleveland in 1951. Now that legacy lives on in tributes to more than 220 performers who defined American pop music, from pioneers such as Les Paul to contemporary artists including Aretha Franklin, ZZ Top and U2. Each year, more inductees are added to the hall of fame, and more fans are lured to town.

Downtown Cleveland rocks these days, and nowhere more than at the Rock and Roll Hall of Fame.

Another Blast from the Past

Hmmm . . . the kid in me must still be in control. All I can think about is an old-fashioned cherry soda—the kind I ordered at the local drugstore when I was a boy. I rediscovered it more than a decade ago in Hudson Village, a small town about 25 miles south of Cleveland that's doing its best to avoid being swallowed by suburbs.

(*Clockwise, from opposite*) At Cleveland's Rock and Roll Hall of Fame and Museum. The Arcade historic shopping mall in Cleveland. Yummy ice cream cones at Saywell's in Hudson Village. The Rock and Roll Hall of Fame.

ON THE FLY

As an Iowa grade-schooler, I got Kitty Hawk, North Carolina, drummed into my brain in conjunction with the Wright brothers. But Orville and Wilbur spent almost their entire lives in Dayton.

The Wright Brothers Interpretive Center, in the Dayton Aviation Heritage National Historic Park, is part of a redevelopment area called Wright-Dunbar, a onetime Dayton "streetcar suburb" and later an African American neighborhood. The Dunbar of Wright-Dunbar is acclaimed Dayton poet Paul Laurence Dunbar, one of America's first African American poets and a lifelong friend of the Wrights.

The restored Wright Cycle Company building stands across from the interpretive center, which is full of aviation exhibits. The old part of the center is a restored commercial building, original to the site, with a corner grocery on the first floor and the Wrights' small job-printing shop above (the brothers were printers before they opened their bicycle shop).

Exhibits tell how the Wrights became obsessed with aviation after reading about others' failed experiments. They decided to try it, applying the same fundamentals they learned from their bicycle work: balance and control. The self-trained engineers then went on to make history on the beach at Kitty Hawk, and the world has been flying ever since.

Dayton has more ties to aviation history than I can hope to explore during my brief stay. I'll be back to visit the other museums in the historical park and the area. Dayton Aviation Heritage National Historic Park (937/225-7705). More information: Dayton/Montgomery County Convention & Visitors Bureau (800/221-8235, daytoncvb.com).

This part of Ohio was known during the Colonial era as the "Western Reserve" of Connecticut. That influence still is clear in Hudson Village: the village green, white-steepled churches, gingerbread-trimmed Victorian and classic Federal-style homes, even the sweeping parklike grounds of the Case Western Reserve Academy (Case Western Reserve University, now located in Cleveland, was founded here). All that has survived, but what about Saywell's Drug Store, with its cozy soda fountain?

Suddenly, there it is, in a deceptively nondescript storefront along the main street. I claim a vinyl-covered stool at the 1939-vintage, black Italian marble counter and order that cherry soda. I can't resist also getting a chocolate phosphate from the high school girl behind the counter as a chaser, because that's an even rarer treat nowadays. The frothy indulgence arrives in a tall glass. It's the genuine article all right—homemade ice cream, lots of fizzy soda water dispensed from one of those long-necked taps, mounds of whipped cream and a maraschino cherry on top.

Even on a weekday afternoon, the place is packed. At the counter and at small tables in the front of this soda fountain, kids in tank tops and shorts, old-timers and a few local businesspeople dig into mounds of ice cream. Best-sellers include standards such as chocolate and vanilla, as well as newer creations such as peanut butter and "moose tracks."

Saywell's has been at this location along North Main Street just off the village green for more than 90 years, operated by descendants of founder Fred Saywell. I was right to be worried. "Development" is rearing its sometimes-ugly head, despite signs such as the one in the front window urging Saywell's customers and passersby to buy from locally owned stores.

Hudson Village preservationists are trying to work out an approach that will retain the identity of their village and still accommodate growth. One example is the Hudson Center development being built across the alley behind Saywell's, designed to mesh architecturally with the rest of the Hudson Village business district.

Co-owner Harvey "Rick" Hanna, Fred's nephew, says the drugstore and soda counter probably will pass from the family when he and his brother John retire. When the time comes, he'd like to sell to someone interested in preserving Saywell's.

Wouldn't it be grand if that's how I find it the next time I return to the Cleveland area—just exactly as it is now?

Cleveland's Theater District

Old World Interlude

German Village is a historic treasure — shops, cafes, well-maintained brick cottages, shady brick streets and a lovingly tended park — almost in the shadow of Ohio's capitol and Columbus' downtown office towers.

hio's capital and the home of Ohio State University is the state's largest city, but it's also friendly and manageable. Citizens have come to count on progress, with an economy and population that grew dependably over the last three decades of the 20th century, while other cities weathered ups and downs. State government, centered in the diminutive 1861 Greek Revival capitol, churns along dependably at the heart of downtown.

Notable additions include the Center of Science and Industry (COSI) downtown; the Arena District, a 95-acre sports and entertainment center with restaurants and nightspots; and thriving Easton Town Center mall in the near northeastern part of the city.

Such comfortable stability is a hallmark of the Midwest. Sure, we're all for moving forward, but there's something to be said for steady progress without radical shifts. This is a city that wins accolades for its livability — from making *Forbes* magazine's list of "best places for business and careers" to being named one of Purina's "healthiest pet cities."

Lest this all sound a bit too bland and predictable, Columbus also is known as a city that reveres the arts. The Columbus Museum of Art houses an acclaimed collection, and the city hosts one of the region's top arts festivals, which fills downtown streets each June. Artists' studios and galleries, as well as shops and cafes, thrive in the Short North Arts District.

It wasn't always so peaceful here, though. The story of the German Village neighborhood is one of this region's most inspiring. It's also emblematic of many comeback neighborhoods across the Midwest. I've visited this enclave south of downtown several times over the years, sometimes wandering streets that seem like a scene from a 1900s postcard, and occasionally stopping in for a hearty meal at Schmidt's Restaurant *und* Sausage Haus (more about that later). Each time, I fall in love with this area all over again.

An Oasis

On this sunny early-summer morning, kids on bicycles pedal past neighbors chatting on the front stoops of compact, brick cottages that line the quiet streets. There are basically four styles of houses. The four-room story-and-a-half Dutch (Deutsch) single is the most common. Another is the Double Dutch, which combines two singles under one roof.

Wrought-iron fences, slate roofs and window boxes overflowing with blooms complete the welcoming picture. Behind the tidy houses, I glimpse compact gardens bursting with color, and practical alleys (remember those?). Shops dot the residential streets. Beyond one leafy, flag-filled courtyard beckons the Book Loft, a

(From top) Schiller Park. Specialties at Schmidt's in German Village.

bookworm's fantasy come true, with 32 rooms and 500,000 titles. Best of all, this community is more than a couple of showcase blocks remaining from a once-thriving neighborhood. It's a district of 1,600 homes, more robust than ever.

Settlement in German Village began in the 1840s, when brewery workers built homes that resembled those they left behind in the Old World. The enclave thrived, with a few grand mansions belonging to the brewmeisters built around Schiller Park, named for the German poet and dramatist Friedrich von Schiller. Proud local Germans erected a statue of Schiller in 1891—then came World War I. The area was renamed Washington Park for a time, then rechristened Schiller Park in 1930.

German-language books were burned in the park, and neighborhood families had to give up their schnauzers, dachshunds and German shepherds. From then, as the saying goes, things went from bad to worse. Prohibition killed the local breweries. Then, German Americans endured another relocation during World War II. Families who'd lived in the community for generations fled to the suburbs.

German Village was just inches from being replaced by a collection of freeways and commercial buildings in the 1960s, when preservationists rallied, led by the late Frank Fetch. Residents still speak his name reverently.

The German Village Society formed to promote preservation and restoration. Since then, German Village has become one of the largest privately owned districts of historic homes (233 acres total) in the National Registry of Historic Places. More than 5,000 people converge on the area for the annual June home tour. Although the society works diligently to retain the area's charm, it also is a real neighborhood where families live, work and play. That makes it even more special.

Perhaps the finest moment in the rebirth came in 1991. The statue of Schiller was rebronzed for its 100th birthday, ending a sad chapter and beginning a bright new era for German Village.

Sauerbraten *und* Strudel

Now, as for Schmidt's: It's no secret in my family that I love German food. It's genetic. Blame my Grandma Hamann. If I lived

near a German restaurant, I'd weigh 300 pounds, so maybe it's best that I get to Schmidt's, a German Village institution, only occasionally.

Polka music blares inside this teeming clone of a Bavarian beer hall, and a lunch crowd that includes neighborhood folks, as well as business types from downtown, deliberates over a menu of schnitzel, brats and spatzels. Can't decide? There's a buffet with all the specialties.

Regulars know to order the Bahama Mama and a cream puff, the restaurant's signature sausage and dessert creations. Choosing from the beer menu is almost as difficult, with selections the likes of Paulaner Hefeweizen and Warsteiner.

As Geoff Schmidt, great-grandson of the founder, brings the sausage platter, complete with applesauce and German potato salad, to the table, he explains why the food is so good here: "We make all our own sausage and our potato salad, too."

Now that I've cast caloric caution to the wind, I end my meal with a huge cream puff and a slice of apple strudel. What can it hurt? Thank goodness I don't get to German Village often enough to find out.

German Village cottages

Taste of Ohio

German Puffed Oven Pancake with Glazed Apples
Cobbler Shop Bed and Breakfast, Zoar

6 tablespoons butter or margarine
4 beaten eggs
1 cup all-purpose flour
1 cup milk
¼ teaspoon ground nutmeg or
    ground cinnamon
    Dash salt
2 tablespoons butter or margarine
3 medium apples, peeled, cored
    and thinly sliced
½ cup raisins and/or dried
    cranberries
½ cup packed brown sugar
¼ teaspoon ground nutmeg or
    ground cinnamon (optional)
2 tablespoons coarsely chopped
    walnuts or pecans (optional)

For batter: Place 6 tablespoons butter in a 10-inch ovenproof skillet (preferably cast iron) in a 400° oven until butter melts. In a medium bowl, beat eggs until combined. Add flour, milk, ¼ teaspoon nutmeg and the salt; beat until smooth. Immediately pour batter into the hot skillet. Bake for 20 to 25 minutes or until puffed and well browned.
For filling: In a medium saucepan, melt the 2 tablespoons butter. Add apples and raisins; cook over medium heat until apples are almost tender; stir frequently. Add the brown sugar and ¼ teaspoon nutmeg. Cook and stir until apples are well coated and glazed. Remove from heat. If you like, stir in the nuts. Set aside.
To serve: Transfer pancake to a large serving platter. Spoon filling into the center of the pancake. If you like, sprinkle with sifted powdered sugar or serve with whipped cream. Serve immediately. Makes 6 servings.

More Favorites

CINCINNATI
Inspired by its German heritage and a southern bent, this gracious city beside the Ohio River is being revitalized. The Cincinnati Reds new Great American Ball Park, on the riverfront beside the NFL Bengals contemporary new home, brings to mind old-time baseball shrines. Next door at the National Underground Railroad Freedom Center's three-building, $110 million complex, state-of-the-art exhibits tell the brave stories of escaping slaves.

Other must-see attractions: the combination zoo/botanical gardens; the Cincinnati Museum Center in the 1933 Art Deco train station; the Mount Adams neighborhood; Newport on the Levee entertainment and shopping complex on the Ohio River's Kentucky bank. Paddle wheelers line up nearby for sightseeing. More information: Greater Cincinnati Convention & Visitors Bureau (800/543-2613, cincyusa.com).

LAKE ERIE SHORE AND ISLANDS
Sand and surf supply the perfect setting for vacationers in the Sandusky Bay area along northwestern Ohio's Lake Erie shore. Discover the busy resort town of Sandusky and the fabled Cedar Point amusement park with 16 roller coasters, 67 other rides, an 18-acre water park and a mile-long beach.

Ferries travel from Sandusky and the peninsula towns of Port Clinton and Marblehead to three of the five main islands offshore: serene Kelleys Island; South Bass Island and its lively village of Put-In-Bay; and Middle Bass Island, with its castlelike Lonz Winery. More information: Ottawa County Visitors Bureau (800/441-1271, lake-erie.com). Sandusky/Erie County Visitors Bureau (800/255-3743, visitohio.com).

HOCKING HILLS
Southeastern Ohio's Hocking Hills provide a glimpse of what much of America looked like before settlers reshaped it. About 50 miles southeast of Columbus, age-old Appalachian foothills, rugged valleys and soft-shouldered ridges transform the landscape. The largest communities—Logan, Nelsonville and Athens—grew on the banks of the area's biggest river, the Hocking. Hocking Hills State Park and the adjacent state forest, about 10,000 acres total, form the centerpiece of this region west of Logan. More information: Hocking Hills Tourism Association (800/462-5464, 1800hocking.com).

HOLMES COUNTY
Life moves at a horse-and-buggy pace in Holmes County, home to the largest Amish settlement anywhere. Just as their ancestors did more than a century ago, the 18,000-plus Amish who live here make and grow what they need and shun the trappings of modern life such as electricity and automobiles.

Plan stops in the towns of Berlin and Walnut Creek, both beehives of shops and restaurants. Many of the businesses close on Sundays, and adult Amish don't wish to be photographed. More information: Holmes County Chamber of Commerce & Tourism Bureau (330/674-3975, holmescountychamber.com).

Travel Journal

VILLAGES THAT TIME FORGOT

Founded in 1817 as a Utopian religious community, Zoar includes a 12-block historic district (12 miles south of Canton). Among the restored buildings, costumed interpreters depict lives of the settlers (800/874-4336). More information: Zoar Village (800/262-6195). Just north of Coshocton (70 miles northeast of Columbus), Roscoe Village recaptures the canal era's 19th-century heyday (800/877-1830).

Featured Stop

The Cobbler Shop Bed and Breakfast In Zoar, an antiques-filled 19th-century home with five guest rooms. $$ (800/287-1547).

Lodgings

Atwood Lake Resort A modern resort with a lake and golf course near New Philadelphia (25 miles south of Canton). $$–$$$ (800/362-6406).
The Inn at Roscoe Village Fifty-one rooms with Shaker-style furnishings along the village's Main Street. $ (800/237-7397).
Springhouse Bed and Breakfast Near Bolivar, a renovated 1857 Greek Revival home overlooking river valley. $$ (330/874-4255).
The Zoar Tavern & Inn In Zoar, five guest rooms with hand-hewn beams, brick-and-stone walls, and antiques. Adjacent is a four-room guest house. $$ (330/874-2170).

Dining

Old Warehouse Restaurant In Roscoe Village, an old mill store and canal-boat loading site serving specialties including rotisserie chicken and rich desserts amid yesteryear atmosphere (740/622-4001).
The Zoar Tavern In Zoar, casual atmosphere for fresh seafood, steaks and hearty sandwiches (330/874-2170).

Side Trip

Schoenbrunn Village Seventeen log buildings and a garden re-create the first settlement of Moravian missionaries, who in 1772 arrived in New Philadelphia (25 miles south of Canton). You also can see the original mission cemetery and tour a museum. Hours vary by season. Admission charged (800/262-6195). At the nearby 1,400-seat amphitheater, *Trumpet in the Land* tells the story of the early Moravians and their leader. The drama by Pulitzer Prize-winning playwright Paul Green runs from mid-June through late August. Admission charged. Ask about bargain nights (330/364-5111).

TOTALLY COOL CLEVELAND

The greater Cleveland area stretches 100 miles along the shore of Lake Erie and about 40 miles inland. An industrial giant from the Victorian age through World War II, the city over the past three decades has reinvented itself with stunning attractions and a thriving cultural and entertainment scene. More information: Convention & Visitors Bureau of Greater Cleveland (800/321-1001, travelcleveland.com).

Featured Stops

Rock and Roll Hall of Fame and Museum Six levels of exhibits and memorabilia honoring legendary musicians, record producers and other music-industry greats. Admission charged (216/781-7625).
Saywell's Drug Store In Hudson Village (25 miles south of Cleveland), an old-fashioned drugstore in a New England-style village (330/653-5411).
Warehouse District A National Historic Landmark of shops, restaurants and nightspots atop a bluff overlooking the Cuyahoga River downtown (216/344-3937).

More Great Stops

Great Lakes Science Center Some 400 hands-on exhibits and demonstrations fill this museum on the Lake Erie shore downtown. You can "touch" a simulated tornado and experience how static electricity makes your hair stand on end. Visitors also can see shows at the Omnimax Theater and daily science demonstrations. Admission charged (216/694-2000).
Playhouse Square Center Downtown, the second-largest performing arts complex in the nation hosting opera, ballet, concerts, comedy and Broadway-style musicals in five restored theaters (216/771-4444).
Shaker Square/Larchmere Boulevard Colonial-style specialty stores, coffeehouses and restaurants clustering around a grassy commons at Shaker Square (seven miles southeast of downtown). Stroll one block north to Larchmere Boulevard, Cleveland's antiques district. More information: Shaker Heights Area Development (216/421-2100).
Tower City Center Downtown, a renovated train depot turned into an upscale indoor shopping center of more than 100 specialty shops, hotels, restaurants (including the only Hard Rock Cafe in Ohio) and an 11-screen movie theater (216/623-4750). Also downtown: the glass-enclosed Galleria at

Erieview, with 17 shops (216/861-4343).
University Circle This cultural district in a park-like setting includes museums, art galleries, restaurants, and medical and educational institutions (four miles east of downtown). The Cleveland Museum of Art features Egyptian artifacts, Renaissance armor and Impressionist works by Monet, Degas and Van Gogh. Other attractions: Cleveland Museum of Natural History, African American Museum and Children's Museum of Cleveland. University Circle, Inc. (216/791-3900).
West Side Market Easily identified by its clocktower, a 1912 landmark that's one of the largest indoor/outdoor markets in the nation, with vendors selling goods from produce to freshly baked breads. Open Mondays, Wednesdays, Fridays and Saturdays (216/664-3387).

Lodgings
Baricelli Inn A three-story 1896 brownstone mansion. Seven rooms decorated with antiques and stained glass. In University Circle, overlooking Little Italy area. $$$$ (216/791-6500).
The Glidden House In the heart of University Circle, a 60-room full-service boutique hotel in a 1910 French Gothic mansion listed on the National Register of Historic Places. $$$$ (216/231-8900).
Renaissance Cleveland In a vintage building located on downtown's Public Square. $$$ (216/696-5600).
Ritz-Carlton Cleveland An elegant hotel in the Tower City Center complex downtown. $$$$ (216/623-1300).

Dining
Blue Point Grille Fresh seafood in the Warehouse District (216/875-7827).
Fahrenheit Serving contemporary American fare in the up-and-coming Tremont neighborhood (216/781-8858).
Great Lakes Brewing Company A casual pub featuring ribs, seafood, pasta and sandwiches in a Victorian building located in a historic neighborhood near downtown (216/771-4404).

AN OLD WORLD INTERLUDE
In central Ohio, Columbus reigns as the state's capital and largest city. More information: Experience Columbus (866/397-2657, experiencecolumbus.com).

Featured Stops
German Village This historic district just south of downtown was built by German immigrants. Today, rehabilitated 19th-century buildings are homes, shops and restaurants. Call about group tours (614/221-8888).
Schmidt's Restaurant *und* **Sausage Haus** In German Village, serving a variety of German specialties such as schnitzel and knockwurst (614/444-6808).
The Book Loft A block-long store in German Village, with new books and music CDs filling 32 rooms (614/464-1774).

More Great Stops
Center of Science and Industry (COSI) This submarine-shaped building downtown, with scores of interactive exhibits, is a combination

In Cleveland's Warehouse District

multimedia playground, thrill ride, time machine and computer fantasyland. Visitors can feel as if they're submerged in a submarine, spin a granite sphere weighing more than two tons and survive a meteor shower in a rocket simulator. Catch shows at the large-screen theater. Admission charged (877/257-2674).
Columbus Zoo and Aquarium Located along the banks of the Scioto River (17 miles northwest of downtown), the zoo is home to more than 750 species from all regions of the world, including the first gorilla born in captivity. Open every day of the year. Admission charged (800/666-5397).

Shopping
Columbus City Center Three-level downtown mall, with more than 110 shops and restaurants, across the street from Ohio's state capitol (614/221-4919).
Easton Town Center An eclectic assortment of specialty shops, restaurants and entertainment venues in a village setting with cobblestone walkways (614/416-7000).

Lodging
Hilton Columbus An upscale, full-service hotel adjacent to Easton Town Center. $$$ (614/414-5000).
The Lofts Hotel A downtown boutique hotel in a renovated 19th-century building with exposed brick and floor-to-ceiling windows. $$$ (800/735-6387).
The Columbus, A Renaissance Hotel The latest downtown addition to the lodging scene (converted from an Adam's Mark Hotel in 2004). $$$ (614/233-7501).

Dining
Buckeye Hall of Fame Café Just north of downtown, a casual eatery filled with Ohio State sports memorabilia (614/291-2233).
Mitchell's Steakhouse An upscale steak house that's a Columbus institution. High ceilings and dark woods creating a warm ambience (614/621-2333). ■

South Dakota

■ The Black Hills, the tallest mountains between the Rockies and the Alps, rise in the southwestern corner of this vast state, a Wild West realm of wilderness, ranches and farms. Most people instantly envision Mount Rushmore when they think of South Dakota—and that monument is just as awesome as everyone expects. But there's much more to see in this surprising state, including an even grander tribute to an Oglala war chief that's taking shape nearby: the massive Crazy Horse Memorial, being sculpted from one of this gold-mining region's pine-studded granite monoliths. In many ways, all of South Dakota is larger than life.

Cathedral Spires in Custer State Park

Mountain Majesties

Breathtaking scenery, one-of-a-kind attractions, plus enough gold-rush lore to thrill any Wild West fan. South Dakota's storied Black Hills region is one of America's favorite vacation destinations. Mine, too.

othing in the Midwest prepares you for the Black Hills, a riot of granite rising from the plains in an area almost half the size of Switzerland, with pine- and spruce-covered peaks soaring from 2,000 to 4,000 feet. These mountains claim the highest point between the Rockies and the Alps (Harney Peak, 7,242 feet above sea level).

The Lakota Sioux held this land sacred and called it *Paha Sapa*, meaning black heights. In their culture, it's the mythical Garden of Eden. Gold miners swarmed here in the mid-1870s, disrupting that paradise. Now, locals mine tourism gold from a mother lode of man-made attractions—some quite stirring. To my mind, not even Mount Rushmore can compete with the majesty of these mountains, canyons, tumbling waterfalls and riffling streams.

Hearts of Gold

Three pockets showcase the hills' varied character: Spearfish Canyon and the Lead-Deadwood area; Mount Rushmore and the Crazy Horse Memorial; Custer State Park and the Needles Highway. Spearfish Canyon National Scenic Byway, threads 19 miles beside an aspen-lined creek teeming with trout. The creek is fed by waterfalls tumbling from rock formations that soar 1,000 feet from the canyon floor.

About halfway into the drive, I turn off at beautiful, log-sided Spearfish Canyon Lodge, the starting point for a short hike up

to Roughlock Falls, named for the way gold-rush wagon drivers had to "rough lock" their wheels and simply skid down the hopelessly steep slopes. Scenes from Kevin Costner's 1990 Western *Dances With Wolves* were filmed here, as well as at other nearby venues.

Across the road, a longer path leads to Spearfish Canyon Falls. For decades, it was just a trickle, until the Homestake Mining Company eliminated an obsolete upstream dam. I pass under boughs of Black Hills spruce, ponderosa pine, quaking aspen, white paper birch, willow and box elder. Plants the Lakota used for food and medicine line the trail: serviceberry, gooseberry, chokeberry. This is a fly fisherman's dream—rainbow, brook and brown trout thrive in Black Hills streams. Hawks, vultures and an eagle or two soar overhead.

Time to continue on the road down the shadowy canyon, past turnoffs with storybook Western names such as Raspberry Gulch Place. Vacation homes and small resorts tuck into the woods, but they're out of sight for the most part. We've photographed some extraordinary scenes here in winter, when snowmobilers rule the canyon. Downhill skiers schuss the runs at Terry Peak and other nearby resorts, reveling in up to 100 annual inches of snow.

On to the twin towns of Lead and Deadwood. In Lead (that's pronounced "leed," named for what miners call a layer of ore),

I begin my tour with bubbly transplanted Texan and Lead booster Phyllis Fleming at the Homestake Visitors Center. The center perches beside the biggest darn hole in the ground I've ever peered down into. The former Homestake open-pit gold mine and its companion underground mine nearby gave this town the unique slogan Phyllis proudly recites: "A mile high, a mile wide, 8,000 feet deep and a heart of gold!"

For decades, Lead was the ultimate company town. The Homestake Mining Company, founded by George Hearst, patriarch of a family now best known for newspapers and magazines, employed as many as 2,000 miners who lived in tiny cottages that still cling to the mountainside. For decades, the paternalistic employer showered its miners with amenities such as free medical care, an opera house, library and opulent high school (outfitted with marble floors, a 1,100-seat theater and three gyms). More than a dozen neighborhood markets kept busy serving a melting pot of immigrant mining families from Wales, Yugoslavia, Finland, Germany, Sweden and Ireland.

The gaping open-pit mine closed (for the second and probably final time) in 1998 after gobbling up half a mountain, followed in 2001 by the closing of the underground mine, a victim of unfavorable gold-mining economics. Lead's population has declined from a peak of 10,000 in its heyday to

(Clockwise, from opposite) The Crazy Horse Memorial. Moon over the Badlands. Cowboys in Deadwood. The old Homestake Mine in Lead. Spearfish Falls.

3,500. Now, Lead pins its hopes on family tourism and a major research project: a center for the study of subatomic particles.

A tour trolley travels up the hillside to the vacated aboveground mine facility. With no pumps in operation, the depths of the lower mine, once the Western Hemisphere's largest, richest and oldest, are flooding at the rate of 500 gallons of water a minute. We see a locker room built for 1,000 miners per shift and 6,000-foot steel cables wound up like so much thread on spools. The cables once dropped miners into the heart of the mountain at 50 miles per hour. In all, 39.8 million ounces of gold were extracted, refined and smelted here.

Two miles from Lead, Deadwood (population 1,400) already has found its new identity: a gambling mecca. A sign reading "Slots! Highest payouts in town!" greets visitors to the once-forlorn gulch where 25,000 wild-eyed gold-seekers stampeded in 1876. Main Street buildings hum with slot machines, video poker and blackjack tables. Legal gambling arrived in 1989, virtually saving Deadwood.

A low-key crowd of vacationers meanders along Main Street, in and out of storefront casinos: the Midnight Star, Lucky Lady, Gold Dust, Hickok's and Miss Kitty's. Souvenir outlets such as Gold Strike Gifts purvey mementos. Foil portraits of John Wayne and Elvis Presley glisten amid a sea of refrigerator magnets, shot glasses and belt buckles.

The Adams Museum downtown tells the stories of old Deadwood, including Wild Bill Hickok and Calamity Jane, the infamous bullwhacker and part-time prostitute who sometimes revealed a heart of, well, gold. Other long-gone, lesser-known Deadwood characters such as Madam DuFran and Poker Alice live on here, too.

Anyone who laments the role of gaming in Deadwood's economic revival has only to study the town's history to realize things are much more righteous now than they were back in the lawless frontier days.

Noble Shrines

The next morning, I rise extra-early for a daybreak glimpse of east-facing Mount Rushmore. At first, I'm frankly disheartened by all the signs along the road: "Incredible Christmas Park!" "Old McDonald's Farm!" "Rapid Ride Go-Carts!"

Then comes the almost signless world of 1.2 million-acre Black Hills National Forest. The commercialism abates, except for a few little shops in Keystone. I round a bend, and suddenly I behold George Washington's noble visage. South Dakota's mind-boggling "Shrine to Democracy" awes me in terms of both its natural setting and its patriotic theme. In 1927, Danish-born sculptor Gutzon Borglum started work on Mount Rushmore National Memorial, commissioned by the state of South Dakota to create a colossal patriotic sculpture to spur tourism. It worked: Three million people now visit annually.

The gray stone peak that Borglum chose for his raw material looms 5,275 feet above

(From left) The presidential visages of Mount Rushmore. Crazy Horse Memorial.

sea level. A scale model that guided Borglum's efforts still is on display in his 1939 studio at the mountain's base. The faces of the four great presidents (Washington, Jefferson, Roosevelt and Lincoln) measure approximately 60 feet from their chins to the tops of their heads. More than 400 people, aching for jobs during the Great Depression, jumped at the chance to assist Borglum over the years — dynamiting, chiseling and smoothing as they dangled from the rock. Those workers included Polish American sculptor Korczak Ziolkowski (KOR-shak Jul-KUF-ski) of Boston, whose own mountain masterpiece, the Crazy Horse Memorial, is taking shape nearby.

No lives were lost creating Rushmore, but some men later died prematurely of silicosis caused by inhaling the granite dust. The unfinished project was suspended in 1941 due to Borglum's death that March, and the U.S. entry into World War II.

Judy Olson, a native South Dakotan, has been visiting Mount Rushmore since her parents brought her here as a 2-year-old. Now, she's one of the unflaggingly pleasant park officers. On the viewing terrace near Rushmore's sleek visitors center, completed several years ago, she reveals inside stories about the monument: Jefferson originally was on Washington's right, but as Jefferson's face neared completion, cracks became apparent and he was "moved" to the space at Washington's left. This helped create the opening that Borglum filled with latecomer Theodore Roosevelt, a personal hero of Borglum's. Judy points out three errant fingers on Lincoln's "chest," where he would have been clutching his coat collar, had the project been completed.

Could Mount Rushmore have been built today? Probably not, for both environmental and cultural reasons. At the time, nobody thought to ask the Lakota how they felt about the idea. How is Mount Rushmore holding up? Pretty well, Judy tells me, considering that the mountain actually consists of 22 separate blocks of granite.

Computer sensors wedged in such undignified niches as President Lincoln's nose monitor minute shifts caused by freezing and thawing. Serious cracks are filled with a form of silicon putty. The mountain itself will be around awhile: It's eroding only about one inch every 10,000 years.

Before I leave, I stroll the half-mile President's Trail, a wooden walkway through the pines and aspens, and listen to others' comments: "I was here as a kid, and I wanted to see it again." . . . "TV just doesn't do this justice." . . . "This is so cool!"

On to another mega sculpture 15 miles southwest: the colossal horseback rendering of the brilliant Oglala war chief, Crazy Horse—hair flowing and one arm pointing out toward the plains (when completed). It's a tribute to all of North America's native peoples. I'd budgeted just a few minutes for gazing at the partially complete image blasted from 6,740-foot-high Thunderhead Mountain. Instead, I spend almost half a day, mesmerized by the awesome scale of the project, the commitment of the Ziolkowski family who are creating it and the tourism empire it has spawned.

Lakota elders, led by Chief Standing Bear, approached Ziolkowski about undertaking the project in 1939. Crazy Horse's face, to date the one complete part of the project, was unveiled in 1998. Ziolkowski and his wife, Ruth, now 78 years old, raised 10 children here, initially in the most primitive of conditions. Today, all but

Custer State Park Game Lodge

three of those children work here, and the sprawling, modern complex near the base of the mountain includes an interpretive center, gift shop, restaurant, library, Native American cultural center and a museum with the Ziolkowskis' first home.

Why Crazy Horse? One reason the elders chose him to represent their people was because of his bravery, evidenced in his role as a key strategist at the Battle of the Little Bighorn. Nobody knows what Crazy Horse really looked like—he permitted no photos and was stabbed in the

back at age 33 by a dastardly U.S. soldier under a truce flag.

Ziolkowski is this project's other hero. He died in 1982 at age 74, his body ravaged by his labors. His bright-eyed, still-dedicated widow says: "My husband believed if you have pride and are willing to work, you can accomplish anything."

When will the work be completed? It's an issue because the scale of this memorial is so astoundingly ambitious. All of Mount Rushmore could fit neatly in Crazy Horse's head. Perhaps one of his 23 grandchildren or a great-grandchild will see the finish, an event that may not happen even in this century. "We're keeping a dream alive," Ruth says.

I'm soon riding up a winding road, past grazing mountain goats. Eight men are working on the mountain today. They'll be blasting soon and, from far below, we'll witness 750 tons of granite fly like a small puff of smoke (thus far, 8 million tons have been blasted from the mountain).

Walking out on the level space that one

The scale … is so astoundingly ambitious —all of Mount Rushmore could fit in Crazy Horse's head.

day will become Crazy Horse's outstretched arm, I turn and face the red granite war chief's haunting glare head-on. His pointing finger alone will be 10 feet wide. The face, burnished smooth with 3,500-degree torches, measures 90 feet high and 55 feet wide. The nose, 27 feet. One eye alone took four and a half months.

Descending the mountain road, I pass the Ziolkowski family tomb, where the sculptor reposes as others carry on his work. The visitors center at the mountain's base tells the story of the Lakota and their

traditions. A university instructor and author, Director Donovin Sprague is a descendant of a Lakota chief, and he's even distantly related to Crazy Horse.

Donovin, who grew up on South Dakota's impoverished Cheyenne Reservation and went on to attend the University of California at Berkeley and the University of South Dakota, comes from one of the poorest counties in the nation, one with a 70 percent unemployment rate. What will turn things around? His one-word answer: education. To that end, the foundation associated with the Crazy Horse Memorial offers annual scholarships to Native American youth in South Dakota.

My last stops in the Black Hills are within Custer State Park, one of America's best wildlife preserves and the home of the scenic Needles Highway. Established in 1919, the state park embraces 71,000 acres of rolling prairie grasslands, ponderosa pine forests and striking granite formations. Two million visitors come every year, hoping to glimpse the 1,500 buffalo that roam the preserve, along with elk, burros, bighorn sheep, deer, pronghorns, antelope and mountain goats.

The park's Needles Highway is my last and most spectacular Black Hills drive. Fourteen miles of knockout vistas everywhere I turn make it hard to focus on the narrow, twisting road punctuated by one-car-wide tunnels carved out of the solid rock. The needlelike spires that give the road its name mingle with giant boulders and round-shouldered mountains, including the area's tallest, Harney Peak.

Three bighorn sheep that act as if they own the road cross my path. I park and climb out on one craggy promontory to survey a vast domain of rock formations and countless pine trees. I'm stunned by the view, even though it's almost standard in this majestic realm.

(*Clockwise*) Tunnel on Needles Highway. Sylvan Lake at Custer State Park. Bighorn sheep, one of many wild species in the park.

Small Pleasures

World War II Memorial and Flaming Fountain

The town of Pierre, near the exact center of sparsely populated South Dakota, may be America's most remote capital. The airport terminal is drugstore size, there's no local TV station, the Federal Express office closes early and there's not a Starbucks in sight. Besides the handsome state capitol, the tallest building in town is five stories high. Yet the capitol grounds are among the nation's most beautiful, the earth-bermed state historical museum is well worth visiting, and people are as friendly as can be.

Pierre's isolation and diminutive size fascinate me. Only one state capital is smaller: Montpelier, Vermont, with 7,500 people. But Montpelier is closer to the Northeast's population centers and has a countywide population of 58,000. Pierre's population is about 13,900, with only 18,300 in the two adjoining counties combined. To shop at a large suburban-type mall, residents head for Sioux Falls (225 miles southeast) or Rapid City (191 miles southwest).

The first thing you need to know about Pierre is that it's pronounced PEER, even though it was named for an early French fur trader, Pierre Choteau, Jr. How many capitals almost straddle two time zones? Although Pierre is Central, Fort Pierre just across the Missouri River is Mountain.

Combative Teton Sioux almost ended the Lewis and Clark expedition in 1804 at the mouth of the Bad River in what's now Fort Pierre, but a calm Indian chief prevailed. These days, outdoor enthusiasts are the first to sing this area's praises. Just seven miles upstream is 230-mile-long Lake Oahe, one of the largest man-made lakes in the nation.

Pierre's centerpiece is its 1910 Indiana limestone capitol, topped with a black copper dome. The dome is testimony to Pierre's environment (pollutants that give weathered copper its greenish patina are absent in Pierre). Restored for the state's 1989 centennial, the capitol is the state's pride and joy, filled with brass, murals, marble and granite.

As appealing as South Dakota's capitol building is, the grounds are even lovelier. In fact, a couple of years ago a national report named this one of the 10 most beautiful lawns in America. Memorials and sculptures honoring servicemen and -women, as well as fallen law enforcement officers and firefighters, dot the 80 acres.

A striking statue, *Fighting Stallions*, pays tribute to Governor George S. Mickelson, two pilots and five aides and business leaders killed in a 1993 plane crash. The grounds are blanketed by trees, many planted by South Dakotans in memory of family members, plus some 25,000 flowers.

This is the heart of downtown, but the serenity isn't confined to the capitol grounds. Residents wouldn't have it any other way, Patty Van Gerpen, director of the South Dakota Office of Tourism, affirms over lattés at a nearby coffee shop. Patty, who grew up on a farm near Aberdeen, says, "I love traveling, but I also love getting home and not seeing any crowds. People aren't walking around with cell phones glued to their ears. We can really experience the outdoors here." More information: Pierre Convention & Tourism Bureau (800/962-2034, pierrechamber.com).

Inside the capitol dome

Taste of South Dakota

Easy Indian Fry Bread
A Native American treat

1 16-ounce package (12) frozen dinner
   rolls, thawed
Cooking oil for shallow-fat frying
Indian Taco Meat Sauce or Cinnamon-
   Sugar Topping (recipes follow)

On a lightly floured surface, roll out
each dough ball into a 6-inch circle.

In a heavy skillet, heat about 1 inch
of cooking oil over medium-high heat to
365°. Fry dough circles, 1 or 2 at a
time, in hot oil about 1 minute or until
bread circles are golden brown, turning
once. Remove with tongs and drain on
paper towels. Keep warm in a 300°
oven while frying remaining circles.

To serve, top with Indian Taco Meat
Sauce or Cinnamon-Sugar Topping.
Serve immediately. Makes 12.

Indian Taco Meat Sauce: In a large
skillet, cook 2 pounds lean ground beef
until meat is brown. Drain off fat. Stir
in one 16-ounce can refried beans,
1 cup tomato juice, 1 cup water, ¼
cup chopped onion, 1 tablespoon taco
seasoning or chili seasoning and
1 teaspoon chili powder. Bring to
boiling; reduce heat. Cover and simmer
30 minutes or until desired consistency.

Spoon over warm fry bread. If you
like, top with dairy sour cream,
shredded cheddar cheese, shredded
lettuce and chopped tomato.

Cinnamon-Sugar Topping: In a small
bowl, combine ½ cup sugar and
2 teaspoons ground cinnamon.
Sprinkle over warm fry bread.

More Favorites

MITCHELL
When you travel west across South Dakota
to the Black Hills, a unique "palace" makes
Mitchell a must stop. This county seat
town of 14,600 sidles up to I-90 about 67
miles west of Sioux Falls.

The community's centerpiece, the Corn
Palace, salutes the rich agricultural region.
Topped with domes, turrets and minarets,
the colorful landmark sprawls across half a
block in the heart of downtown. Using
thousands of bushels of corn, grasses and
grains, crews create new murals on the
exterior every spring. Civic boosters built
the original structure in 1892, 10 years
after the town was founded, trying to lure
the state capital to Mitchell.

Be sure to stop by the Enchanted World
Doll Museum in a castle, complete with
moat and drawbridge, across from the
Corn Palace. The museum displays more
than 5,000 dolls—antique to modern—
from 125 countries.

Around downtown, which encompasses
a 15-block historic district, visitors can
browse a scattering of antiques stores, galleries and gift shops featuring local art. The
giant Cabela's World's Foremost Outfitter
on the opposite side of I-90 stocks every
kind of fishing, hunting and outdoor gear.
More information: Corn Palace Convention & Visitors Bureau (866/273-2676,
cornpalace.com).

SIOUX FALLS
You'll feel right at home in easygoing Sioux
Falls, the eastern gateway to South Dakota.
Just 20 miles from the Minnesota and
Iowa state lines, this pretty community of
138,000 beside the Big Sioux River also
ranks as the largest city in the Dakotas.

Trolleys resembling old-time streetcars
travel around downtown among museums,
specialty shops, galleries and antiques
stores in historic buildings. Prairie Star
Gallery sells Plains Indian art, Holsen Hus
stocks Scandinavian goods, and Mrs.
Murphy's Irish Gifts markets Emerald Isle
imports. For downtown dining, choose
from delis, special-occasion Minerva's,
Surf's Up for fresh seafood, and Touch of
Europe, specializing in Eastern dishes.

The region's heritage unfolds at the 1890
Old Courthouse Museum, among vintage
rose quartzite buildings that highlight
downtown. Discover more reminders of
earlier times at the nearby Pettigrew Home
& Museum, an architectural masterpiece.

Downtown's four-story Washington
Pavilion of Arts and Science is the city's
cultural hub, where visitors can touch a
simulated tornado and "fly" the space
shuttle at the Kirby Science Discovery
Center. The Husby Performing Arts
Center, home of the South Dakota Symphony, also hosts touring Broadway-style
shows. The Visual Arts Center includes six
galleries of changing exhibits, a permanent
collection of regional artists' works and the
Children's Studio for hands-on activities.

West of downtown at the Great Plains
Zoo, observe animals from around the
world living in natural settings. Trolleys
stop at Falls Park, where the five-story
observation tower at the visitors center
reveals a skyline panorama. Park trails lead
past the Falls of the Big Sioux, a great spot
to watch the sunset. More information:
Sioux Falls Convention & Visitors Bureau
(800/333-2072, siouxfallscvb.com).

Travel Journal

MOUNTAIN MAJESTIES

Natural wonders and man-made attractions abound in southwestern South Dakota, where the Black Hills stretch about 100 miles along the Wyoming state line. Deep pine forests, which appear black in the shadows and give the hills their name, climb craggy peaks that surround still, blue lakes. Rapid City serves as the area's hub, with shopping, attractions, and plenty of dining and lodging choices. More information: Black Hills Badlands & Lakes Association (605/355-3600, blackhillsbadlands.com).

Featured Stops

Crazy Horse Memorial Mountain carving in progress of Oglala chief Crazy Horse astride

Homestake Gold Mine, Lead

a horse (four miles north of the town of Custer). Visitors now can view the 88-foot-tall face of the warrior. When complete, the carving will be the world's largest sculpture (563 feet high and 641 feet long). The memorial also includes the Sculptor's Studio Home and the Indian Museum of North America. Admission charged; children age 6 and younger free (605/673-4681).
Custer State Park With four resorts, including the historic State Game Lodge and Sylvan Lake Lodge beside beautiful Sylvan Lake *(see lodgings section)*, four lakes, miles of trails, guided interpretive walks and kids' activities such as gold-panning excursions (20 miles south of Rapid City). Also, boating, swimming, horseback riding, fishing and rock climbing. The 71,000-acre park is home to about 1,500 buffalo, one of the world's largest herds, plus bighorn sheep, elk, coyotes and burros (605/255-4515).
Deadwood A historic gold-rush town, now a haven for gamblers with casinos along Main Street, plus Midnight Star, a restaurant and casino actor Kevin Costner owns (40 miles northwest of Rapid City). Attractions range from panning for gold at a historic mine to viewing a reenactment of the trial of Jack McCall for murdering Wild Bill Hickok. Visitors can try their luck at more than 80 gambling halls (800/999-1876, deadwood.org).
Homestake Gold Mine In Lead, with a visitors center, observation deck and guided tours. Homestake, once the largest underground gold mine in the Western Hemisphere, operated from 1876 to 2001. Admission charged for one-hour guided tour; children age 6 and younger free (605/584-3110).

Mammoth Site, Hot Springs

Mount Rushmore National Memorial Sixty-foot-high sculptures of the faces of four U.S. presidents: Washington, Jefferson, Theodore Roosevelt and Lincoln, carved into a mountain (20 miles southwest of Rapid City). With a visitors center, sculptor Gutzon Borglum's former studio and the President's Trail, which winds to the base of the monument (605/574-2523).
Spearfish Canyon National Scenic Byway Two-lane, 19-mile road winding between the towns of Spearfish and Cheyenne Crossing, past dramatic cliffs, waterfalls and canyon walls (605/642-8166).
Spearfish Canyon Lodge Log-and-stone inn amid the canyon along the Spearfish Creek. With a huge fireplace in the soaring lobby and guest rooms trimmed in pine. $$$–$$$$ (877/975-6343). The lodge's creekside Latchstring Restaurant for dishes such as pan-fried trout and buffalo steaks, plus a spectacular view (605/584-3333).

More Great Stops

Badlands National Park Vast 244,000-acre preserve of knifelike spires, steep canyons and buttes in shades of brown, pink and gray (60 miles east of Rapid City). With eight well-marked hiking trails along the Badlands Loop road, a scenic drive (605/433-5361).

Black Hills Central Railroad/The 1880 Train Round-trip ride between Hill City and Keystone in vintage cars pulled by a steam locomotive. Admission charged; children age 3 and younger free (866/367-1880).

George S. Mickelson Trail Crushed limestone hiking and bicycling path winding 109 miles from Deadwood to Edgemont. Fourteen trailheads scattered along the route (605/584-3896).

Jewel Cave National Monument West of the town of Custer, tours into the second-longest cave in the nation, with chambers lined with jewel-like calcite crystals. Admission charged (605/673-2288).

Journey Museum In Rapid City, interactive exhibits, holographs and historic collections tracing the development of the region from

Rock climbing, Custer State Park

the days of the dinosaurs to South Dakota statehood. Emphasizes the cultural contributions of Native Americans. Admission charged; children age 10 and younger free (605/394-6923).

Mammoth Site In Hot Springs, the world's largest mammoth research facility, with a full-size model of a mammoth skeleton and tours of an active fossil dig. Admission charged; children age 4 and younger free (605/745-6017).

Wall Drug Sprawling stop along I-90 that's part drugstore and part carnival, with goods from exhibits and souvenirs to food. Famous for funny signs along the interstate (605/279-2175).

Wind Cave National Park South of Custer State Park, tours of caves of "boxwork" formation, along with prairie dog towns, bison and elk. Admission charged; children age 5 and younger free (605/745-4600).

Shopping

Hill City With Main Street galleries selling traditional Western and modern works (800/888-1798).

Jewelry factories and showrooms Dozens in Rapid City and along State-16 on the way to Mount Rushmore. Leading retailers include Mount Rushmore Black Hills Gold (605/343-7099); Gold Diggers (605/341-9655); and Stamper Black Hills Gold Jewelry Manufacturing (605/342-0751).

Legends & Legacies In Spearfish, for handmade log and oak furniture, throws, quilts, pottery, paintings and other artwork (605/642-9196).

Lodging

Chain motels in Keystone, Spearfish, Deadwood and Rapid City.

Bullock Hotel In Deadwood, elegant historic landmark hotel in a restored 1895 building constructed of native sandstone. With original woodwork and Victorian decor. $–$$$$ (800/336-1876).

Custer State Park Resorts Four properties in the park: Sylvan Lake, Blue Bell and Legion

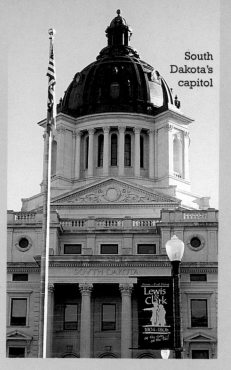

South Dakota's capitol

lodges and State Game Lodge. Lodge and motel rooms, plus cabins. $$–$$$$ (800/658-3530).

Flying B Ranch Bed and Breakfast On a 3,500-acre working ranch near Rapid City, three suites with Old West atmosphere and modern amenities. $$$$ (605/342-5324).

Strutton Inn Bed & Breakfast Victorian-style inn near Custer. $$–$$$ (800/226-2611).

Dining

Cheyenne Crossing Cafe Near Lead, a general store and cafe known for hearty breakfasts of sourdough pancakes or biscuits and gravy, as well as regional specialties such as Indian tacos (605/584-3510).

Deadwood Social Club For pasta, buffalo ribeyes and salmon (605/578-3346).

Jakes In Deadwood, serving American cuisine in a brick dining room with two fireplaces and soaring French windows (605/578-1555).

Saloon No. 10 Buffalo burgers at a favorite Deadwood watering hole (605/578-1533). ■

Wisconsin

■ Artfully sculpted by prehistoric glaciers, Wisconsin is as pretty a state to drive through as any I've traveled. Neat, tidy and prosperous cities and towns still reflect Wisconsin's Old World sense of craftsmanship and order. But new ethnic enclaves are adding welcome diversity to this German- and Scandinavian-dominated region. For travelers, Wisconsin offers wide-ranging sights and experiences: New England-like harbor villages, rustic north-woods resort communities and idyllic farm-country landscapes. Pity the lactose-intolerant when they visit Wisconsin: Not loading up on butterfat in almost any form is considered almost as heretical as not rooting for the Green Bay Packers.

Ephraim, from Eagle Harbor

Beguiling Peninsula

Door County is "the Cape Cod of the Midwest"—and much more. This Lake Michigan peninsula is unique, with steeple-crowned villages, picturesque orchard country and shimmering harbors filled with sailboats.

The village of Ephraim, viewed from a sailboat on Eagle Harbor, epitomizes Door County. The steeple of the Moravian church rises above the treetops of a green hillside spangled with neat white frame inns, shops and homes. Devout German Moravians founded the settlement in 1853. It's one of a string of postcard-pretty villages that includes Fish Creek, Egg Harbor, Gills Rock, Sister Bay and Ellison Bay on the familiar Green Bay side of this 75-mile-long peninsula that juts into Lake Michigan.

Chicagoans, many of whom own second homes here, constitute a substantial share of the county's visitors. I see the appeal. It's hard to imagine a place further removed from a hectic urban lifestyle. The 28,000 people who reside here year-round vigilantly guard their piece of paradise and its 300 miles of shoreline bounded by Green Bay on the west and Lake Michigan on the east. I don't recall seeing a single chain store, fast-food franchise or billboard north of Sturgeon Bay, the hardworking shipbuilding town near the county's base.

A tonic for the soul, Door County is serene harbors, small towns, sailboats and orchards lining quiet country roads. I think my blood pressure drops 10 points every time I visit. After the initial decompression, this civilized playground offers plenty to do, from sailing, bicycling and golfing on 10 public courses to theater and lots of art galleries and crafts shops. It's easy to understand why creative types thrive here.

Door County takes its name from "Death's Door," the stormy straits between the peninsula's tip at Gills Rock and Washington Island, about six miles offshore. Legends about the name abound. Over the years, scores of ships sank (an average of two weekly in the 1870s!) in the same treacherous waters. In 1881, the Sturgeon Bay Ship Canal afforded a calmer, much safer passage and more direct route to Green Bay.

Door County Flavors

New Englanders founded many of the villages, but Scandinavians followed close behind, lured by the familiar climate, rocky shoreline and, at that time, flourishing fishing and lumbering industries. Today, tourism dominates the economy, and the Scandinavian influence is obvious at places such as Al Johnson's Swedish Restaurant.

Ask anyone who's vacationed in Door County, and they'll recall it as the place with the goats on the roof. Al Johnson, who opened his restaurant in 1949, commissioned a local architect to design the present Scandinavian-style log structure, which was fabricated in Norway and reassembled in Sister Bay—complete with a grass roof. Rolf Johnson, Al's son who manages the kitchen, relates the story over coffee and some creamy rice pudding.

Al's friend Winkie Larson presented Al with critters of some sort each year for a birthday gift. One year, the gift was several goats, and Winkie put the goats on the restaurant roof. The rest is Door County legend. Today, four to seven goats graze contentedly on the roof during the day. At night, the goats are loaded in a truck and taken to a nearby farm. In the restaurant, diners partake of heavenly Swedish meatballs (600 pounds per week), limpa bread, and other specialties served by waitresses wearing Scandinavian costumes.

Seaquist Orchards Market north of Sister Bay serves the all-time best cherry pie I've ever tasted anywhere, and the farm store sells cherry filling. During peak season, the Seaquists bake and sell more than 700 cherry pies a week.

The farm produces several million pounds of cherries a year. Fruit trees thrive here, because Lake Michigan moderates the climate. The soil, considered poor for other crops, is perfect for growing cherries. With such an abundant crop, the Seaquists creatively make and market cherry everything: cherry jalapeño salsa, cherry syrup, cherry vinaigrette dressing, cherry fudge and dozens of other cherry creations.

The White Gull Inn, a 19th-century white clapboard Greek Revival restored as an elegant bed and breakfast, is a Door County landmark. Founded in 1896, the inn is now a compound of several similar

(Clockwise, from opposite) Cherries for sale at Seaquist Orchards. View from Peninsula State Park. Smiling servers at Al Johnson's goat-topped restaurant. Wilson's, a favorite with Door County vacationers. The finale of the fish boil at the White Gull Inn.

Taste of Wisconsin

Cherry and Cream Cheese-Stuffed French Toast

White Gull Inn, Fish Creek

> 2 3-ounce packages cream cheese
> 1½ cups fresh or frozen (thawed) pitted, tart red cherries
> ¼ cup granulated sugar
> ¼ cup whipping cream
> 1 12-ounce loaf challah bread, brioche or French bread
> 7 eggs
> 1 teaspoon vanilla (optional)
> ¼ teaspoon ground cinnamon

In a mixing bowl, beat cream cheese, ¾ cup of the cherries, the granulated sugar and the whipping cream with an electric mixer on medium speed until combined. Set aside.

Trim ends from bread loaf. Cut into 1½-inch-thick slices. Cut a pocket in each slice by making a cut from the top three-quarters down the middle of slice. (Bread will appear to be 2 slices, but will be joined at bottom.) Fill each pocket with about ¼ cup of the cream cheese mixture. Gently press slices together, evenly distributing the filling.

In large bowl, beat together eggs, vanilla and cinnamon. Using tongs, dip the filled bread slices in the egg mixture, being careful not to squeeze out the filling. Coat both sides well.

Heat a lightly greased griddle over medium heat. Cook slices for 2 to 3 minutes on each side or until golden brown. To serve, sprinkle with sifted powdered sugar and top with remaining cherries. Serve with maple syrup. Makes 6 servings.

The stony shoreline of Schoolhouse Beach

houselike buildings grouped around a maple-shaded terrace. A 1947 Chevrolet "woodie" used for transporting guests is parked in the driveway. The inn is known for another local tradition: the fish boil, a whitefish feast that started, depending on who's talking, with the county's fishermen, its Scandinavians or its lumberjacks.

When the hour arrives, a strolling accordionist plays Lawrence Welk-type tunes to the delight of 75 or so guests. Then, sturdy Master Boiler Marc Paulson, who's been at this since 1977, patiently explains the basics, as diners listen attentively, sipping wine and beer.

He says the success of the boil depends on how well he controls the fire. He uses good hardwood, puts the potatoes in the kettle first, then the whitefish—30 pounds in all. He adds 10 pounds of salt to hasten the boiling (the salt doesn't affect the final flavor). As the finale, he pours a quart of kerosene onto the fire beneath the kettle. Whoosh! The nasty-tasting fish oils that have collected atop the bubbling cauldron vanish in a column of fire (don't try this at home!). It's time to head into the inn's dining room.

Diners have the option of drenching the mild-as-it-gets whitefish with melted butter provided at the table. Pumpkin, lemon and cherry-walnut breads and coleslaw complete the meal. Dessert, of course, is a generous slice of—you guessed it!—Door County cherry pie à la mode.

Island Time

Our final Door County adventure begins at Northport Pier, where we board the car ferry for the 30-minute ride to Washington Island. The clouds clear as we start our brisk trip across "Death's Door." The Washington Island Ferry Line's five boats, one of them an icebreaker, operate year-round, rarely missing a run despite rough waters and frequent storms.

Beneath these waters lie hundreds of sunken ships. Captain Dick Purinton explains to the passengers how challenging the currents are here and how much the water depths vary. But the crossing is about the only way to reach Washington Island, 22 miles around with only 650 year-round residents, but many more summer visitors. About 100 K–12 students attend the island's single school.

The island claims to be the nation's largest Icelandic settlement, with the first Icelanders arriving in 1870 and others following until about the turn of the 20th century. As you read mailboxes, you'll see a good share of names such as Jorgensen, Bjarnarson and Gunnlaughsson.

A breathtaking vista (in terms of both the view and the hike up the steps) of farms, woods and shoreline unfolds from atop Lookout Tower in Mountain Park. This peaceful, prosperous landscape and the respect for their Scandinavian ancestors inspired Trinity Evangelical Lutheran Church to build a Norwegian *stavkirke* (church), modeled after a famous 11th-century structure in Norway. Constructed entirely of wood, with elaborate carvings and 9,800 shingles, the building resembles a huge Viking ship tilted upright.

Centuries of waves and ice created another island landmark, Schoolhouse Beach. Legions of round stones, fallen from a nearby cliff and smoothed by littoral action, pile up on this stretch of shore and lie under the glass-clear water.

An interior road leads to Sievers Looms and School of Fiber Arts, a nationally renowned crafts learning center that began as a loom-making business. Although the school still makes and markets weaving equipment, some 50 instructors and 650 students show up annually to study here as well. For a weekend or a week from late May through October, students immerse themselves in basketry, knitting, weaving, carving and more. Some of their creations are for sale in the shop at the school.

Another brief stop introduces me to Icelandic horses. After visiting Iceland in 1965, some area residents thought it would be fitting to bring to the island the ponylike horses, with their thick manes and tails and long forelocks. Today, Laurie Veness, a childhood visitor to the island who relocated here from Evanston, Illinois, breeds the tranquil yet amazingly responsive horses at her stable and riding school. I'm surprised to learn these pint-size stalwarts can carry as much as 300 pounds for 50 miles!

As we rush to catch the ferry back to the peninsula, I have to stop at Nelsen's Hall, where I become a card-carrying member (one of 10,000 new members per year) of the legendary World-Famous Bitters Club. During Prohibition, Tom Nelsen circumvented the law by serving 90-proof bitters "for medicinal purposes

Dessert, of course, is a generous slice of—you guessed it!—Door County cherry pie à la mode.

only" in his tavern. I know bitters only as a flavoring used in various mixed drinks (with gin, for example).

After the bartender "signs" my membership card by sticking her thumb in my shot glass and fingerprinting my card (surely she washed her hands first), I down the contents. How can I describe the sensation? Impossible. At any rate, I think I'll stick with my Jack Daniel's.

Tom's approach helped ensure the position of Nelsen's Hall as Wisconsin's oldest continually operating tavern. Furthermore, locals insist that Tom Nelsen made it to the ripe old age of 90, drinking his medicinal bitters every day! I suspect that the true tonic is the good life here on the island and in Door County.

(From top) Checking out the *stavkirke*, a Norwegian-style church. An Icelandic horse on Washington Island.

New Milwaukee

Staid, Old World Milwaukee has added enchiladas and fajitas to its menu of sauerbraten and Wiener Schnitzel. And an amazing, contemporary art museum on the lakefront downtown actually "flaps" its sleek rooftop wings.

Milwaukee. Beer and bowling capital of America. Home of Richie and the Fonz, Laverne and Shirley. Motorcycles, bratwurst and kielbasa. Blue collar to the core. Well, not quite.

There's only one major brewer in town these days (Miller, which lends its name to Miller Park, the Milwaukee Brewers' convertible-top stadium). Schlitz, Blatz, Pabst and most of the other "beers that made Milwaukee famous" are history. Although you can still rattle the pins at the nation's oldest bowling alley (the Holler House along Lincoln Avenue), this city also is home to an array of cultural attractions, including one of the most innovative art museums anywhere.

They do make Harley-Davidson motorcycles and Briggs and Stratton engines, but this manufacturing powerhouse also claims plenty of data processing, insurance, mutual-fund and printing enterprises. At one time, German Americans accounted for more than a third of Milwaukee's residents, and the city was nicknamed the German Athens of America. The Irish and Poles left their marks here too. Today, African Americans, Hispanics and Asian Americans have made Milwaukee a cultural rainbow.

This is a city of minorities: No one racial group claims more than half the population of Milwaukee proper. But the hometown of Spencer Tracy, Liberace and Tom Snyder hasn't forgotten its roots entirely. To many natives, a water fountain still is a "bubbler," a soft drink is a "soda" and Kopp's frozen custard is the treat of choice.

Known to the native Potowatami as *Milliocki* (gathering place by the waters), Milwaukee was settled by Yankees who arrived via the Erie Canal and Lake Michigan to where three rivers converge: the Milwaukee, the Menomonee and the Kinnickinnic. For a time, the city overshadowed Chicago, just 90 miles south. When the great fire swept Chicago in 1871, Milwaukee brewers nobly rushed barrels of their finest to the thirsty firefighters. Then, they eagerly usurped Chicago's smoldering breweries to rule the industry. Ultimately, railroads and the stockyards gave Chicago the edge over its Wisconsin rival.

Today, Milwaukee claims 630,000 residents (1.6 million in the metro area). Although it may not rival Chicago in size, it offers many of the same lures on a less daunting scale: a gorgeous lakefront and great museums, entertainment and dining. The city is also known for clean government, partly a legacy of three German American socialist mayors.

Neighborhood Revivals

This is a tidy city with great architectural bones. Old World stonemasons crafted towering landmarks such as the 1895 Old City Hall, a pie-shaped Flemish Renais-sance structure. The Milwaukee River, with its vibrant, redeveloped RiverWalk, runs through the heart of the business district.

The 1893 Romanesque Revival Pfister Hotel, just three blocks from the lake downtown, always has been my first choice here. I love the three-story, barrel-vaulted lobby ceiling, with its chubby cherubs and extravagant Victorian gilt adornments. Crowning the grand marble staircase is the legend *Salve* (meaning both welcome and farewell in Latin).

To get my bearings, I start with a drive through neighborhoods that almost encircle the compact downtown. The Brady Street Italian neighborhood became home to Milwaukee's flower children in the 1960s and '70s. Now it's been reclaimed by some great Italian bakeries, groceries and restaurants. New condominiums, townhouses and apartments are sprouting up around once-forlorn Brewers Hill, where brewery owners and laborers lived side by side a century ago.

The Water Street entertainment district showcases the baroque 1895 Pabst Theatre and the modern Marcus Center for Performing Arts. Cobblestoned Old World Third Street beckons with shops selling sausages, cheeses, chocolate and spices. Mader's landmark restaurant serves sauerbraten and apple strudel among beer steins and Teutonic artwork.

The former warehouses and factories of

(Clockwise, from opposite) The "wings" of the Milwaukee Art Museum. Downtown, one of Milwaukee's numerous sculptures. A specialty at La Fuente. In the Milwaukee Art Museum. Ratzsch's German restaurant

(From left) Lobby ceiling at the Pfister Hotel. Lunching along the RiverWalk. Dining room at the Pabst Mansion. Saluting a statue of Hermes at Villa Terrace.

the Historic Third Ward are alive with lofts, condos, music venues, shops, restaurants and art galleries. The neighborhood also houses offices of many of the city's architects and advertising agencies.

Time to park the car and start exploring on foot! I stroll the Shops of Grand Avenue, a four-block enclosed mall with the likes of Old Navy, Sam Goody, TJ Maxx and Linens 'n Things, plus the historic Plankinton Arcade. Then I descend a flight of stairs on Wisconsin Avenue to the RiverWalk, lined with shops and eateries. At the Rock

craft docked right in the middle of downtown, high-rises looming all around. Soon, he's grilling lunch. "Salmon," he says. "Just caught them in the lake."

Bill Heller and his wife, Lee, live in suburban Wauwatosa, but spend many weekends aboard their boat here. When they're not boating, the Hellers sample downtown Milwaukee's dining and entertainment. Soon, they're feasting on that fresh-caught salmon and chardonnay, prior to watching the Packers game. Not a bad way to spend a sunny afternoon in the heart of the city.

small crowd gathers. We're all waiting for the "performance" to begin. Soon, Spanish architect Santiago Calatrava's dazzling white creation—with a "wingspan" larger than that of a 747—"flaps" its metal wings like a giant seagull getting ready to fly off over Lake Michigan.

This museum has a fantastic trove of art, but it's the new entry pavilion that's stolen the show since it was completed in 2001. According to the architect, those "wings" that open each morning and close each evening (with a just-for-fun "flap" at noon), both control light inside and create a giant moving sculpture.

Inside, the permanent collections—housed for the most part in an existing wing designed by Eero Saarinen—are just as intriguing. My favorites: works by Georgia O'Keeffe, a native of Sun Prairie, Wisconsin; an American folk art collection of weathervanes and whirligigs; the riotously colorful Haitian collection, donated by a Milwaukee couple.

Soon, they're feasting on that fresh-caught salmon and chardonnay . . . Not a bad way to spend a sunny afternoon in the city . . .

Bottom Brewery, fans are gathering for the Packers game that starts in an hour. On the terrace, I lunch on a huge salad and a local microbrew called Sprecher's, watching kayakers paddle by. Tour boats pass, the *Edelweiss I* and *Edelweiss II,* passengers waving.

A few steps away, down another landing, I see a fisherman cleaning his catch aboard his cabin cruiser, one of a string of pleasure

A few minutes later, I'm standing at the end of a walkway beside a big sunburst sculpture, admiring the most amazing art museum building I've ever seen. It's the Quadracci Pavilion of the Milwaukee Art Museum (named for Milwaukee's late printing magnate, Harry Quadracci), which features an incredible moving sunscreen called the Burke *Brise Soleil*. A

Old World and New

A short drive from downtown, two grand homes are reminders of Milwaukee's past. Villa Terrace, an Italian Renaissance-style

1920s mansion, stands on a bluff over-looking Lake Michigan. From the Terrace Avenue side, you would hardly guess what's in store behind the wrought-iron gates. The home looks unprepossessing. An ancient statue of Hermes and a fountain in the boxwood-filled courtyard leads my eye directly through the house to Lake Michigan. This nonprofit decorative-arts museum contains many furnishings representing the 15th to the 20th centuries that belonged to its original owners, Lloyd and Agnes Smith. Architecture and design students now study here.

I walk out onto the terrace to take in the view. Just a few years ago, overgrown gardens completely obscured the hillside. Then, volunteers stepped in and created a horticultural miracle: 16th-century formal Italian gardens complete with water steps that burble down the hillside. A tiny incline tram takes visitors down to the lower lawn.

The Smiths (he was president of A.O. Smith Company, the world's largest manufacturer of automobile frames) honeymooned in Italy and wanted to recapture the romance of the trip in their new home. David Adler, a leading residential architect of the day, surpassed their expectations.

Formally planted roses, hydrangeas, arctic willows, ornamental grasses, yews, honeysuckle and sumacs gracefully step down the hillside and onto the lower lawn—all re-creating the look of a formal Italian garden with plants that can withstand Wisconsin winters.

About a mile west of downtown along Wisconsin Avenue, just past the 12,000 student Marquette University campus, is another home that speaks to Milwaukee's rich history. The tan brick, 1892 Flemish Revival Renaissance Pabst Mansion was built by Milwaukee's most famous beer baron, Captain Frederick Pabst.

From the outside, I feel like I'm looking at a storybook castle. Old World craftsmen took two years to build and furnish this home, at a then-extravagant price tag of $250,000. Rooms represent German Renaissance, Venetian, English Regency and French styles of various periods. Mrs. Pabst's absolutely over-the-top French parlor is a riot of red fabric and gilt. Enough German heritage, even for me!

I head to the Fifth and National neighborhood within the historic Walker's Point district just south of downtown. My Milwaukee guidebook lists four German

restaurants and 18 Mexican restaurants. Times are changing, especially here. Mexicans started settling in Milwaukee to help make up for a labor shortage in the 1920s. In the 1990s alone, Wisconsin's Hispanic population doubled, and 12 percent of Milwaukeeans now are of Hispanic origin. The United Community Center in Walker's Point is one of the largest Latino community centers in the nation, offering neighborhood residents an array of educational, athletic, arts and social services.

In the shadow of an old Catholic church steeple, a tiled fountain bubbles in a busy courtyard filled with colorful canopies at La Fuente (The Fountain) Mexican restaurant. Sipping on a perfect margarita and nibbling an incredible shrimp soup, I survey the growing crowd: a mix of businesspeople, college students and suburban families, many of them Latino.

There's an array of Mexican restaurants in this neighborhood, plus a Mexican market and bars where you can hear mariachi music. After dinner, heading back to the Pfister, I note the signs: Acapulco, Conejito's Place, Pedrano's, Botanas, La Perla, the Gaucho Grill. It's a new Milwaukee, indeed.

Designed for Luxury

Looking for world-class pampering—unforgettable lodgings, excellent dining, top-notch golf and shopping? Head for this plumbing-fixture factory. Then, cross the street and be amazed by The American Club Resort.

At the Kohler Design Center, I nestle (with permission) into an original Kohler Company bathtub dating from the turn of the last century. An improbable transaction launched the company that made this tub and millions of bathtubs, sinks, toilets and every other imaginable plumbing fixture.

In exchange for the grand sum of 14 chickens, a Wisconsin farmer asked Austrian immigrant John Michael Kohler to retrofit one of the hog troughs he had been manufacturing into a bathtub, complete with a porcelain surface inside and claw feet. The rest, as they say, is history. Today, the Kohler Company product roster includes generators, engines, home furnishings, decorative tiles, plumbing fixtures—and hospitality.

John Michael Kohler, who came to the U.S. from Austria when he was a child, began manufacturing agricultural supplies in 1873. His sons, Robert and Walter (the latter a Wisconsin governor), nurtured the company's plumbing line. Now, grandson Herbert V. "Herb" Kohler, his wife, Natalie Black, and their three children are involved in every facet of the $3 billion company. They employ 25,000 people around the globe, and mastermind it all from this postcard-pretty village just west of Sheboygan.

As the Kohler Company grew in the early 1900s, so did its appetite for workers. Young men from central and eastern Europe arrived in droves to work in the Kohler factory. To assist those immigrants on the road to U.S. citizenship, the Kohlers built The American Club and launched adjoining Kohler Village in 1917, across the street from their behemoth factory.

For the grand sum of $27.50 weekly, American Club guests got all the hearty food they could eat, twice-weekly English lessons, laundry service, a barbershop and recreational facilities—including a billiards room and bowling alley.

The gracefully designed American Club was and still is a classic. The red brick building has a steeply pitched slate roof, rows of tiny European-style dormers and, inside, lots of rich oak paneling. During much of the last century, American flags fluttered patriotically, and rousing marches blared on the Victrola at mealtimes.

When many early American Club residents became citizens, married and had families, the Kohlers founded the neighboring planned community. Attractive, affordable single-family houses in a park-like setting became home for the workers.

Reinventing the Club

By the 1970s, The American Club had served its original purpose, and times had changed. Herb Kohler envisioned a first-class luxury resort in the former dormitory. In 1981, The American Club, then and now the Midwest's only AAA Five-Diamond resort, opened to serve a new clientele and has been an elegant success ever since. The carefully manicured village of 2,000 residents, more appealing than ever, boasts curving, shady sidewalks that pass 1920s-vintage cottage-style homes.

I've visited here many times over the years, in every season, often with my wife, Julie. It's the extraordinary Old World attention to detail that sets this place apart.

A circular drive, surrounded by carefully tended trees, shrubs, flowers and native grasses, leads to the entrance, where a troop of bellhops ushers guests under the distinctive green canopy. My room, one of 239, is in the Carriage House across the parking lot. The block-long vintage commercial building formerly housed shops and the village post office; it now offers luxurious rooms and suites, among amenities such as the Kohler Waters Spa and the Kohler Design Center.

I quickly unpack. If only I had time to relax in that inviting whirlpool or take a self-indulgent shower with jets massaging me from every direction. But duty calls! It's off to dinner at the Immigrant Room in the lower level of the main building.

This posh dining facility pays homage to those workers from many countries who first lived in this historic building, with rooms richly decorated to reflect themes from Germany, Normandy, France, Holland, England and Denmark. My associates and I are served a fabulous, five-course

(Clockwise, from
opposite) Lounging
in one of the first
Kohler tubs. The
American Club
Resort. The
Immigrant Room
and Winery's
cheese course.
The greens of
holes No. 9 and 18
at Whistling Straits.
The Greenhouse,
a stained-glass
solarium imported
from England.

(From left) Cottage-style homes in Kohler Village. The "Great Wall of China" in the Kohler Design Center.

meal. We choose our wine from among 700 selections with help from the wine steward, and enjoy impeccable service.

An unanticipated dining interlude just before dessert is our most memorable course: the cheeses. Of course, Wisconsin and cheese are as inseparable as Nebraska and beef. Chef Gregg Wangard explains that there are 350 cheeses made from the rich milk produced by Wisconsin's very contented dairy cows, which dine in grassy pastures nurtured by the state's rich glacial soils. Chef Wangard's mission is to elevate palates beyond squeaky cheese curds, cheddars and Colby Jacks with his collection of approximately 30 artisanal cheeses.

True masters, Chef Wangard explains, craft artisanal cheeses in very limited quantities. He offers a cheddar that's been aged 10 years, a Pleasant Ridge Reserve made exclusively with milk taken during the summer months, and a Grand Crusuroix Gruyère aged in a copper vat.

Dessert is served in the stained-glass greenhouse, which formerly was a conservatory in a children's hospital in England. Even though The American Club has been expanded three times in recent years, additions are absolutely seamless, with imaginatively landscaped courtyards tucked between various wings. Throughout, I note the similar brick, oak paneling, slate roofs, and style of copper downspouts.

Alice Edland, in charge of hospitality and real estate at the Kohler Company, explains the prevailing Kohler philosophy of gracious living. It encompasses home design ideas, fine cuisine, world-class landscaping and architecture, unsurpassed golf and soothing spa treatments. The concept also inspires classes and seminars held year-round at The American Club, with distinguished guest speakers edifying guests about topics from chocolate to yoga.

Having completed his first 50-year plan, devised by Frederick Law Olmsted, the design genius behind New York's Central Park, Kohler embarked in 1967 upon a second 50-year plan, created by the Frank Lloyd Wright Foundation.

Just blocks from The American Club are the Shops at Woodlake, a collection of approximately 30 home furnishings, accessories and clothing boutiques and restaurants, in addition to the 121-room Inn on Woodlake, a newer, moderately priced Kohler lodging. Just beyond Wood Lake, new houses and condominiums have sprouted, as both year-round and second homes, in the woods and along small lakes and accessible to Kohler golf courses.

First-Class Pampering

In desperate need of a back massage after spending the better part of two weeks behind the wheel on this extended road trip, I head to the Kohler Waters Spa in the lower level of the Carriage House. This is more than your typical health club.

I'm greeted by images of Roman temples, with ancient-looking columns and a long pool in the center. Guests in terrycloth robes in the coed part of the spa relax on chaises. I'm led into a massage room lit with dozens of small candles and a fireplace. Mark starts kneading my aching neck and shoulders and, in seconds, I'm ready to drop into a deep sleep.

But no! Time to move on to my next stop. If only I could devote more time to properly researching the whirlpool, plunge pool, steam room and sauna.

Director Jean Kolb says that male golfers who come to Kohler love to loosen up with the flexibility massage. There's even a treatment for golfers' feet, one of 50 pampering spa services. Jean suggests I try an exfoliation session, but I don't want to sign up for anything that sounds like a landscaping project.

Upstairs in the Carriage House, the Kohler Design Center is a fascinating collection of Kohler Company current product displays, memorabilia and design inspirations. The "Great Wall of China," made up of colorful Kohler plumbing fixtures, is dazzling.

Kohler's gracious living concept extends outdoors, and many visitors come here just to study the breathtaking landscaping and gardens. But the four acclaimed Pete Dye-designed golf courses are the biggest lure so much so that I feel guilty not being a golfer. Instead, I've tagged along and enjoyed the splendid courses with business associates and friends, who attest that the two wooded courses at Blackwolf Run (as well as the two new ones at Whistling Straits along Lake Michigan) are unsurpassed. Blackwolf Run hosted the Women's PGA Championship in 1998, and Whistling Straits hosted the Men's PGA Championship in 2004.

A flock of black-faced sheep groom Whistling Straits, a links-style golf course that hugs two miles of Lake Michigan shoreline. According to experts, the dunes, grasslands and four streams make this one of the most challenging layouts anywhere.

The course's new-but-old-looking limestone clubhouse and nearby stone barn look as if they came directly from Ireland. Indeed, a dozen of the caddies are Irish men. I overhear golfers laughing out loud at the pleasure and pain of this supremely challenging course.

I didn't make it to one of the places on my list: River Wildlife, the 500-acre wilderness preserve with 20 miles of groomed trails. There's never enough time for all the activities and pampering possible at this one-of-a-kind retreat.

CEDARBURG

About 20 miles north of Milwaukee, Cedarburg (population 11,000) is worth a stop. Once, this historic suburb boasted five busy mills along picturesque Cedar Creek. Two of them still survive. The main 1864 Cedar Creek Settlement building is a former woolen mill that churned out uniforms and socks for Union soldiers during the Civil War. Now, it houses shops selling home accessories and artisans' works.

The other survivor of the milling era, the 1855 Cedarburg Mill, is now home to a microbrewery. Once, early settlers took refuge from a threatened Indian attack behind the mill's stout walls. Cedarburg was settled by German and Irish immigrants who knew how to fashion solid buildings from locally quarried limestone.

The Washington Avenue Historic District is lined with Cedarburg's characteristic white-trimmed limestone shops, inns and cottages, crowned by the hilltop steeple of historic St. Francis Borgia Catholic Church. There's an active arts community here, and a popular September Wine and Harvest Festival.

More than a dozen eateries, ranging from coffeehouses and taverns to special-occasion restaurants, cater to almost every taste. Klug's Creekside Inn, a Cedarburg institution for more than 50 years, specializes in German fare.

There's an old-fashioned Main Street feeling here, even though the ever-encroaching suburban McMansion developments are all around. Many of these old limestone buildings, built by those craftsmen, probably will outlast the new houses going up all around. More information: Cedarburg Chamber of Commerce (800/237-2874, cedarburg.org).

ST. CROIX RIVER VALLEY

The copper-colored ribbon of the lower St. Croix River, a National Scenic Riverway, carves a 52-mile-long swath between Minnesota and Wisconsin. It starts at St. Croix Falls and tiny Taylors Falls on opposite banks, then flows south to Hastings, Minnesota, and Prescott, Wisconsin, where the St. Croix tumbles into the Mississippi River. Towns with the feeling of yesterday cling to the banks, as canoes, kayaks and powerboats of all sizes glide past.

In the mid-1880s, logs jammed the St. Croix, bound for some 130 sawmills along its banks. Lumber barons built solid brick buildings and opulent mansions, many now bed and breakfasts. Antiques shops, galleries and restaurants line the streets, once domains of rowdy lumberjacks. Thousands of reforested acres along the St. Croix are protected in six state parks and as part of the riverway system.

A half hour east of the Twin Cities, Hudson is a showcase of Victorian architecture. The riverfront beach park makes a perfect spot for a swim and picnic.

At St. Croix Falls, headquarters of the National Scenic Riverway, the river rushes through a rocky gorge called the Dalles. On tour-boat rides, natural sculptures loom overhead. You also can rent canoes and kayaks for river outings.

More information: Hudson (800/657-6775, hudsonwi.org). St. Croix Falls (800/222-7655, polkcountytourism.com).

Weird and Wonderful

"House on the Rock, 9 miles!" . . . "House on the Rock, 5 miles!" . . . "House on the Rock!" Slightly mysterious road signs lettered in a vaguely Oriental script beckon, as I drive across the green hills and valleys of southwestern Wisconsin. I turn off the highway into a vast parking lot canopied by abundant birches, evergreens and hardwoods that discreetly veil the contemporary stone and wood buildings I'm here to see. It's all getting more mysterious. Huge, phantasmagoric flowerpots stand sentinel. A sign reads: "Where imagination comes to life."

These days, "the Rock" is a collection of collections: the original hilltop retreat with its incredible Infinity Room, 17 other structures housing untold collections and displays, and 200 acres with 285 varieties of plants, most not native to the area. It's all a weird little world unto itself, owned by the Donaldson family of Janesville, Wisconsin. Businessman Art Donaldson was a longtime friend and associate of the self-driven imaginative genius behind this place: Alex Jordan (1914–1989).

Jordan, who grew up in Madison, began his monument to creativity in the early 1940s during weekend visits to the valley he'd hiked as a kid near his grandmother's home. The son of a builder, Jordan hadn't quite found his niche in life. Then, a 60-foot outcropping called Deer Shelter Rock caught his fancy. He put up a tent on one of his visits, then leased and later purchased the land. Soon he was single-handedly constructing a permanent weekend house atop the rock. Passersby couldn't resist pulling over for a look. In 1961, Jordan started charging a modest admission (50 cents back then; it's a rather amazing $19.50 now). The project grew—and grew. Soon came the collections and a bizarre assortment of exhibits.

Like the gatekeeper of the Emerald City, an assistant opens the main doors. My first stop is that Infinity Room, a 218-foot-long, needlelike projection that cantilevers 156 feet above the craggy, forested valley. More than 3,200 panes of glass frame incredible panoramic views. The room seems to extend forever, exactly the effect Jordan wanted.

Back inside, I wander through the original retreat that started it all. I move along down through a labyrinth and secluded rooms. Pneumatically operated musical instruments play tunes. Pretty strange. A network of adjoining unadorned metal structures brim with collections: cars, coaches, planes, weapons, dolls and dollhouses, paperweights, miniature circuses, mechanical banks, Oriental art, stained-glass lamps, china, silver, calliopes, butterflies. There's the world's largest carousel: 20,000 red and white lights, 89 chandeliers, 269 handcrafted animals—no horses, but lions, tigers, zebras, dragons and more. My favorite exhibit? "The Mikado," a wall filled with Oriental lanterns and figures playing tambourines, bells and cymbals around a huge Japanese drummer with a Fu Manchu mustache and ominously waggling eyebrows, who pounds away on a kettle drum. The music is the *Danse Macabre*. Don't recall that one from school? You would if you heard it played in this setting, I assure you. House on the Rock (608/935-3639, thehouseontherock.com).

"The Mikado" at House on the Rock

Travel Journal

BEGUILING PENINSULA

More than 300 miles of shoreline edge Door County, a narrow 75-mile-long peninsula between Green Bay and Lake Michigan in Wisconsin's northeastern corner (180 miles north of Milwaukee). Boxy white frame shops and cafes line the streets of New England-like harbor towns such as Fish Creek and Ephraim. Cherry orchards, open fields and deep forests cover the interior of this distinct piece of land that juts into Lake Michigan. Outdoor enthusiasts flock to the county's beaches, 11 golf courses and five state parks. More information: Door County Chamber of Commerce (920/743-4456, doorcounty.com).

Featured Stops

Al Johnson's Swedish Restaurant & Butiks Serving limpa (a rye bread made with molasses), Swedish meatballs and Lake Michigan whitefish in a Sister Bay log cabin. Famous for grass-munching goats on its sod roof (920/854-2626).

Nelsen's Hall On Washington Island, an 1899 building housing a popular tavern and serving as the island's social center (920/847-2496).

Seaquist Orchards Farm Market Two miles north of Sister Bay, one of Wisconsin's largest cherry and apple orchards, with a shop, bakery, greenhouse and playground (800/732-8850).

Sievers School of Fiber Arts On Washington Island, an internationally known arts-and-crafts school (920/847-2264).

Washington Island A 30-minute ferry ride from the peninsula's northern tip to the island. Washington Island Chamber of Commerce (920/847-2179, washingtonisland.com).

White Gull Inn In Fish Creek, renowned for its fish boil. Popular for candlelight dinners and for breakfasts of homemade granola and cherry-stuffed French toast. Reservations recommended for fish boil and dinner. $$$-$$$$ (888/364-9542).

More Great Stops

Door County Maritime Museum On the lakefront in Sturgeon Bay, with a focus on local shipbuilding, refurbished pilothouse from the steamer *Elba*, and an extensive local lighthouse display including a working fourth-order Fresnel lens. Admission charged (920/743-5958).

Main Street, Fish Creek

Door County Trolley Forty-five-minute narrated scenic tour of Door County, daily June through October. Departs from Orchard Country Winery along State-42, a half mile south of Fish Creek (920/868-1100).

Peninsula State Park Between Fish Creek and Ephraim, one of Wisconsin's largest state parks. Also an 18-hole golf course, hiking and bicycling trails and nearly 500 campsites. Other highlights: Eagle Bluff Lighthouse, nature programs and musical theater performances during the summer. Twice voted favorite Midwest state park by *Midwest Living*® magazine readers (920/868-3258).

Simon Creek Vineyard and Winery North of Sturgeon Bay, the largest vineyard in Wisconsin, producing chardonnay, merlot and other popular wines. Opened in 2003. Free guided tours of the wine-making facilities ending with a tasting (920/746-9307).

Whitefish Dunes State Park Dunes and hiking trails along a secluded Lake Michigan beach (between Sturgeon Bay and Jacksonport). Observation deck at Old Baldy, the park's tallest dune (920/823-2400).

Shopping

Founder's Square In Fish Creek, about a dozen shops in original and reconstructed settlers' buildings scattered along a shady cedar-bark path. Fish Creek Information Center (920/868-2316).

Frogtown Framing & Gallery Door County and other regional artists' works on display. In Baileys Harbor, complete custom framing service (920/839-2566).

Jack Anderson Gallery In Sister Bay, a large gallery operated by one of Door County's best-known artists. Also on display and for sale, originals and prints by a variety of Midwest artists (920/854-5161).

Lodging

Alpine Resort In Egg Harbor, full-service resort, cottages, homes and hotel rooms. With pool, golf course and tennis court. $$ (920/868-3000).

Edgewater Resort In Ephraim, vintage white clapboard resort with a breezy upscale flair. $ (920/854-2734).

Glidden Lodge Beach Resort Near Jacksonport, a family favorite with spacious one- to three-bedroom condominiums along a secluded stretch of Lake Michigan shore. With private beach and indoor pool. $$$ (888/281-1127).

Dining

Florian II **Lakeshore Rib and Steakhouse** In Baileys Harbor, featuring ribs and steaks in a casual setting with a stunning lake view (920/839-2361).

Inn at Cedar Crossing Fine dining in an 1884 restored brick building in Sturgeon Bay (920/743-4249).

Old Post Office Restaurant Traditional fish boil and home-cooked breakfasts featuring cherry pancakes, overlooking Eagle Harbor in Ephraim (920/854-4034).

Sister Bay Cafe Specializing in homestyle Scandinavian dishes such as heart waffles and *lapskaus* (920/854-2429).

Town Hall Bakery & Daily Special In Jacksonport's onetime city hall, innovative sandwiches and salads, freshly baked scones, cherry-oatmeal cookies and other treats (920/823-2116).

NEW MILWAUKEE

On the shores of Lake Michigan in southern Wisconsin, this city is shedding its brew-and-brats image and building a new, upscale reputation with revitalized neighborhoods, a lively arts scene and cutting-edge architecture. But Milwaukee's many ethnic distinctions remain, with traditional celebrations, storefront restaurants and a summerlong schedule of festivals. More information: Greater Milwaukee Convention & Visitors Bureau (800/554-1448, milwaukee.org).

Featured Stops

Captain Frederick Pabst Mansion Opulent beer baron's home built in 1892, with stained glass, intricate hand-wrought metalwork and exquisitely carved paneling. Admission charged (414/931-0808).

Historic Third Ward Downtown A 12-square-block enclave of restored 1890s warehouses housing boutiques, art galleries and cafes. Also, the Milwaukee Institute of Art & Design and Broadway Theatre Center (414/273-1173).

Kopp's Frozen Custard A Milwaukee institution with three locations (414/961-3288 in Glendale, closest to downtown).

La Fuente Serving Mexican specialties, such as shrimp soup topped with avocado, in a lively setting (414/271-8595).

Mader's German Restaurant Since 1902, serving traditional German fare along Old World Third Street. Specialties include standards such as Bavarian sauerbraten and red cabbage, pork shank, and Wiener Schnitzel (414/271-3377).

Milwaukee Art Museum About 20,000 works from antiquity to present, including renowned collections of American decorative arts, German Expressionism and folk and Haitian art. With a 90-foot-high glass-walled reception hall enclosed by a white steel rooftop sunscreen that looks like a giant water bird. Admission charged (414/224-3200).

Old World Third Street Downtown, the historic hub of the city's German community, with restaurants, 19th-century storefronts and cobblestone streets, plus the Milwaukee County Historical Center. More information: Greater Milwaukee Convention & Visitors Bureau (800/554-1448).

Pfister Hotel Downtown, an elegant, antiques-filled hotel open since 1893. The restored Victorian landmark has the largest collection of 19th-century paintings in any hotel in the world. $$$$; ask about packages (800/558-8222).

RiverWalk Following both sides of the Milwaukee River through the heart of downtown, linking cafes, microbreweries, green spaces and revitalized neighborhoods.

Sculpture along the Milwaukee RiverWalk

Information: Greater Milwaukee Convention & Visitors Bureau (800/554-1448).

Shops of Grand Avenue Downtown, more than 90 shops and restaurants, including locally owned stores, as well as popular chain retailers such as Old Navy and Dress Barn (414/224-0655).

Villa Terrace Decorative Arts Museum Italian Renaissance-style villa built in 1923, featuring decorative arts from the 15th to 20th centuries, wrought-iron artwork and a formal garden. Admission charged (414/271-3656).

More Great Stops

Discovery World–The James Lovell Museum of Science, Economics and Technology Downtown, with more than 150 interactive exhibits. Admission charged (414/765-9966).

Harley-Davidson One-hour factory-floor tour Monday through Friday at regular intervals between 9:30 a.m. and 1 p.m. Tour free but tickets required. Available on a first-come, first-served basis beginning at 9 a.m. (877/883-1450).

Miller Brewing Company Visitor Center and Gift Shop Free tours showing how beer is made, followed by a beer tasting, Monday through Saturday (414/931-2337).

Pere Marquette Park On the west bank of the Milwaukee River downtown, with lush lawns and an old-fashioned gazebo. At the park's dock, visitors can rent boats or board the 40-foot *Brew City Queen* for sight-seeing tours (414/257-6100).

Shopping

Usinger's Famous Sausage Old World Third Street's famous sausage maker. The store, which sells more than 70 varieties of sausage, still looks like it did when it was built in 1906, with tile floors and marble counters (414/276-9100).

Lodging

Best Western Inn Towne Hotel Near the RiverWalk along Old World Third Street, with recently remodeled rooms and the Speak Easy 710 Grill. $$ (414/224-8400).

Hilton Milwaukee City Center Downtown hotel near the RiverWalk, with a kid-pleasing indoor water park. $$$–$$$$ (414/271-7250).

Hotel Metro Convenient location near Lake Michigan downtown, an upscale Art Deco boutique hotel with suites and fireplaces. $$$$ (877/638-7620).

Wyndham Milwaukee Center Hotel Newer hotel near the RiverWalk and convenient to shopping areas. $$$ (414/276-8686).

Dining

Bartolotta's Lake Park Bistro Known for French cuisine, on a bluff overlooking Lake Michigan (414/962-6300).

Coquette Café In the Third Ward, for bistro-style lunches with outdoor seating in season (414/291-2655).

Karl Ratzsch's Venerable traditional German restaurant, where dirndl-skirted waitresses serve Wiener Schnitzel and other specialties in a classic late-19th-century setting (414/276-2720).

Milwaukee Ale House Microbrews and a variety of American specialties in the Historic Third Ward (414/226-2337).

Third Ward Caffé Italian specialties, including more than 20 pasta dishes (414/224-0895).

DESIGNED FOR LUXURY

Before being transformed into a premier resort, The American Club was a boardinghouse for immigrants working at the Kohler Company, the well-known plumbing products manufacturer. Golf now stars at this first-class resort, created in 1981.

The American Club Resort today forms the centerpiece of the Village of Kohler, a recreational, retail and restaurant community near Sheboygan that resembles an Old World village (55 miles north of Milwaukee). The 239-room American Club, listed on the National Register of Historic Places, is housed in a Tudor-style building with an exterior of rough-textured red brick and rows of dormers. The well-appointed interior includes handcrafted woodwork, gleaming brass and elegant bathrooms. $$$–$$$$; ask about packages (866/847-4856).

In addition to The American Club, Kohler Village encompasses more than two dozen specialty stores, four acclaimed 18-hole golf courses, a sports and fitness club with tennis courts and swimming pools, a 500-acre preserve with hiking trails and a river for fishing and canoeing, a spa, seven restaurants and a design center *(see below)*.

The four Pete Dye-designed golf courses—two at forested Blackwolf Run, two at the new Whistling Straits along Lake Michigan—draw golfers from all across the nation.

The Shops at Woodlake is a collection of approximately 30 home furnishings, accessories and clothing boutiques and restaurants. The 121-room Inn on Woodlake, overlooking a spring-fed lake and with its own beach, provides a newer, more moderately priced Kohler lodging option. $$, includes Continental breakfast; ask about packages (866/847-4856).

Kohler Design Center A three-level showroom filled with upscale, cutting-edge plumbing fixtures and faucets.

Information about Kohler Village: Destination Kohler (800/344-2838). ∎

The clubhouse at Whistling Straits Golf Course

Contributors

DAN KAERCHER

Editor-in-chief of *Midwest Living®* since the magazine's inception in 1987, Dan Kaercher has been a writer and editor with Meredith Corporation in Des Moines, Iowa, since 1972. He's a former features editor for Meredith's *Better Homes and Gardens®* magazine and served on the startup teams of several other Meredith titles. Dan has lived in the Midwest almost his entire life, primarily in Iowa and Nebraska. He is a journalism graduate of the University of Nebraska at Omaha. Dan and his wife, Julie, reside in the Des Moines suburb of Urbandale. They are the parents of two grown children and have one grandson. Dan enjoys swimming, reading and gardening. Outside the Midwest, his favorite place to travel is Mexico.

BOB STEFKO

In addition to *Midwest Living,* the wide-ranging work of photographer Bob Stefko has appeared in many national magazines, from *Gourmet* to *Forbes*. Bob's fine-art images are exhibited in several permanent collections, including The Ogden Museum of Southern Art. A native of Ohio, Bob now lives in Evanston, Illinois with his wife, Holly, and their three parrots. Regarding the images from this project, Bob says his favorites are of Michigan's Pictured Rocks and South Dakota's Badlands.

PETER TUBBS

Videographer Peter Tubbs, who documented Dan Kaercher's entire 10,000-mile journey for Iowa Public Television, is a veteran of both news and corporate broadcasting. A native Iowan, Peter is a graduate of Iowa State University and lives in Dallas Center, Iowa. He and his wife, Joanne, have a 3-year-old daughter. Peter likes telling the stories of the Midwest's people and places through the eyes of his video camera. He and his wife are avid bicyclists and music fans.

LOVE THE HEARTLAND?

Enjoy even more of its heart and soul with every colorful issue of *Midwest Living®* magazine. It's like having your personal guide delivered to your doorstep. Whether you hit the road or stay close to home, you'll always get the best of the Midwest to choose from—pretty backroads and quaint little towns, cozy dining experiences and mouthwatering recipes, charming bed-and-breakfasts and fun-filled festivals. *Midwest Living* does all the work. You get all the ideas, information and inspiration. That way you can plan your most successful trip ever. What better way to get the most out of your precious vacation days—and dollars!

There's never been a better time to start planning your next getaway. Call 1-800-374-9378 today. Or, visit us on the Web at www.MidwestLiving.com.

HELP US KEEP THIS GUIDE UP TO DATE

Every effort has been made by the authors and editors to make this guide as accurate and useful as possible. However, many things can change after a guide is published—establishments close, phone numbers change, hiking trails are rerouted, facilities come under new management, etc.

We would love to hear from you concerning your experiences with this guide and how you feel it could be made better and be kept up to date. While we may not be able to respond to all comments and suggestions, we'll take them to heart and we'll also make certain to share them with the authors. Please send your comments and suggestions to the following address:

The Globe Pequot Press
Reader Response/Editorial Department
P.O. Box 480
Guilford, CT 06437

Or you may e-mail us at: editorial@GlobePequot.com

Thanks for your input, and happy travels!

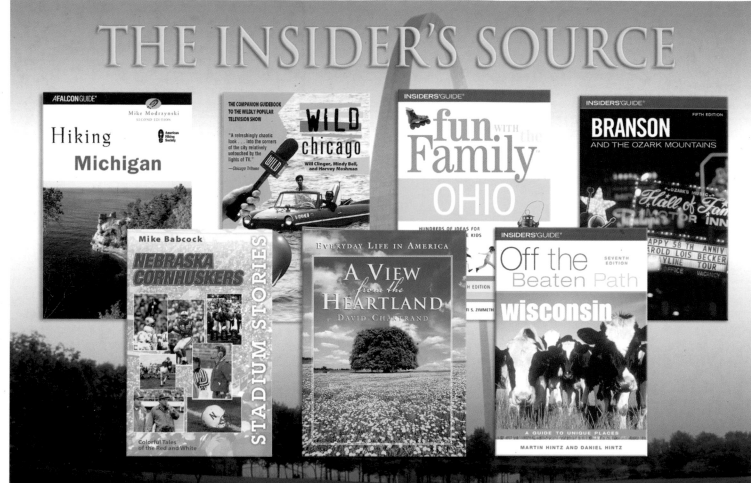